Till the Boys Come Home

DEDICATION

To Efa and Joe, who served on the Home Front, to R.J., who served at Sea, and to our children, Sian and Gareth, to our granddaughters Jessica and Rebecca and to all who served in 'The Great War' on land, air and sea and on the Home Front.

Robert James Holt (father of co-author Tonie Holt) who joined the Royal Marines as a bandboy in 1914 at the age of 14 and served on HMS *Inflexible* at the Battle of Jutland one year later. '*I didn't see a thing*', he said, '*I was below decks.' British: (Pub. T. Humphries, Southsea)*

Till the Boys Come Home

THE FIRST WORLD WAR THROUGH ITS PICTURE POSTCARDS

Tonie and Valmai Holt

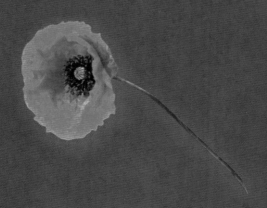

Pen & Sword
MILITARY

First published 1977 by Macdonald & Jane's Publishers Ltd.
This updated edition 2014, published
by Pen & Sword Military
an imprint of
Pen & Sword Books Ltd
47 Church Street
Barnsley
South Yorkshire
S70 2AS

ISBN 978 1 47382 352 5

Typeset in Ehrhardt by
Mac Style Ltd, Bridlington, East Yorkshire
Printed and bound in India by Replika Press Pvt Ltd

Pen & Sword Books Ltd incorporates the imprints of Pen & Sword Archaeology, Atlas,
Aviation, Battleground, Discovery, Family History, History, Maritime, Military, Naval,
Politics, Railways, Select, Transport, True Crime, and Fiction, Frontline Books, Leo Cooper,
Praetorian Press, Seaforth Publishing and Wharncliffe.

For a complete list of Pen & Sword titles please contact
PEN & SWORD BOOKS LIMITED
47 Church Street, Barnsley, South Yorkshire, S70 2AS, England
E-mail: enquiries@pen-and-sword.co.uk
Website: www.pen-and-sword.co.uk

Foreword to 2014 Edition

Below is the original Foreword to the 1977 Edition. It was written by WW1 veteran writer and journalist, Eric Hiscock. He was then in the public eye for his supposedly realistic and autobiographical account of his WW1 experience as an under-age soldier, *The Bells of Hell Go Ting-a-Ling-a-Ling*, also published that year. Today it is rated as highly exaggerated, controversial, somewhat unreliable factually, and, among other criticisms, obsessed with homosexuality. It is still a cracking good read – and he *was* actually there!

WHEN THE BOYS COME HOME.

QUAND LES POILUS RETOURNERONS.

By well-known and prolific artist of chubby children, Mabel Lucie Attwell. Many of the boys didn't come home until 1920. *British.*

Foreword to 1977 Edition

When I left home in 1915 to join the 29th Battalion, Royal Fusiliers, there was an album in the house nearly full of postcards. They had been sent to me, my brother or sister, or my parents by schoolfriends, relations, or sometimes by chance acquaintances met on seaside holidays. Nobody flew to Corfu those days. More than forty years later I read a novel of Graham Greene's, *Our Man In Havana*, in which a character observes: 'A picture-postcard is a symbol of loneliness.' Looking through this quite remarkable collection of cards of nations at war I can only conclude, if Graham Greene's character was right, there were an awful lot of lonely people in the world during 1914-1918. There were, of course. We were lonely in the trenches. Comradeship that arrived with dirt, danger and death, helped enormously, but it was the post from home that made such a degraded form of life endurable. There are many postcards in this book, so energetically collected and so brilliantly presented by Tonie and Valmai Holt, that I recognise. Some, especially the Austrian artist, Raphael Kirchner's, I remember seeing on the damp walls of dugouts, wartime pin-ups that brought with their *La Vie Parisienne* near-nudity a moment or two of relief from the rat-infested, water-logged, mud-filled holes that sheltered men from the mad, death-dealing outside world of Nomansland. We, on the other hand, could send back only those printed, monosyllabic Field Postcards (I am well, I am in receipt of your letter, I am wounded' – or words like that) except when, out of the Front Line, in some small, shell-shocked village, it was still possible to buy, for a few centimes, some sentimental postcard printed in Paris. Such shy-making cards have, inevitably, been corraled in this volume by the Holts. The card-sending habit died, in the main, when the Great War ended and stamps for cards went up from a halfpenny to a penny. Now there will be no time for sending such blatantly propagandist, heart-stirring, comic messages in any future war. Nuclear fission will not allow leisure enough for loving messages.

Such a thought helps to make this book the treasure house it is. There can never be another like it. It represents an innocent industry that was buried along with most of the recipients of the postcard pictured here.

Eric Hiscock

ERIC HISCOCK

Contents

Authors' Introduction

NOTE TO 2014 EDITION

By the time the 100th Anniversary of the WW1 Armistice is reached in 2018, every one of the some 750 original postcards in this book will also be at least 100 years old. No longer will they be just, scraps of paper, but treasured historical documents, unwitting contemporary observers of the war in all of its aspects.

This completely revised edition contains many new images from both sides, some of them extremely rare and valuable propaganda cards

The universality of information via the internet has enabled us to expand some of the picture captions beyond what we were able to do with the first edition, but we have left the central narrative untouched.

Internet sites like e-bay and a variety of international auction houses, have brought the value and significance of the contemporary picture postcard to a wider audience including schoolchildren, and these simple pictures, sometimes with their poignant messages, are a wonderful introduction to the young of the price that was paid for the freedoms that we enjoy today.

In 1914, much to his later embarrassment, H.G. Wells, then revered as Britain's foremost man of letters, called the Great War 'The War that will end War'. We know now that it was simply the beginning of technological warfare that has today reached a level of development where any nuclear power has the capability of annihilating millions perhaps even of ending our world. Between 1914 and 1919, the years of holocaust, many irreplaceable things died. Almost an entire generation of the manhood of the combatant nations was killed. Certain national

An extremely rare card showing the arrest of Archduke Franz Ferdinand of Austria's would-be assassinator, '*The Bomb-thrower, Cabrinovic*' on June 28 1914 at Sarajevo. Cabrinovic's bomb missed the Archduke and, despite swallowing a cyanide capsule and jumping into the *River Miljacka*, this member of the Black Hand secret organisation was fished out and arrested. *Austrian.*

Der Bombenwerfer Čabrinovič.

attitudes and beliefs began to die after the War, such as the British jingoism of blind faith unto death for King and Country. Others disappeared altogether, for example, a narrow moral code about women and their place in society. The end of the War was the end of an era.

With the end of that era came the demise of a phenomenon in the history of communication – the picture postcard.

The postcard was born at the Wiener Neustadt Military Academy in Austria in 1869. Dr Emanuel Hermann, a professor at the Academy, suggested the idea, and the world's first postcards were issued on 1 October 1869. The object of the exercise was to increase the business of the post office by encouraging people to write to each other more often. This encouragement took the form of a special reduced price for sending the new postcard, which was less than a letter.

The idea worked, and when Britain's first postcards were issued one year later on 1 October 1870, half a million passed through the post office at St Martins Le Grand on that first day. At the beginning in Britain, cards were only available at post offices and were printed by Messrs De La Rue under an exclusive contract. They were made of plain light buff cardboard, 122mm by 88mm, and one side carried a pre-printed stamp and space for the address, while the other provided room for the message.

Entrepreneurs rose and flourished, making and losing fortunes. In Britain the Prime Minister, Mr Gladstone, loved the postcard and said so. De La Rue clung tenaciously to their monopoly while other publishers seethed. On the Continent greater freedoms allowed the use of the cards for advertisement purposes and, gradually over the first 30 years, the idea of putting pictures onto the cards took shape. By the beginning of the twentieth century the picture postcard was a major communication medium and art form. It recorded political events, personalities, daily news, wars, holidays, indeed every human activity. There were no telephones, no mass produced cameras; there was no radio and the postcard was the Victorian television. In Britain alone in 1900 over 500 million cards were used during the year. There were postcard clubs, postcard exhibitions, postcard machines, postcard magazines, special postcard post boxes, postcard pens, postcard wallets, postcard importers and above all postcard collectors. The cards were Status symbols, recording the ability of the wealthy to travel. They were windows on an exciting world outside the knowledge of most ordinary people; they were contemporary, cheap and collectable. In Germany, where excellent printing processes and a freer commercial climate had produced the most rapid postcard development, the collecting craze was known as 'The Plague' and newspapers commented that Europe would be drowned under a sea of postcards.

Erzherzog-Thronfolger Franz Ferdinand und Gemahlin Herzogin Sophie von Hohenberg gefallen durch Mörderhand am 28. Juni 1914 in Sarajevo.

Mourning card for the Archduke and his morganatic wife, Sophie. *Austrian.*

The famous '*Scrap of Paper*' London Treaty of 1839. Seals of the signatories: Palmerston (Britain), Sylvain de Weyer (Belgium), Senfft (Austria), H. Sebastiani (France), von Bulow (Prussia) and Pozzo di Bergo (Russia). The strip of paper which is just wrapped around the card explains that all the profits from the sale of these postcards will be given to the National Relief Fund (formed after an appeal from the Prince of Wales on 7 August 1914) and the Belgian Relief Fund. It is quite remarkable that the strip, which is not stuck in any way, is still on the card after 100 years. *British: (Pub. C. W. Faulkner & Co.)*

THE " SCRAP OF PAPER "
Guaranteeing the Independence and Neutrality of Belgium.

THE "SCRAP OF PAPER."

The whole of the profit which we derive from the sale of these cards will be given to the National Relief Fund and the Belgian Relief Fund.

C. W. FAULKNER & CO., Ltd.

(With acknowledgments to the Parliamentary Recruiting Committee)

The signatures of the representatives of the six Powers who were parties to the famous Treaty of 1839. The signatories are : Palmerston (Great Britain), Sylvain Van De Weyer (Belgium), Senfft (Austria), H. Sebastiani (France), Bülow (Prussia), and Pozzo di Bergo (Russia).

Reproduced from the Original Document

From 1914 to 1918 Europe was crowded with soldiers far from home, and they not only sent cards but received them too. It was a period in which the postcard industry reached its zenith.

By 1917 the British Forces postal services alone employed over 4,000 men handling almost 2 million letters and postcards a day. The soldiers liked the postcards. They were colourful and the pictures could often speak better for them than they could for themselves. In France picture postcard shops were everywhere in the villages just behind the lines and Tommy out of the trenches searched the shelves anxiously for something suitable to send home. The cards showing scenes from the War that Tommy received from home (notably those in the excellent official *Daily Mail* War Series) were often the most accurate and up–to–date information that he ever had as to what was going on around him. At home the pace of the War made letter-writing difficult and the postcard suited the need for haste. Collecting still went on, indeed even increased; even Royalty collected postcards.

Throughout Europe people communicated by postcard and, in doing so, created an historical record of their life and times and hence of the Great War – both from the 'picture side' of the cards and, equally importantly, from the written messages on the reverse. Many of these messages, which range from the poignant to the banal, are featured in this book.

The technical advances in communication forced by the War – the radio and telephone – and the social changes that made people generally more knowledgeable of the world about them, plus the raising of the postcard postage rate by 100% in 1918 to 1d, finished the picture postcard almost overnight. The years of the War had been its summit of achievement, its heyday; the flame had burnt brightest at the end.

Today the significance of the picture postcard as a social document is becoming realised. It provides an extraordinarily vivid contemporary record of the world of over 60 years ago. Today, once more, the same cards are being collected. Picture postcards are becoming valuable, and in particular the period of the First World War is attracting more and more attention. Almost every home in Europe will have somewhere in its family an old picture postcard that could form the basis of a collection, whether for interest only, or for serious study and for investment. The field of research is especially wide open for those interested in discovering more about the artists who became famous for their postcards, but apparently for little else. The postcard makes a natural vehicle for the small, fascinating word pictures of the amusing, sorrowful, terrible and wonderful stories that were contrasting fragments of the 'Great War'. The dramatis personae of these cameos include the great leaders and the common men of the times.

When Germany invaded Belgium in 1914, Britain declared war because she had a treaty with Belgium to defend her frontiers and protect her neutrality. The Imperial German Chancellor could not understand Britain going to war over what he is reported to have called 'a scrap of paper'. It is ironic that the following years of struggle and Germany's ultimate downfall are so graphically recorded on millions of scraps of paper known as picture postcards.

Tonie and Valmai Holt

1 The Nations & the Men who Went to War

Together we Fight for the
Cause and the Right.

The Nations

The summer of 1914 was exceptionally hot. In retrospect it is easy to imagine that the sultry, oppressive heat seemed to breed feelings of sinister foreboding and evil to come. Certainly resignation to the idea that war was inevitable prevailed in the mutually distrustful climate of European politics, which has often been likened to an expectant powder keg, with the igniting spark the assassination of the heir to the Austrian throne. Once the gunpowder had exploded, the affected Nations behaved like collapsing pieces in a game of dominoes, as one by one they entered the War – and were immortalised on picture postcards as they did so.

1

1 The British bulldog personifies the fighting spirit. Posted 10 July 1916. *British: (Pub. Smith Bros., Croydon.)*

2 Switzerland, who officially remained neutral, says in effect to a menacing Germany, *'Be careful, I'm armed'. Swiss: Political card by M. Radiguet. 1914.*

3 Card by much sought–after 'glamour' and military artist, Xavier Sager. Caption reads, *'Brotherly charity to the Heroes'* (of Serbia) and message in English on reverse from a husband at the front to his wife reads. *'Wish to God it would end, that's what we want.' French: (Pub. Noyer.) Passed by Censor 1020. March 1918.*

2

auy head. la
chante fraternelle.

3

WE DON'T WANT TO FIGHT.
BUT BY JINGO. IF WE DO.
WE'VE GOT MEN, AND COIN
AND SHIPS, AND GUNS,
TO SEE IT THROUGH,
AND THROUGH & THROUGH.

4

4 Canada, India, Australia – the Dominion countries – rally behind Great Britain. The verse is from the song sung in 1878 by supporters of Beaconsfield's pro-Turkish policy that started the word 'Jingoism' and that nearly brought Britain to war with Russia. The jingoistic mood was strong in the early months of the War, and was a throwback to the fervent patriotism fired by Kipling's verses in the Boer War. As the character of the War changed from a bright, noble crusade to a dreary and dangerous existence in the trenches, jingoism died. It was killed by the awful reality of trench warfare. *British: (Pub. Inter-Art Co. Patriotic Series.)*

As the assassination was committed by Serbs, *Serbia* could be regarded as the first link in the chain. The political scene in Serbia was extremely shaky after the recent Albanian campaign, with nationalist feeling running high. Its strength was demonstrated by the two Serbian students, Princip and Cabrinovic, who successfully carried out the nationalist plot by shooting the Arch Duke Francis Ferdinand and his wife on 28 June at Sarajevo.

Long fearful of nationalist movements in her creaking Empire, composed of a variety of cultures, *Austro-Hungary* saw the assassination as a serious threat. She responded on 23 July by offering Serbia an ultimatum, on which the British Foreign Secretary, Sir Edward Grey, commented: 'I have never before seen one State address to another independent State a document of so formidable a character'. It was obviously designed to be unacceptable. Serbia's reply was evasive and she offered to submit any outstanding points to the Hague Tribunal. But Austro-Hungary rejected this proposal and on 28 July formally declared war on Serbia. Fearing the worst outcome, Nicola Pasic, one of the founders of the Serbian Radical Party who remained Prime Minister throughout the War, had already ordered mobilisation.

VIVE L'AMÉRIQUE
AMERICA FOR EVER

5

5 Card from the popular artist, Xavier Sager's *Amitié Franco-Americaine*' Series. Posted 1 September 1917. French morale in 1917 was at an all-time low, following the springtime mutinies in the Army. America's involvement provided a badly-needed boost to the war-weary *Poilu* and the under-nourished civilian alike. *French: Sent to his wife by Sapper Stacy. Passed by Censor 2678.*

6 Vitriolic political cartoon of Sir Edward Grey, *Warmonger and Mass-Murderer'*. The devil admits that even he can learn something from this young man. Surprisingly, this Field Postcard was sold in aid of the Red Cross. The mass of the German people genuinely believed that Britain had started the War and that Foreign Secretary Grey (in reality mild-mannered and peace-loving) was a prime instigator. *German: Artist Hermann Lorch.*

7 Artist Agnes Richardson. Posted 5 April 1918. America's long-awaited entry into the War on 6 April 1917 was greeted with as much enthusiasm in Britain as it was in France. It was the culmination of Winston Churchill's campaign, when First Lord of the Admiralty, to embroil her. It has even been suggested that the *Lusitania* tragedy was engineered to force America's hand. *British: (Pub. Inter-Art Co.)*

Austro-Hungary acted after full consultation with her ally, Germany. Germany took her support further by sending ultimata to *France* and *Russia* on 31 July. The next day, President Poincaré (who had hurriedly returned from a state visit to Russia) ordered general mobilization. That same evening, news of what was regarded as a declaration of war reached a St. Petersburg riven with angry demonstrations. The news quickly changed the mood of the workers, who joined cheering crowds outside the French and Serbian Embassies and the Winter Palace. War fever was as euphoric in Russia as in Europe. Mobilization started immediately and enthusiastically – much to the surprise of German military pundits who had planned the defeat of France before her cumbersome Russian ally could be ready.

On 2 August *Turkey* signed a treaty pledging her entry into the War on Germany's side. After the first Allied successes, however, Turkey shied from her responsibilities, but in late October, Germany drove her reluctantly into action. The Turkish fleet bombarded Odessa, forcing the Allies to declare war on Turkey. Turkey's greatest contribution to the Central Powers was that her participation led to the disastrous Allied campaign in the Dardanelles.

Engl. Minister Grey
(Kriegsverbrecher und Massenmörder)

Junge, Junge! von Dir
"kann ich noch was lernen"!!

6

"I have waited for you so long!"

7

8 Serbia in the beautiful hand-painted '*Aux Alliés Human Butterfly*' series of the Allies. This imaginative series is enthusiastically sought-after by postcard collectors. A full set would add a premium to the value of the individual cards. *French: (Pub. L. Géligné.)*

9 Hand-painted '*Human Butterfly*' from '*Aux Alliés*' Series. Portugal, *Britain's oldest ally.* In 1899 ancient treaties of alliance were reaffirmed in secret between Britain (under Lord Balfour) and Portugal (then still a monarchy under Carlos). On 7 August 1914 Portugal proclaimed its adhesion to the English Alliance and became actively involved in November 1914 with an attack on German S.W. Africa. Sent from the BEF Jan 1917. Passed by Censor 3468. *French: (Pub. L. Marotte, Paris.)*

10 Hand-painted '*Human Butterfly*' from *French Aux Alliés* Series of Japan with a poignant message on the reverse, '*…am afraid you will think I am not very cheerful but it is hard to look at things in a different light to what I do as thing stand now, they have not got a very cheerful outlook, but let us hope for better days to come in the near future. Please do not think dear that I always look at the black side of things but one must sometimes, even if it is only to realise fully the enormous task we have undertaken and all it means to us if we come through on top. And I might add that it is my firm belief that we shall eventually.' Sent in an envelope.* French: (Pub. L. Géligné.)

11 From same Hand-Painted French series of *Aux Alliés* as the charming Butterfly cards. Cleverly drawn, it portrays Austrian Emperor Franz Joseph as a wasp impaled on a sword, in a strikingly contrasting and cruel style. *French: (Pub. L. Géligné.)*

Serbie

Portugal   Portugal

12

9

Japon

Autriche

14

Great Britain

15

Italy

16

France

17

Britain, surprised during her August Bank Holiday Weekend, was the next to enter. Preoccupied with problems nearer home, like the Irish Question and Women's Suffrage, she was nevertheless shocked by Germany's violation of Belgium's neutrality – which she had pledged to preserve on the famous 'scrap of paper'. An ultimatum was sent to Germany to exhort her to respect Belgium's position on Tuesday 4 August and an answer was demanded by 11.00pm. No answer came. Britain was at war. The crowds were hysterical with patriotic fervour, but for Sir Edward Grey, who had strived to regain the old concept of 'a concert of Europe' it was a sad moment. 'The lamps are going out all over Europe, we shall not see them lit in our lifetime', he predicted.

The Commonwealth naturally supported Britain's war effort: Canadians, Anzacs and the Indians whose colourful cavalry seemed so incongruous round the muddy trenches of France and Belgium.

Montenegro had flirted with unity with Serbia before the War broke out and therefore supported her as a matter of course, although, after the invasion by Austro-Hungary in the bitter winter of 1915–1916, Prince Nicholas tried to negotiate terms with the Central Powers and eventually fled to Italy.

Portugal, a new and shaky Republic since its revolution in 1910, nevertheless proclaimed her support of her ancient ally, England, and sent an expedition on 11 September 1914 to reinforce her Colonies in S.W. Africa. But it was not until after Portugal seized German ships in Portuguese ports in February 1916 that Germany actually declared war on Portugal on 9 March 1916. In 1917 Portugal sent an expeditionary force to the Western Front under General Fernando Tamagnini de Abreu.

Japan declared war on Germany in late August 1914. Her main motive was to acquire German possessions in the Far East and to expand her influence over China. Her contribution, however, was slight.

Bulgaria joined the Central Powers in October 1915, quickly helping to effect the defeat of Serbia in the second Central Powers Campaign.

12 Official Swiss Red Cross Card by Eug. Burnand, showing neutral Switzerland as a refugee. Dated I August 1917. The reverse shows a picture of Henri Dunant, founder of the Red Cross. As a young soldier in the Battle of Solferino 1859, Dunant was so horrified by the plight of the unattended wounded that he organised a band of helpers from local townspeople. After a four year campaign he formed '... *a society in every country when nations are at peace, in which men and women could be organised and trained* so *that they could give aid to the wounded in time of war*'. At the outbreak of World War I the International Prisoners of War Agency in Geneva, with a staff of over 1,000, was opened by the Society which had become known as the Red Cross. It was to help evacuate civilians from occupied zones and to repatriate wounded soldiers. Posted in Switzerland Xmas 1917. *Swiss: (Pub. Pretz.)*

13 Card depicting Japan, one of our Allies since a treaty of 1902. Japan offered to enter the war on the Allies' side if it could take German Pacific territories. As early as 7 August 1914 the Japanese fleet destroyed German ships in Chinese waters and formally declared war on Germany on 23 August, and later on Austria-Hungary. She continued to offer naval and war supplies assistance throughout the war. Artist H.G.C. Marsh Lambert. *Posted Feb 1916. British: (Pub. A.E. Davis & Co, London.)*

14 A delightful and rare example of a German version of the more typical allied style of girl's head. This kind of card rarely found its way to Allied countries and is still difficult to find. *German.*

15 Dated 22 April 1916, the message reads, '...*I reckon they're a decent set*'. No such ship as the H.M.S. *Great Britain* actually took part in the War. The card was sent to 'Kate' in April 1916. *British: (Pub. Vivian Mansell.)*

Belgium.

18

Russia.

19

16 Although Italy had signed the 'Triple Alliance' of 1882 with Germany and Austria-Hungary, she did not join the Central Powers in August 1914 because of Austria's designs on minority Italian territories such as Trieste. She had signed also the 'Triple Entente' between Britain, France and Russia in a supplementary agreement which also included Portugal. *British: (Pub. Vivian Mansell.)*

17 France in revolutionary attire. '*At last I have completed the set*', reads the message. Present-day collectors will appreciate the feeling. This British publisher produced the most prolific and highly-rated series of girls' heads with a patriotic theme. Sent May 1916. *British: (Pub. Vivian Mansell.)*

18 Belgium, overrun by the invading German army in the first days of the War, has every reason to look wistful. Posted 11 November 1914. The sender would have been more than wistful if she had known that it would be another four years to the day before the fighting would stop. *British: ('The Allies' Series. Pub. James Henderson.)*

19 Russia. In accord with the terms of the 'Triple Entente' of 31 August 1907, Tsar Nicholas II led his country into the war, suffering heavy losses in the first battles at the Masurian Lakes and Tannenburg, provoking social unrest and distrust of the Romanovs (mainly due to the influence of Rasputin, who ironically, had advised against Russia entering a war that was bound to end in disaster for her.) Following the Bolshevik Revolution of 1917, the Treaty of Brest-Litovsk of 3 March 1918 finally led to a cessation of hostilities with the Central Powers and the massacre of the Royal Family on 17 July of that year. *British: (Pub. James Henderson.) 1914.*

20 From series 'The Allies' depicting Serbia with a wild gipsy touch. The romantic image associated with this vigorous little country helped fan the fund-raising efforts of Britain's voluntary team of aristocratic lady enthusiasts. Measures ranging from lecture tours to bazaars were quickly organized. *British: (Pub. James Henderson) 1914.*

21 Elegant, fur-clad Russia with her troops marching in the background. Early belief in the ability of the Russian forces to win battles by massive numerical superiority alone, known as the *Russian Steam Roller* was quickly dispelled. In their defeat at the Battle of Tannenburg in the first month of the War the Russians were reported to have lost 10 of their soldiers to every 1 German. *British: (Pub. Vivian Mansell) by E.C. Brinsley.*

22 Hatband of the famous *Iron Duke'*. The message reads, '*... am having a lovely time now. Life is worth living. My old boy is taking me everywhere. Theatres, Zigzag, Chu Chin Chow, Canadian War Pictures'* obviously a great leave! Posted 4 September 1917. *British: (Pub. Vivian Mansell) by Joyce Averell.*

23 France depicted with *'bonnet rouge'* and *fleur-de-lis* – the contrasting symbols of the revolutionary working class and the ancient monarchy. *Posted March 1916. British: (Pub. Vivian Mansell) by E. C. Brinsley.*

24 Belgium. Posted 10 May 1916. Although these colourful series were in the shops immediately after the outbreak of War, showing how quickly publishers could respond, they were still as popular two years later. *British: (Pub. Vivian Mansell)*

25 Unusually for this series, which normally portrays girls, Italy is depicted as a dashing young *Bersaglieri* (Rifleman). In reality the pictorial promise was not fulfilled. Italy's first offensive in May 1915 against the Austrians on the Isonzo Front under General Cadorna was a failure, despite their overall 3 to 1 numerical superiority. *British: (Pub. Vivian Mansell.)*

Servia.

20

Russia

21

England

22

France

23

Belgium

24

Italy

25

Italy

26

MY COUNTRY, 'TIS OF THEE

27

SERBIA.—"Freedom for ever!"

28

Serbie - Servia.

29

"We are coming, brothers, coming,
A hundred thousand strong!"

"Voici la République sœur,
Avec vous, frères d'armes, de cœur!"

30

26 Italy in a more traditional 'Allied' representation. *Posted May 1916. British: (Pub. Vivian Mansell.).*

27 The song 'My country 'tis of thee', also known as 'America', with lyrics by Samuel F. South and sung to the same tune as the British National Anthem, was used as the American National Anthem until replaced by the 'Star Spangled Banner' in 1931. It is still sung at many patriotic functions, such as the 1st inauguration of Pres Obama. *Posted March 1918. British: Artist Ellem. (Pub. Photochrom Co.)*

28 Serbia was often known for propaganda purposes as *'Poor Little Serbia'*, just like 'Poor Little Belgium'. By Arthur Butcher from the *United Six'* Series. At this stage, the other *'five'* would be, France, Russia, Belgium, Britain and Japan. *Posted May 1916. British: (Pub. Inter-Art Co.)*

29 Serbian soldier in Salonika, 1917, epitomising the spirit of his country. The Artist, Drack-Oub (pseudonym and anagram for his surname, Antoine Bouchard), was serving as a Reserve *Sous-Lieutenant* in the Zouaves when he went to Salonika. In the '20s and '30s he was well-known for his North-African ethnic caricatures and illustrations for the Fables of La Fontaine with 'patois' captions. Born in Saumur in 1879, he died in Algeria in 1942. *French: (Pub. Camis, Strasburg.)*

30 The spirit of America, backed by modern war birds, hurries to join the fray. Sent on Active Service, passed by Censor 3211, posted 12 June 1918. The first two lines of the quoted song are variations on the popular Civil War song, *'We are coming Father Abraham* [Lincoln], *300,000* [or sometimes 600,000] *strong…'* *British: (Pub. Inter-Art Co.)*

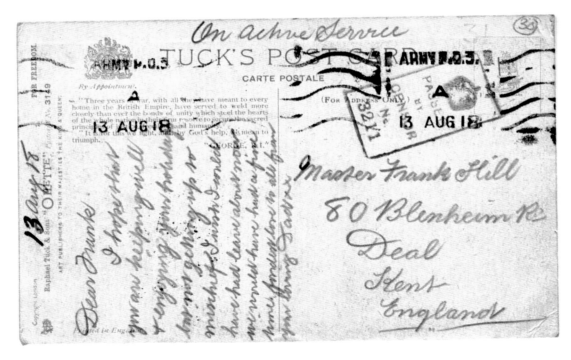

31 The front bears the Flags of the Allies. The reverse bears a printed message from King George. '*Three years of War with all they have meant to every home in the British Empire, have served to weld more closely than ever the bonds of unity which steel the hearts of the whole nation in their firm resolve to secure the sacred principles of justice, freedom and humanity. It is for this we fight and, by God's help, we mean to triumph.*' Sent on Active Service 13 August 1918, passed by Censor 3211 (see card 30). *British: (Pub. Tuck.)*

32

33

34

32 The flags of the Allies. The reverse reads, *'German View of Treaties. "A Scrap of Paper"'*. The Imperial Chancellor is said to have expressed inability to understand the attitude of England and to have exclaimed, *"Why should you make war on us for a scrap of paper."* Sir Edward Goschen is reported to have replied that he understood the German Statesmen's inability to comprehend British action, but that England attached importance to the *'scrap of paper because it bore her signature as well as that of Germany.'* *The scrap of paper of course guaranteed Belgian neutrality. British: (Pub. Birn Bros.)*

33 French propaganda card. The German soldier boastingly lists the numbers of men and equipment they have. The French soldier's dismissive reply politely translated equates to *'So what? Clear off.' French.*

34 *Feldpostkarte.* As the Germans overran Belgium, so refugees fled into neutral Holland, and to stop the flow and to reduce the manpower needed to guard the border, the Germans built a lethal double line 2,000 volt electric fence which ran for over 100 miles. Here the poor cat is being electrified and the sentry really does not need to say *'Halt who goes there'*! The sign on the barbed wire proclaims, *'High tension electricity. Danger of death'*. See also card 232. *German.*

THE CANADIANS.

From North to South, from East
    to West,
The Canadians give their very
    best,
Leaving their homes forsaking all
Responding nobly to the call
Of King and Country, round the flag
They rally grandly; do they lag?
No! The trumpet calls, and off
    they go
To help their brothers, downhearted
    No!

G.L.H

ST. GEORGE FOR MERRY
    ENGLAND
ST. ANDREW FOR THE SCOT,
ST. PATRICK FOR OLD
    IRELAND—
THEY HAVE HELPED US
    HAVE THEY NOT?
THEY HAVE LIFTED US TO
    HONOUR
THEY HAVE HELPED TO
    MAKE US FREE
FOR THE UNION IS ENGLAND
    AND ENGLAND—
    UNITY!
        CLEMENT SCOTT.

"UNITED WE STAND"
"SHOULDER TO SHOULDER AND SWORD WITHIN HAND"

35

36

The Glory of a
Lion is his
Mane.

COPYRIGHT.

37

35 Canadian support for 'The Motherland' was virtually instant and unanimous when war broke out. Prime Minister Robert Borden authorised mobilisation and thousands flocked to recruit. By October 1914 the 1st Contingent of the Canadian Expeditionary Force crossed the Atlantic. After training on Salisbury Plain, the first troops to land on the Continent in December 1914 were Princess Patricia's Canadian Light Infantry. From then on the Canadians fought with bravery in many theatres. Statistics vary but it is estimated that out of a force of some 620,000, their casualties were c67,000 killed, with c172,000 wounded. *British: (Pub. E.Mack, Hampstead.)*

36 7th Hussars, 3rd Dragoon Guards, Life Guards, Seaforth Highlanders, Gordon Highlanders, Royal Horse Artillery, Royal Scots Fusiliers, 16th Lancers – all united to fight for England. Many of these famous Regiments won new battle honours in the next four years. *British*: (*Pub. Rotary Photo Co.)*

37 *'A tribute to our colonies'* by William Armitage. This well known novelty card spells out the words, *Canada, India, Australia, New Zealand and African Colonies'* in the lion's mane with the comment that 'the mane protects the lion.' *British: (Pub. Boots the Chemist.)*

38

39

38 Generals from Belgium, Russia, France, Britain, Italy, Japan and Serbia 'unite against the *Barbarians*'. Posted 30 July 1915 from Army Post Office 3, with the BEF in France. The representation of the Germans as barbarians was a main plank of Allied propaganda. *French: Artist Albert Beerts. Passed by Censor 1332.*

39 The Allies. Left to right are German, Bulgarian, Turkish and Austrian boy soldiers depicting the Central Powers. Posted 18 August 1916. *German.*

Italy followed a devious path in 1914. She had formed the Triple Alliance with Germany and Austro-Hungary who assumed that she would be on their side. They scathingly condemned her perfidy when, after coldly bargaining with both sides, she eventually decided that her territorial interests would best be served by signing a secret treaty in London with France, Russia and Britain on 26 April 1915. She declared war on Austro-Hungary in May 1915 and finally on Germany in May 1916.

Greece's route was also tortuous. King Constantine was pro-German, expected a German victory and favoured neutrality, while his Prime Minister, Venizelos, had territorial ambitions in Bulgaria and Turkey and Allied sympathies. When Constantine abdicated, Venizelos brought Greece in with the Allies in 1917.

Like Greece, *Rumania* coveted territory in Hungary and Bulgaria and, encouraged by Allied successes on several fronts, declared war on Germany in late August 1916. She contributed little to the Allied cause and by the end of the year was overrun by German forces.

The final entry into the Great War which had the most significant effect on its course was that of the *United States of America*. Until their entry the War was essentially European – all other non-European combatants, like the Commonwealth countries, were under the leadership of a European power. America's interests and prosperity were closely bound with Europe, however, and she found her early 'neutrality' difficult to maintain, especially when the British Blockade of Germany affected her trade. President Wilson's dilemma was to protect America's rights on the high seas without violating her neutrality. Britain's propaganda machine finally proved more effective than Germany's in whipping up American feelings.

The sinking of the *Lusitania* with loss of American life began to make President Wilson's neutral stand untenable, and when five American ships were torpedoed in March by U boats, Wilson decided : It is a fearful thing to lead this great, peaceful people into war, but the right is more precious than peace', and declared war on Germany on 6 April 1917.

Her entry was just in time to mobilise, train and despatch troops to the Front to balance the Allied loss of another power – *Russia*. The Bolshevik revolution in October 1917 effectively ended Russia's participation in the Great War. On 3 December Lenin's Government signed an Armistice with the Central Powers and on 3 March 1918 the Treaty of Brest Litovsk was signed. It deprived Russia of her Baltic Provinces, the Ukraine and some of the Caucasian border lands. Its terms were harsh, but Russia had no choice, as she desperately needed to end her participation in the crippling War.

As this lethal game of dominoes was being played out, symbolic representations of the combatants were soon appearing on postcards on sale in all the countries concerned. The most usual and attractive form taken – especially by British publishers like A. Vivian Mansell and James Henderson – was that of portraits of pretty girls or children in national costume. They showed archetypal national characteristics – mysterious Japan, gay Italy, proud gipsy Serbia, brave little Belgium, alluring France and regal Russia – and many artists produced such series, like E. C. Brinsley, Flora White and Sager in France. But the obvious way of depicting a nation was by showing its flag.

The Central Powers used the United flag theme on greetings cards, for Christmas, Easter and the New Year.

America's eventual entry into the War was greeted by an exuberant spate of cards showing the Stars and Stripes. It was now added to the array of Allied flags or was carried aloft by heroic American maidens. *We have waited for you so long* and *Last, but not Least*, were popular captions on French and British postcards.

40

41

40 The Allies are shown as England, France, Belgium, Russia, Servia, Japan and Italy – but as yet no America. *British: (Pub. J. Salmon.)*

41 Showing the flags of Russia – Imperial, National and Naval – posted 30 December 1915. During 1915 the Germans had adopted an aggressive attitude towards the Russians as opposed to their defensive attitude on the Western Front. Over Christmas 1915, General Falkenhayn, the German Chief of Staff, believing that the heavy Russian losses and impending internal political strife would now keep the Russians quiet, recommended that the German offensive in 1916 be switched to the West. *British: (Pub. W. N. Sharpe.)*

42 The heads of State of Great Britain, France, Russia and Belgium. Posted 23 September 1914. *British: The Great War. Series 1. (Pub. Jarrolds.)*

42

The final Allied version showed Serbia, Russia, France, Great Britain, Belgium, Italy, Portugal, Rumania, Montenegro, Japan, the U.S.A. – and even Cuba and Panama! On the Central Powers' side, the flags of Austro-Hungary, Germany, Turkey and Bulgaria waved together – while Switzerland and her protecting neutrality were wooed by both sides.

The leaders were also grouped together on postcards; *All against the Barbarians*, proclaimed Allied cards, while the Central Powers pointed out the apparent unfairness of *Four Against Eight* (as it was in 1915).

Mostly, these prolific series of colourful flags and pretty girls in costume, which were produced at the outbreak of hostilities and as each new country came into the War, appear ironic in their naive innocence to those who know the full story of the horror that was to come in the next four years.

43

43 Uncle Sam repays Lafayette for his help. On 13 June 1777 the impetuous 19-year old French aristocrat arrived in America with a small group of friends to fight in the War of Independence, where he served as a Major General through several bloody campaigns. Returning briefly to France he obtained further support from France in October 1778. His efforts were crowned by the defeat of the British at Yorktown in October 1781. France never forgot their debt to this gallant French Marquis. *American: (Pub. Merval Corp, N.Y.)*

44 France honours her Allies, especially the French Colonials from North Africa and the British Indian forces. An estimated 500,000 French Colonials were deployed, some as fighting forces, others as labourers, of whom some 71,000 were kia or mia. They came from Algeria, Madagascar, Morocco, Senegal and Tunisia. Gradually their colourful (but conspicuous) uniforms were changed to khaki. *French: (Pub. unmarked.)*

44

The Men who Went to War

In 1914 people still thought that wars were won by Great Captains, by individuals whose personal qualities alone would virtually decide the outcome. This belief, common to all the combatants, was strongly reflected in their picture postcards. Royalty, Presidents, Prime Ministers, leaders of the Church, personalities of all sorts had been popular subjects on cards for over a decade. Now the familiar figures began to appear in uniform and were joined by new ones, by Generals, by Admirals, all emphasizing the national characteristics of their Nation. The French saw President Poincaré as their 'Royal' figurehead. The mystical elements of *Honneur* and *La Patrie* coupled with waving banners, are typical ingredients of the French cards, reflecting their policy of basing their tactics upon the moral *élan* of attack. The Germans relied heavily upon the Kaiser, who even in family groups with his six sons retains a severe unsmiling image. Born with a paralysed left arm, his head tilted to the left and deaf in the left ear, the Kaiser perhaps found it difficult to smile. When he was four years old, he was forced to wear a strong girdle around his middle to which was fixed a steel rod reaching up the spine, with a collar in front to grip the neck. This was only one of many painful treatments he endured throughout his childhood. The severity of his image softens a little, however, when coupled with the pictures of Emperor Franz Joseph, generally looking bearded and benign.

UNSER STEUERMANN.
UES' VATERLAND MAGST RÜHIG SEIN.

The British Royal Family struck a true British compromise in their card portraits. They were softer than the Germans, but less extroverted than the French. At Christmas 1914 every soldier and sailor received a present from Princess Mary – a beautiful brass box containing chocolate and tobacco. The lid was embossed with the Princess's head and acknowledged Belgium, Japan, Russia, Montenegro, Serbia and France. With the box, the soldiers and sailors received a postcard of the King and Queen, the King in naval or military uniform as appropriate. These postcards and brass boxes can still be found today, often in perfect condition. The gift reflected the general belief that the War would be over in six months: but by 1915 there would be too many soldiers and sailors and too little brass for such a gesture.

The British Empire made a major contribution to the Allied cause: India's participation was second only to that of the U.K. Imperial Indian State Princes, such as

NICOLAS II, EMPEREUR DE RUSSIE   GEORGE V, ROI D'ANGLETERRE   ALBERT, ROI DES BELGES
152. NOS FRÈRES D'ARMES

46

WORLD WAR 1914~1916.

EGYPT 1882-96   INDIA 1902-08
KHARTUM 1898   ATBARA 1898
OMDURMAN 1898   SOUDAN 1885
S. AFRICA 1899-1902   THE NILE 1885

24ᵗʰ JUNE 1850. ~   ~ 5ᵗʰ JUNE 1916.

FIELD-MARSHAL EARL KITCHENER.
PERISHED WITH THE SINKING OF H.M.S. HAMPSHIRE.
5ᵗʰ JUNE 1916.
7626. K.   ROTARY PHOTO. E.C.

47

691.L.   GENERAL LEMAN.   SEAGLES POSTCARDS.
THE GALLANT BELGIAN COMMANDER AND DEFENDER OF LIÈGE.

48

45 The Kaiser at the wheel of the SMS *Hohenzollern* – 'Our Helmsman'. During the War, lumbago and rheumatism were added to the many disabilities he had suffered since birth, notably a withered left arm. Despite his handicaps – or perhaps even as a result of the disciplines he was forced to employ to overcome them – the Kaiser cut a fine figure, especially when posing for artist and photographers. *German: (Pub: Adolf Engel, Berlin.)*

46 *'Our Brothers in Arms'*. Notice the extraordinary family resemblance between Nicholas II (on the left) and King George V who were cousins. *French: from a painting. Posted 31 March 1915. Passed by Censor C98*

47 Kitchener Memorial card, June 1916. The Hero of Egypt, India and South Africa, Kitchener was England's most distinguished soldier. When he was appointed Secretary for War in August 1914 it was the first time in Britain's history that a soldier had total charge of the country's War effort. He was one the few 'experts' to realize that the War would last beyond Christmas 1914. He was drowned when HMS *Hampshire* sank on 5 June 1916. *British: (Pub. Rotary Photo Co.)*

48 General Leman, son of the Director of the
Brussels Military school, completed the building
of the forts at Liège and by skilful movement of
a small force within the defences, delayed the
advance of the German armies in 1914. *British:
(Pub. Beagles.)*

49 General Sir John French commanded the
B.E.F. in France throughout the retreat from
Mons. During the Retreat he asked Kitchener's
permission to withdraw his weary forces from the
line. Kitchener refused. French's controversial
love letters to his mistress in England at the time
were auctioned at Sotheby's in 1976. *British: (Pub.
Valentine.)*

50 British soldiers and sailors received a gift from
H.R.H. Princess Mary's Fund at Christmas 1914.
The gift comprised a small brass tin containing
cigarettes and tobacco (or chocolates for non-
smokers) and this postcard. Sailors received a
postcard showing the King in Naval uniform.
British: (Official Christmas Card.)

49

50

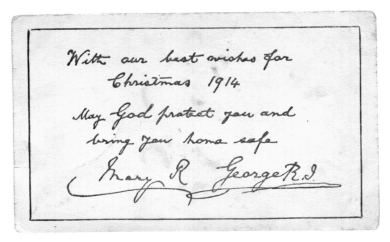

51

52

53

51 The reverse of 50, showing the Royal couple's Christmas message.

52 The Leaders of the Allies. 'Honour. Fatherland. Strength in Union'. *French: 1914.*

53 Eleftherios Venizelos was Prime Minister of Greece 1910-1920. Credited with being "the maker of modern Greece", he brought his country into the war on the side of the Allies. This led to 'The Schism' that tore the country apart as King Constantine wished to remain neutral (his wife was German). *Italian.*

54 Generalfeldmarshall von Hindenburg with his Staff. To his right is Generalleutnant Ludendorff (No 1), to his left Oberstleutnant Hoffmann (No 2) – a bomb-thrower's dream gathering. Recalled from retirement in 1914, Hindenburg was appointed Chief of the German General Staff in 1916. This gave him great military and political power. *German. Photo Kuhlewindt.*

55 Official card to raise funds for the Red Cross. The Kaiser (left) and Emperor Franz Joseph. Red Cross cards were issued by both sides and would form the theme of an interesting and valuable collection. *German.*

the Maharajahs of Gwalior and Kishangarh, offered money, horses, men, themselves and even ships, which were 'graciously accepted' by H.M. King George. Beagles, the prolific publishers of Royal photographic postcards, produced many series of the personalities of the War and a complete collection of Allied leaders could be put together even today.

One degree behind the Royalty came the military and civilian leaders. In Germany Hindenburg, Ludendorff, Moltke and von Falkenhayn were the favourites, but above all it was Hindenburg. In August 1914 Hindenburg was sent, with Ludendorff as his Chief of Staff, to the Russian

Generalfeldmarschall von Hindenburg
mit seinem engeren Stabe.
(1) Generalleutnant Ludendorf, (2) Oberstleutnant Hoffmann.

54

55

56

57

Hon. Major-General
H.H. Maharaja
Sir Pratap Singh
Bahadur,
G.C.S.I., K.C.B.

58

56 Prince Alexander was appointed Regent In June 1914, a period when he was suspected of being a member of the Serbian Black Hand (qv). He became titular Commander in Chief of the Serbian Army when war broke out. The Serbs fought gallantly in the first months of the war but the army was driven out of the country in 1915 to exile in Corfu. They recovered to fight in Salonika in 1918. Independence was gained in December 1918 and in 1921 Alexander came to the throne and changed the country's name to Yugoslavia. He was assassinated on a State Visit to France in 1934. *British: (Pub. Beagles.)*

57 The Maharajah used some of his immense wealth to support the Empire's war effort, providing 'thousands of horses', men and funding for a hospital ship and convalescent home. His loyalty was rewarded with Hon doctorates from Cambridge, Oxford and Edinburgh Universities. *British: (Pub. Beagles.)*

58 The much-decorated HH Maharajah Sir Pratap Singh, Baradur of Idar, was a career officer in the Indian Army. A close friend of the British Royal Family he commanded his forces in Flanders in 1914-15 at the age of 70. Created Lt-General in 1915 he later fought in Palestine. Posted 19 December 1914. *British: (Pub. A & C Black. 'Our Indian Armies Series.)*

59 *Men of the Moment'* was a catch phrase of 1914. Here a selection of timely military and naval high-ranking officers surround HM King George V and the serving Royal Princes. *British.*

Gen. Sir H. Smith Dorrien.

Lord Kitchener.

Field-Marshal Sir John French.

H.R.H. Prince of Wales.

H.M. King George V.

Prince Albert.

Admiral Sir W. May.

Admiral Sir John R Jellicoe.

Admiral Sir John Fisher.

MEN OF THE MOMENT

59

Front. Two Russian armies under Generals Samsonov and Rennenkampf were advancing into East Prussia, pushing back the Germans. Within two weeks Hindenburg defeated the Russians at Tannenberg and he immediately became the most popular man in Germany. An enormous wooden statue was erected to him in Berlin into which his admirers drove thousands of nails. They paid one mark for each nail and the money went to war charities.

Von Moltke was the nephew of the famous Count von Moltke, who achieved fame in the Franco-German War of 1870 and who died in 1891. In 1914 Moltke was already 66 years old, and in ill health, yet he was placed in charge of German operations. The plan of invasion, known as the Schlieffen Plan, was bold and simple. This plan might well have finished the War in a few weeks, but Moltke baulked at violating Dutch neutrality, reduced the concentration of force against the right wing in France and advanced east of Paris. Early in November 1914 his health failed and he was relieved of his post. He died on 18 June 1916.

60 With Von Hindenburg
is Graf Frans Conrad Von
Hötzendorf, the somewhat
conservative and often
controversial military strategist
of the Austro-Hungarian
Army. His onslaught on
Serbia in 1914 was long and
initially very costly. When
the new Charles 1 succeeded
in November 1916 (the last
Austro-Hungarian Emperor)
he took overall command of the
Army and Conrad was reduced
to commanding an Army Group
on the Italian front until mid–
1918. *Austrian: (Pub. WRB &
Co, Wien.) Artist R.A. Höger.*

61 General Haig commanded
the B.E.F. First Corps in
1914 and went on to become
Commander in Chief. The
message on the reverse is
from someone trying to avoid
conscription and says, '*... shall
be pleased when I know definitely
that I am exempt*'. What a card
to choose! Posted February
1918. *British: (Pub. Beagles.)*

62 General Smith-Dorrien
commanded the B.E.F. Second
Corps which stopped von Kluck
at Mons. Smith-Dorrien's
personality was an important
factor in the maintenance of
the morale of his men during
the long Retreat that followed
Mons. Frederick Coleman, an
American civilian volunteer
who took part in the retreat as
a driver, remembers. '*It was
good to see Smith-Dorrien's face
and hear his voice… As he looked
my way he smiled… It was of
inestimable value that morning…
Smith-Dorrien's smile. It put heart
into many a man.*' Posted 15 July
1919. British: (Pub. Beagles.)

R. A. HÖGER pinx.   Hötzendorf-Hindenburg.

60

GENERAL SIR DOUGLAS HAIG.

61

691.S.   GENERAL SIR H. L. SMITH-DORRIEN.
THE HERO OF THE BRILLIANT RETREAT.

"*I cannot close the brief account of this glorious stand
of the British troops without putting on record my deep
appreciation of the valuable services rendered by General
Sir Horace Smith-Dorrien.*

*I say without hesitation that the saving of the left
wing of the Army under my command on the morning of
the 26th August could never have been accomplished
unless a commander of rare and unusual coolness, intre-
pidity, and determination had been present to personally
conduct the operation."*   — Sir John French to Lord Kitchener.

62

Eric von Falkenhayn, a Prussian General, succeeded von Moltke as Chief of the General Staff of the Army in November 1914. He was instrumental in planning the successful Russian campaigns of 1914 and 1915, and for the over-running of Serbia in the winter of 1915–16. He advocated the attack on Verdun and was blamed when the attack failed. In August and September 1916 the Germans and Austrians agreed to the establishment of a General Supreme Command with the Kaiser at its head, Hindenburg signed the agreement for the Germans and took the place of Falkenhayn as Chief of the General Staff.

It is interesting to note that most of the postcards available today are of Commanders who featured early on in the War. Presumably more cards were produced of them than of the many lesser Generals that followed in the subsequent years, or perhaps, as the slaughter mounted, Generals became less popular. A novel collection may be made by gathering together cards of individuals who were adversaries in a particular battle or campaign. General von Kluck and General Smith-Dorrien provide an example of this. General von Kluck commanded the German First Army: his aggressive advance through Belgium was stopped at Mons by the newly arrived B.E.F. Commanded by Sir John French. The British were greatly outnumbered. It was their skill with their rifles that won the day and enabled them to fire so rapidly that the Germans believed that they were using machine guns. Von Kluck himself described the B.E.F. as 'incomparable'.

Two days later, on 27 August, General Horace Smith-Dorrien with his Second British Corps fought the biggest battle the British Army had fought since Waterloo, successfully disengaging his troops from von Kluck's forces. This began the historic retreat from Mons, which ended at

63

63 Machine-woven silk card of George V. Throughout the War King George and Queen Mary set a personal example in all things – including strict observance of rationing, digging for victory and total abstinence from alcohol. *French.*

64 Embroidered silk card, with hand-tinted photo inset of King Victor Emmanuel of Italy. Victor Emmanuel took an active part in the War, moving to the Front when Italy declared War on Austria, where he remained until the Armistice. He visited the trenches and hospitals and shared the hardships of his soldiers. *French.*

65 Machine-woven silk card. *'Papa'* Joffre created Plan 17, the French defence against the German invasion. He held strategic responsibility for perpetuating the outmoded French belief in the use of waves of men in frontal attacks, despite the readily apparent superiority of the machine gun over the infantry. Although considered a hero for his successful defence of the Marne, he was eventually removed from command following the disasters at Verdun in 1916. *French.*

64

65

GENERAL-COLONEL von KLUCK

66

67

(Titelblatt aus der Münchner „Jugend" 1914 Nr. 51.)

66 Von Kluck commanded the extreme right wing of the German forces and pursued the B.E.F. from Mons to the Marne. His forces were directly opposed to those of Smith-Dorrien. The Tommies called him 'Old one o'clock'. Hand-written note on reverse says, '*Reported captured many times.*' *American: (Pub. HH Co, N Y.)*

67 General von Hindenburg who, as a result of his victory over the Russian forces under Rennenkampf at Tannenburg, was made Field Marshal and Supreme Commander of the German Forces. Portrait by Angelo Janke which formed the title page of the magazine, *Jugend*, in 1914. Posted 3 June 1916. *German. (Pub. Knorr & Hirth, Munich.)*

GENERALS OF THE BRITISH ARMY. *Portraits by Francis Dodd.*

Lieut.-Gen. The Rt. Hon. JAN C. SMUTS,
P.C., K.C., M.L.A., Companion of Honour,

who, formerly in arms against the British, commanded the Southern Armies, which in 1915 swept the south of German S.W. Africa, and later the Expeditionary Force which in the spring and summer of 1916 drove the Germans off British territory, and penned them into a small area in the south of German East Africa.

68

GENERALS OF THE BRITISH ARMY. *Portraits by Francis Dodd.*

General The Hon. SIR J. H. G. BYNG,
K.C.B., K.C.M.G., M.V.O.,

who commanded the Canadian Corps when it took Courcelette in the Battle of the Somme, and later when it stormed Vimy Ridge. Under his command, the Third Army made a memorable advance in the neighbourhood of Cambrai in November, 1917.

69

GENERALS OF THE BRITISH ARMY. *Portraits by Francis Dodd.*

Lieut.-General SIR W. N. CONGREVE,
V.C., K.C.B., M.V.O.,

who commanded the XIII Corps at the capture of Montauban and Longueval and in the desperate fighting at Guillemont in the Battle of the Somme.

70

GENERALS OF THE BRITISH ARMY. *Portraits by Francis Dodd.*

Lieut.-General SIR H. E. WATTS,
K.C.B., C.M.G.,

who commanded the famous 7th Division in the Battle of the Somme, when it captured Mametz and Bazentin le Petit.

71

73

GENERALS OF THE BRITISH ARMY.   *Portraits by Francis Dodd.*

General SIR H. S. HORNE, K.C.B.,

who commanded the First Army which captured Vimy Ridge with
11,000 German prisoners and over 100 guns in April, 1917.   He is one
of the few Artillery Generals.

72

GENERALS OF THE BRITISH ARMY.   *Portraits by Francis Dodd.*

General SIR E. H. ALLENBY,
G.C.M.G., K.C.B.

who, after a victorious career on the Western Front, commanded the
British Army which took Beersheba, Gaza and Jerusalem in the
Autumn of 1917.

68, 69, 70, 71, 72, 73 Examples of a superb
series illustrating Generals and Admirals
of the British Army by portraitist Francis
Dodd RA. Dodd replaced his brother-in-
law Muirhead Bone as Official War Artist
(appointed by the War Propaganda Bureau).
No. 70 is General Congreve VC whose son
'Billy' also won the VC and was killed in
France. *British.*

the Marne, where the tide of invasion was turned. General Smith-Dorrien played a very personal part in the battle and in the retreat, constantly riding amongst his troops and encouraging them.

The B.E.F. Consisted of two Corps, Smith-Dorrien's and the First Corps under General Sir Douglas Haig. Haig was not confident in French's ability to command the B.E.F. In December 1975 the Imperial War Museum bought at Sotheby's, 99 love letters written by Sir John French during his command of the B.E.F. They were addressed to his mistress, Mrs. Winifred Bennett, and were said to contain details of troop movements and of the itineraries of wartime leaders who visited him, including King George. After the disastrous battle of Loos in December 1915 French was relieved of his command and replaced by Haig. General Sir Douglas Haig was an extremely thorough, clear-thinking though stubborn cavalryman, who after the War was blamed for the heavy casualties in his Somme and Passchendaele offensives. Although the Somme and Passchendaele had not been tactical successes, they had a strategic importance in that the German losses in men, in particular junior N.C.O.'s, were large enough to affect the overall pool of manpower. One of Clausewitz's 'Principles of War', most of which are still taught in the British Army today, is 'Maintain the Aim', i.e. always bear in mind the ultimate objective. Haig achieved a significant step forward in the ultimate objective of defeating Germany, not by winning ground, but by killing German soldiers. The German well of manpower was much smaller than the combined strength of the Allies, and though British and German losses were roughly equal, the Germans were far less able to stand the loss of men on a national basis than the Allies. Some authorities believe that without the 400,000 casualties sustained on the Somme, the Germans could have continued the War into 1919.

Haig was made a Field Marshal in 1917 and on his retirement in 1921 he became the first President of the British Legion.

General John Pershing commanded the American Expeditionary Force when it arrived in France in 1917. Haig was impressed by Pershing's A.D.C., whom he described as a 'fire-eater, and longs for a fray'. That A.D.C was Captain George Patton, who in the Second World War was to earn the nickname 'Pell Mell Patton' because of his aggressive armoured advances. General Pershing rose from humble beginnings. He saw service against the Indians, Apaches and Sioux, and commanded the Mexican campaign against Francisco Villa. In France he insisted upon maintaining the separate identity of the American forces and it was not until September 1918 that the longed for independent American battlefield victory took place on the Saint Mihiel Salient. National pride and prestige were satisfied at last and Pershing's army grew to over four million men. In 1919 in recognition of his achievements, Congress created for him the rank of General of the Armies, making him the highest ranking military officer in American history.

General Joffre had a humble start too, like Pershing, and rose to the highest command. He took part in the defence of Paris in 1870 and was trained as a military engineer. The French plan of campaign in the event of a war with Germany, known as Plan 17, was laid by Joffre as Chief of the General Staff and when war broke out he became Commander in Chief of the Armies. The early failures in battle contrasted strongly with the optimistic forecasts. This 'let-down' roused public opinion against Joffre, but the successful stand on the Marne made him a hero. Nevertheless, the inadequate preparations for Verdun in 1916 and the disasters on the Somme, again raised opinion against him and he was replaced by General Nivelle in December 1916. He was, however, generally regarded affectionately and known as 'Papa Joffre'. On his replacement he received the honorary title of Marshal of France.

France's most famous soldier was Field Marshal Ferdinand Foch, whose greatest asset was his ability to persuade the Allied military commanders to work together, a position strongly similar to that of General Eisenhower 40 years later. In April 1917 he became Chief of

Command of the Allied Armies and by his strength of will gained the maximum cooperation between General Pétain commanding the French, Haig commanding the British and Pershing commanding the Americans. It was Foch who headed the Allied delegation which presented the Armistice terms to the German envoys in the Forest of Compiègne on 8 November and who successfully concluded the negotiations resulting in the German signature. He received the acclaim of Europe as the man who had secured victory, became a Marshal of France, a British Field Marshal, a Polish Marshal and later a member of the Académie Française.

While Haig eventually became the British military figurehead, during the first two years of the War it had been Lord Kitchener who had represented the Nation's image of its fighting forces. Born in County Kerry in 1850 he entered the Army through the Royal Military Academy, Woolwich, and like Joffre joined the Engineers. He commanded the victorious force at Omdurman in 1898 for which he was raised to the peerage and, following a spell as Chief of Staff to Lord Roberts in South Africa, he commanded the forces there from 1900 until the end of the War in 1902. He was an extremely thorough and far sighted individual with great administrative ability, developed through service in Egypt and India. On 6 August 1914 Kitchener became Secretary for War, thus taking complete control of the war effort away from civilian authority, and immediately planned for a three year war. In this approach he was almost entirely alone as most people believed that the War would be over by Christmas.

Kitchener's recruiting campaign was superb. The now familiar poster, with pointing finger and eyes that follow the onlooker, together with his stirring appeals to the Nation,

Prince George wounded.   S Tchernoff

GENERAL VON RENNENKAMPF.

CROQUIS DE GUERRE 1915

Le " Landsturm " de Berlin se met en route
pour la Guerre

423

76

74 Prince George of Greece shared his father King Constantine's sympathies with the Central Powers and had served in the Prussian Guard. In June 1917 George followed his father into exile and was denied accession to the throne. Finally, following a complicated series of events when his younger brother Alexander, who succeeded to the throne, died of septicemia from a monkey bite in October 1920, his father was then re-instated only to abdicate again in September 1922. George then became King of Greece. Russian artist Samsom Tchernoff also depicted the sufferings of Serbia and its Royal family. *Probably American.*

75 General Rennenkampf, commanding the Russian forces with General Samsonov in Prussia, was defeated at Tannenburg by Hindenburg and Ludendorff. *British: (Pub. Tuck.) Notabilities Series. Card No. 4321.*

76 Excited German conscripts en route from Berlin to Paris and the war. Note the caricature of Joffre being drawn on the bustling carriage and their shaven heads. The message on the back is written by a *Poilu 'in my trench'* to his *'Dear Wife'* and his little daughter. He misses his family and dreads the winter

The flag he loves is the flag you love,
He swore its honor to defend.
One hundred million Americans
Will back him to the very end!

77

GUERRE 1914-17

Le Maréchal JOFFRE et le Général PERSHING

(Ph. M. D d'après l'Illustration)

78

ahead, but he must *'accept his fate'*. One wonders if they were ever reunited... *French. Used 11 November 1915.*

77 Thomas Woodrow Wilson, 28th President of the United States, who strove to keep America neutral. The German U-Boat campaign and the sinking of the *Lusitania* forced his declaration of war on Germany. His preference for peace did not change, however, and led to his formulation of the famous '14 Points' as the basis for peace terms. *American: (Pub. Buck. New York.) Flag Series No. 4.*

brought men flocking to the recruiting stations. His breadth of responsibility was enormous and included the provision of guns and ammunition for the new and constantly growing army. Some criticism has been levelled at him over the so-called shell scandal of 1916 when it was widely reported that the British armies were short of ammunition. A further great asset of his was his personal contact with and influence over the leaders of France and Russia, and it was at the request of the Tsar that he sailed from Scapa Flow for Russia on the cruiser *Hampshire* on 5 June 1916. The ship struck a mine in the Channel and Kitchener and 800 officers and men were drowned. There were 12 survivors. The Queen Mother immediately headed an organization to place a memorial to Kitchener in St. Paul's Cathedral and the amazing sum of over £700,000 poured in from all over the Empire in answer to her appeal. The picture postcard industry reacted immediately and black-bordered cards of Kitchener were on sale in a few days and these became treasured inspiring mementoes for individuals and households around the country.

Civilian leaders, too, featured strongly on early postcards, generally posing in an impressive manner. Warlike connections usually guaranteed a politician a place on a card, but as the

Rt. Hon. Winston S. Churchill,
First Lord of the Admiralty.

EMPRUNT DE LA LIBÉRATION
Les Vainqueurs de la Marne 1914-1918

MARECHAL FOCH
né à Tarbes (Hautes-Pyrénées)
Général Commandant d'Armée

Maréchal Commandant en Chef les Armées alliées

114   Son Altesse Royale Léopold
DUC DE BRABANT (*Août 1915*)   GALLI PARIS

81

78 General Pershing became the highest ranking military officer in American history. Known as '*Black Jack*', a veteran of the Indian Wars and the Mexican Campaign, Pershing strove to retain the U.S. forces as an independent command on the Western Front. At one time his chauffeur in France was the future air ace, Eddie Rickenbacker. Here he is greeted by Marshal Joffre. *French: (Sold at the Musée de l'Armée in aid of the wounded and mutilated.)*

79 A rare picture. Churchill, who was First Lord of the Admiralty in 1914, ordered Naval Mobilization before War was declared and without waiting for Cabinet authority. He was involved in controversy over the Dardanelles campaign, which he had promoted, and when left out of the Coalition Government in 1915, served in the trenches in Belgium at 'Plugstreet'. In the autumn of 1916 he returned to Parliamentary life and was appointed Minister of Munitions under Lloyd George and had a great deal to do with the development of the tank. *Posted 26 September 1914. British: (Pub. Valentine.).*

80 Field Marshal Foch became supreme Commander of the Allied forces, although his objectives during the latter part of the War were frequently questioned by Generals Haig and Pershing. He was later appointed President of the Allied Military Committee which administered the terms of the Armistice at about the time that this card was published. *French, official card raising a 5.65% War Loan.*

81 Drawing by Maurice Pepin, a popular artist who normally drew glamorous pin-ups. The message reads, '*... by the time you get this we shall be around the fighting zone again.*' Leopold is shown here as the Duke of Brabant. At the tender age of 13 in August 1915 he was 'presented' by his parents to the Belgian 3rd Division of the Belgian Army, became King of the Belgians in 1934, was captured by the Germans in World War Two and abdicated in favour of his son, Baudouin, in 1951. *French: (Pub. S. Herbert. Paris.)*

82 Moody Italian soldier by sought-after Artist Umberto Brunelleschi, who made his reputation as illustrator and designer in Paris before returning to Italy in 1914 to serve in the Italian Army. After the war he returned to Paris, designing costumes and sets for many prestigious stage productions and Josephine Baker's costumes. *Italian: Official card for the Italian 3rd Army.*

83 Jolly German soldier with his sausage and his stein of beer. Reverse printed with words and music for a chorus of '*Leichte Wahl*', literally translated as '*Easy Choice*', a typical soldiers' song. *German: (Pub. C. G. Roder, Leipzig.)*

83A Powerful image of 3rd Bavarian Inf. Regt (of Prinz Karl von Bayern), commemorating their fallen comrades. At first glance this has an air of modernity, much like a WW2 image, but it is clearly posted on 10.1.18 with a regimental imprint. *German: (Pub. Ph. J. Pfeiffer, Augsburg.)*

84 Somewhat posed Italian Fusilier mounts a 'lightening attack', his comrades hiding in the rocky hillside behind him. On the reverse a French soldier in Rome in 1916 complains to his mother about his lack of letters, and assumes she is still 'in a bad mood'! Regular letters from home are a major plank of morale in all armies. Posted 10 June 1916. *Italian: (Pub. STA.)*

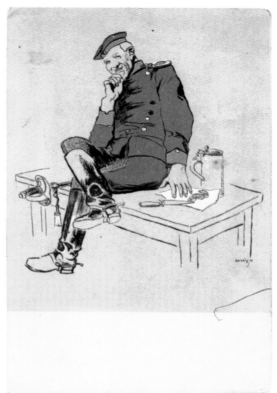

83

84

83A

85

War progressed and life at home became harder, the number of individuals popular enough to feature on cards gradually diminished.

A man most difficult to find on 1914-18 postcards is the young Winston Churchill. At the outbreak of the War he was First Lord of the Admiralty, a post he was to return to again on the first day of the Second World War in 1939. He was strongly blamed for the failure of the Dardanelles campaign which he had sponsored and was left out of the Coalition Government formed in 1915. He served in the trenches in France as a Lieutenant Colonel in the 6th Royal Scots Fusiliers from 1915 until the autumn of 1916 but returned to parliamentary duties as Minister of Munitions under Lloyd George and had much to do with the development of the tank.

It is intriguing to reflect that while Churchill was in the trenches, a few miles away in the German trenches was the man who, almost half a century later, would lead Germany against Britain, a Britain led by Churchill. Adolph Hitler was in the first battle of Ypres and after two years' continuous service in the trenches, was wounded in October 1916. Another pair of future enemies were also cutting their teeth in France: Montgomery, serving with the Royal Warwickshire Regiment, was in the retreat from Mons, won the D.S.O. and was wounded in the chest in October 1914, one month after the man he was to confront in Africa in the 1940 s was wounded in the leg. That man was Erwin Rommel who enlisted with the 6th Wurttemberg Regiment, served on both Western and Eastern Fronts and went on to win the *Pour le Mérite* in action against the Italians.

The mass of men who went to war were soldiers, whose epitaph in all western countries is embodied in the grave of the Unknown Soldier: one soldier who characterises a Nation.

This is the way most soldiers were seen in the early heady days before the War became a grim reality nobody wanted. Thus the artists recorded what they saw through nationalistic

85 A cheery group of Royal Engineer Glee Party members. Probably in a training camp in the UK. *British.*

86 Picture by local photographer. Most camps had their own photographer. Sid sends his portrait to his 'old chum', 2nd Lt F.E. Barker of the 'West Cum Yeomanry'. *British.*

87 Young Leonard trains for the coming war. He writes to his Ma about being swamped out in camp and complains at having to leave his rifle behind in the Church Room. In Newfoundland many of the newly formed Newfoundland Regiment were volunteers from the Brigade. In the UK a battalion of the KRRC was formed from the Brigade. *British.* *(Pub. Johnson Riddle & Co, London.)*

88 German soldier, with flowers on his *pickelhaube*, bids farewell to his family. New Year card. *German: (Pub. Ottmar Zieher, Munchen.)*

86

87

88

89 *'A la Frontière'*. Swiss sentry patrolling the Swiss Border. Field Postcard for the Red Cross. 1914–1915. *Swiss. (Pub. E. Goetz, Luzern.)*

90 Uncle Sam ignores the eager under-age soldier dying to join up, in what was at that time a subtle hint to older youngsters to do just that. An appeal to Patriotism was a major feature of recruitment campaigns – notice the flag. *American.*

91, 92, 93, 94, 95, 96, 97, 98, 99, 100 Examples of a magnificent 1914/5 series of heads by Emile Dupuis who sketched the fighting soldiers of both sides. There are three main series. *Nos Alliés* (Our Allies); *Nos Poilus* (Our Hairy Ones); *Leurs Caboches* (Their Thick Skulls). Dupuis also made comments upon the contrasts between the occupied countries and the neutrals such as Holland, Switzerland and Norway. *French.*

89

eyes. A magnificent series of such representations is that produced by the French artist Emile Dupuis. The most well known sets of 'Dupuis Heads' were produced between 1914 and 1915 in three main series – *Nos Alliés* (Our Alliés), *Nos Poilus* (Our -French – Soldiers) and *Leurs Cabochos* (Their – German – Soldiers). Each nation had its artistic interpretation of its national soldier, but so did each soldier have his idea of his own new found identity. The War to most of them was an opportunity for adventure, a chance to escape from poverty and unemployment. They found and thrived upon a sense of belonging, of camaraderie and discovered a personal identity that was new and exhilarating. Photographers set up studios around the training camps, snapping thousands of picture postcards which, in many cases, were the first photographs the

90

subjects would have had taken. Whole families would enlist and send their group picture back to the parents at home. Individuals would proudly pose in their new uniform, vaunting their newly formed identity. Often the uniform would be their finest suit of clothes. Often it would also prove to be their last. Soldiers of many nationalities provided endless material for the photographer: all proud comrades in arms, all knowing that God was on their side, all knowing their cause was right, set out to fight, believing in their leaders and prepared to die for their country. Those were the men who went to war in the early days. The glamour was soon to fade, the enthusiasm to die, until by War's end, Britain would be the only country at war in 1914 whose fighting soldiers had not mutinied.

Em. Dupuis

Nich
Oct 1914

Infanterie Serbe

91

Em. Dupuis

Cettigné
1914

Infanterie Monténégrine

92

95

Em. Dupuis

Paschendaele
Nov. 1914

Cavalerie indienne

93

Em. Dupuis

Villers-Cotterets
1914

Arras
Février 1915

Infanterie Anglaise

94

96

officier d'infanterie (allemand)

97

Soldat d'infanterie (Landsturm bavarois)

98

Soldat d'infanterie (Landsturm allemand)

99

officier de Uhlan (allemand)

100

101 By WW1 the 'Zouzous' or 'Zouaves' were a mixture of conscripted North Africans and Europeans from mainland France. Their colourful, distinctive, traditional uniforms and elaborate drill were extremely popular during the American Civil War and was adopted by many units, notably the 72nd Pennsylvanians at Gettysburg. Passed by Censor 346, 21 October 1915. *French*.

101

102 '"The War" was like one enormous club to the officers and soldiers who fought in it. Membership of this club set them apart from the civilians at home who had no true conception or understanding of the horrors of the fighting. The club spirit is plainly evident here. The Brigade, a Territorial Force, was part of the 67th Division. *British: (Pub: Allwork Bros., Tonbridge.)*

102

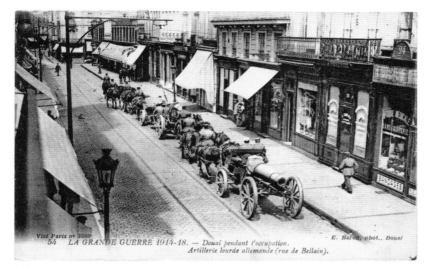

Visé Paris nº 3569
54 LA GRANDE GUERRE 1914-18. — Douai pendant l'occupation.
Artillerie lourde allemande (rue de Bellain).
E. Baron, phot., Douai

103

103 German artillery entering Douai under occupation. The photographer, E. Baron of Douai, has taken his shot from the rear of the column, indicating that it was surreptitiously obtained. Four horses are needed to pull one gun – even on pavé. *French: (Pub. Lévy Fils, Paris.)*

New Zealand Contingent passing the Law Courts London

104

104 New Zealand sent a full division as her contribution to the Allied Cause. The New Zealanders fought through some of the War's bloodiest campaigns – against the Turks in Gallipoli in 1915, and in the Ypres Salient, especially in the Passchendaele Offensive of 1917 – with exceptional courage. *British: World War Series.*

105 The Wurtembergers marching through Spa in Belgium en route to France. They arrived on the Somme in September 1914 and their daily life and battles up to July 1916 have been documented in a wonderful collection of 62 water colours by German War Artist, Albert Heim, which was exhibited by art dealers Abott & Holder in January 2013. *French: (Pub: Pays de France. 1914.)*

57. Guerre 1914. — SPA. — Défilé de Wurtembourgeois.
"Ed. Pays de France"

169   L'ARMÉE FRANÇAISE. — *Groupe de Chasseurs Alpins en tenue de campagne.* — LL.

106 French Alpine Troops or '*Chasseurs Alpins*'. The word '*chasseur*' originally applied to light infantry or cavalry regiments. At the beginning of the War there were 30 battalions of chasseurs, of which 12 were '*Chasseurs Alpins*', specially trained and equipped for mountain warfare. The origin of the 'Alpins' lies in the perceived need to protect the mountainous border from ambitious Italians. *French: (Pub. prolific photographer, Louis Lévy.)*

Officiers Anglais prenant le thé sur la route | English officers having tea on the way

107 'Everything stops for tea'. British officers live out the cliché with their French liaison officer en route. *French: (Pub. E L. D.)*

108 The Egyptian Expeditionary Force was formed in March 1916, initially to protect the Suez Canal. They subsequently fought in the Sinai and Palestine against the Turks. This card probably shows the Mountain Battery with the camels carrying light field guns. *British / Egyptian: ('Pub. E. Morhig. The English Pharmacy, Khartoum.)*

109 The wealthy Indian Princes and Maharajahs were quick and generous in answering Britain's call to her Dominions for assistance when war broke out. Caption reads: 'Many of the brave chiefs are on active service with the Indian troops In the Great War against Germany and Austria.' *British: (Pub. Beagles.)*

2 Propaganda: Patriotism & Hatred

Im Einverständnis
mit dem Central-
Comitee vom
RotenKreuz
zu
essen
Gunsten

Welcome from Ostend
to the British Troops

THE TRUTH
ABOUT
GERMAN
ATROCITIES

No. 43.

Founded
on the Report
of the Committee

 german

1915

n ein Deutscher,
ne Farben

The Patriotism

It requires strong motivation to make normal, industrious, peace-loving peoples engage whole-heartedly in war against other peoples like themselves. It requires a fierce emotional reason to persuade man joyously to kill his fellow man, or be killed by him; or woman to take pride and encourage her son or husband in taking life or sacrificing life. It requires a unity and steadfastness of purpose to make civilians endure the hardships, privations and tremendous effort required to maintain the war effort

Propaganda is the tool Governments employ to persuade their nations to support them in waging war, and to justify to the rest of the world the rightness and fairness of a particular country's entry into, and continued waging of, war. Propaganda is necessary in two phases: firstly, when war is declared, the Government has to have the active approval of the populace to set the war machinery effectively and enthusiastically in motion. Secondly, propaganda is needed not only to maintain the effort of troops and civilians, but also to keep up morale when things go badly or last for a long time. Machineries for the dissemination of propaganda were set up with varying degrees of efficiency in the main combatant countries. In his post-war memoirs, General Ludendorff credited the British machinery with far more effect than the German, to the extent of seeing it as the Allies' most powerful weapon. As Britain had no popular emotional reason to go to war with Germany, it was therefore immediately necessary to set up an organization to create such a reason artificially. Asquith, followed by Lloyd George, experimented with a series of Bureaux and Departments, with a rapid turnover of Directors. These included the Chancellor of the Duchy of Lancaster, Colonel John Buchan, Beaverbrook, Northcliffe and Sir Edward Carson. Germany was slower to act, showed a total lack of cohesion between the various departments involved, military and civil, and frequently put out contradictory stories as we shall see.

France's *Maison de la Presse* pulled heavily on the heartstrings of its people and the world with the Alsace-Lorraine crusade and, characteristically, French propaganda featured abstract ideals rather than concrete realities. Russia pursued her normal policy of keeping the peasants in total ignorance as she

The KING'S MESSAGE TO HIS ARMY.

BUCKINGHAM PALACE.

You are leaving home to fight for the safety and honour of my Empire.

Belgium, whose country we are pledged to defend, has been attacked, and France is about to be invaded by the same powerful foe.

I have implicit confidence in you, my soldiers. Duty is your watchword, and I know your duty will be nobly done.

I shall follow your every movement with deepest interest, and mark with eager satisfaction your daily progress. Indeed, your welfare will never be absent from my thoughts.

I pray God to bless you and guard you, and bring you back victorious.

GEORGE R.I.

"THIS LITTLE PIG STAYED AT HOME"

111

EN ATTENDANT PAPA! IL FAUT QUE JE PROTÈGE MAMAN, MAINTENANT
WAITING FOR DADDY.
I MUST TAKE CARE OF MUMMY NOW! No. 2

112

"FALL IN AND FOLLOW ME"

113

110 '*War Series No. 1821*'. Message on reverse reads, '*I thought this was rather good.*' *Posted 3 February 1915. British: (Pub. The Regent Pub. Co.)*

111 Artist 'AE', well known for his comic postcards. The pressure to enlist is strong. The message on the reverse reads, '*Who is not going to be a soldier? British: (Pub. Wildt & Kray.)*

112 From the Patriotic Series by Lawson Wood. The bilingual caption indicates that it was also produced for the French market. Posted on 16 July 1915 from '*Somewhere in France on Active Service*' from a father to '*My Darling Sonny, I hope you are quite well and that you will soon be like this picture. I am just as eager to come back home to you again.*' *British: (Pub. Dobson. Molle & Co.) Passed by Censor 1040.*

113 Aptly named '*Armageddon*' series. No. 21. Posted 3 December 1914. It is said that in the first month of Kitchene 's recruiting campaign 100,000 enrolled. *Posted December 1914. British.*

UP GUARDS AND AT 'EM.

114

WHEN YOU'RE READY, KAISER.

115

flung them to death in their thousands at the better equipped and trained enemy, and made little attempt to communicate with the outside world.

Because of her neutrality during the first years, the U.S.A. was a battle ground for the opposing propaganda messages of the Allies and the Central Powers. Germany wanted to keep her out, Britain wanted to bring her in. This was further complicated by the fact that the intelligent attempts of Germany's Ambassador in Washington, Count Bernstoff, were often thwarted by conflicting stories from the Berlin War Ministry.

The first propaganda campaign relied heavily in all the principal nations on a strong feeling prevalent in each of them: patriotism. It was the ideal ground for cultivating the seed of war fever. Once planted, the seed thrived like a lethal Jack's beanstalk, and the rush to the recruiting stations in Britain (where

114 Patriotic Series. No. 804. The famous slogan of the Guards – led by Britannia. It is a variation on an exhortation by Wellington to his troops at Waterloo. *British : (Pub. Inter-Art Co.)*

115 Ludgate Series No. 702 by T. Gilson, well-known humorous postcard artist. *Posted 21 December 1915. British: (Pub. E. I. H. & Co.)*

116 Bert Thomas's casual and good-humoured Tommy typifies the gutsy spirit of the British Army. Posted 22 December 1914. The caption on the reverse reads, '*Specially drawn by Mr. Bert Thomas for the 'Weekly Dispatch' Tobacco Fund, Carmelite House, London* E.C. *Every 6d will gladden the heart of a hero.*' The drawing first appeared in December 1914 and over the next four years it helped to raise £250,000. The artist, Bert Thomas, served in the Artists' Rifles. *British: (Pub. Gale & Polden, Aldershot.)*

117 From the Patriotic Series by Lawson Wood, who served in the Royal Flying Corps, plane-spotting from balloons, and was decorated for valour by the French. After the War he went on to become one of Britain's most popular comic artists, especially with his famous '*Gran'pop*' (a humorous chimpanzee) series. He died in 1957. *British: (Pub. Dobson. Molle & Co.)*

118 M. Boulanger's representation of the battered area protected by the impassable *Poilu*. The 1916 fighting at Verdun, which preceded the Battle of the Somme, was amongst the worst of the war but the Germans never took the town. The sender has written in another popular French slogan, '*On les aura*' (We'll get 'em'!) 17/2/18 on the reverse. *French.*

119 Famous military artist Harry Payne helps the recruiting campaign with heavy pressure. The seated civilian is being asked, '*What are you doing to guard the homes of England?*' On the reverse is printed a poem entitled *Fall In*, by Harold Begbie:

> *Why do they call, Sonny, why do they call*
> *For men who are brave and strong?*
> *Is it naught to you if your country fall.*
> *And Right is smashed by Wrong?*
> *Is it football still and the picture show.*
> *The pub and betting odds.*
> *When your brothers stand to the tyrant's blow*
> *And England's call is God's?'*

The card is dedicated to Earl Roberts. *British: (Pub. Tuck.)*

120 Patriotic Series No. 2574. Posted 3 April 1915. Note the heartfelt message added by the sender, '*Oh let it be soon. 1915.*' The Kaiser's ambition is cut down to size. *British: (Pub. Philco.)*

121 Fine novelty card, a montage made from stamps. Note the postmark – Army Post Office No. 2. For security reasons, numbers, not names, were used. Each Army Post Office or Field Post Office had its own number and postmark. Enthusiasts collect good 'strikes' (clear impressions of the postmark) of all the different numbers. *Posted 29 December 1915 from the YMCA. French. Passed by Censor 1076..*

122 The uniform of the British Convalescent soldier. Message on reverse reads, '*Dear Gran, Am not on crutches yet, but am going to have a try today.*' One theory for the origin of this popular cry is that it may have originated from a popular song written by Arthur Boyton in 1914. *British: (Pub. /. Salmon, Sevenoaks.)*

there was as yet no conscription) and to the conscription check-in stations in France and Germany, started in earnest as each country declared war.

The postcard was the ideal vehicle for the propagandists, especially during this first patriotic wave, disseminating their message so widely and in such vast numbers. The public obligingly distributed this message for their Governments. Cards in their millions were sent to the lads at the Front, from the Front to the loved ones at home, and between friends at home. The result was total mass coverage at no cost to the Government whatsoever, sometimes with a total unawareness of the significance of the card, that was often bought for its colourful picture alone.

The popular artists who designed peacetime postcards were soon helping Governments to put their propaganda message over. In Britain, Henry Newbolt and humorous artists like T. Gilson and L. Biggar turned their talents to more sterling stuff. Mailik, the artist who in peacetime portrayed Christian virtues such as Faith, Hope and Charity, or gentle landscapes, did the same in Germany and Emile Dupuis in France. Soon postcards appeared which appealed to the loyalty of the peoples. Loyalty, to one's country and Nationalism, to the symbols and representations of Nationalism and, most especially, to the Flag, was portrayed in a variety of imaginative ways. France was particularly effective at portraying with fervour the glorious concept of pride in the Flag – whether her own or her Allies. Loyalty to one's leaders was strongly tied to allegiance to the Flag and to one's Allies and even towns vied to prove their loyalty to the Cause and to their national Allies by printing patriotic postcards featuring their local enthusiasm. Pride in the Army in general and to the individual Regiments in particular encouraged the youth of the nations to respond to such powerful appeals as Kitchener's accusatory *Your King and Country Need You* campaign. The populace also responded to appeals to honour concepts, alliances and treaties.

116

118

119

"'ARF A 'MO' KAISER!"

DUTY AND HONOUR
BID US PART.   No. 5

THE DREAM   THE REALITY.

Are we downhearted at
Beaufort Hospital? No!

122

123

Are We down-hearted? NO!

Our foes may be many; but to each other we're true
Soldier, and Sailor and Colonial too

124

125

126

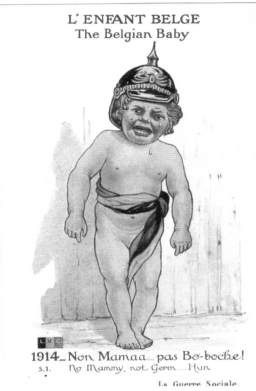

127

128

Internal political differences and fights for political freedoms (involving socialism and the establishment) were submerged before the greater cause of national peace and freedom through victory. This temporary unity was known as the *Union Sacrée* in France and as the *Burgirieden* in Germany, and it rallied people to support the national effort. The people were constantly reminded of their formal ties and agreements with their Allies, such as the 'Triple Alliance' between Russia, France and Britain, the *Entente Cordiale* between France and Britain and, above all, of the treaty scorned by Germany as a 'scrap of paper' whereby Britain guaranteed Belgian neutrality. Slogans and rallying cries encouraging patriotism and comradeship were strongly used on all sides to whip up enthusiasm and fervour. National characteristics coloured the nature of these cries to a large extent.

123 '*I am a German*' a popular patriotic catch phrase. The song verse below literally translated begins, '*I will away be brave and fear no enemy*'. This could be considered as the German equivalent of the British Bamforth postcard series. Feldpostkexp. 14th Inf Div. 21.6.15. *German.*

124 Ernest Ibbotson, artist of a fine series of military postcards for the same publisher showing all the different regiments of the British Army, with his version of Britain's favourite rallying cry. *Posted 17 August 1915. British: (Pub. Gale & Polden.)*

125 Card No. 8834. C. E. Shepheard's Anzac takes up the popular cry. Another theory for the origin of this cry is that it was created as a political slogan just after the turn of the century and became popularly used in songs in the early years of the war. Posted 23 June 1916. *British: (Pub. Tuck.)*

126 Conscription did not start in Britain until January 1916, so the need for recruits was strong. Government propaganda was aimed at persuading or embarrassing men to join up and a separate department was set up to devise words and images to do that. *British: (Pub. A. Adlington.) 1914.*

127 '*La Guerre Sociale*' *(The Social War)*. A Belgian baby, forced in 1914 to wear a German pickelhaube, protests, '*No, Mummy… not German, not a Hun (Boche).*' The country fears the consequences of the German occupation. *Belgian: (Pub. L.V.C. – logo in colours of the Belgian flag.)*

128 Designed and printed in Faversham, Kent. Anti-German feeling had to be whipped up in the early days and even the Old Testament was called upon (…dwell in the tents of Shem). *British.*

129 '*The German Eagle flaps its wings. It fights for right and it will succeed.*' Posted 27.10.14. *German: (Pub. Hermann Wolff, Berlin.)*

DER DEUTSCHE AAR REGT MÄCHTIG SEINE SCHWINGEN, ER KÄMPFT FÜR'S RECHT, UND ES WIRD GELINGEN!!

129

German slogans tended to be serious and fearsome. *Gott strafe England* (God Punish England) was the most powerful one of all. It became a standard greeting, opened telephone conversations and had a standard reply, *Er Strate Es* (May He Punish It). It was not taken too seriously in England or France, and Tommy made many jokes about 'strafing' any everyday object that annoyed him. *Deutschland Über Alles*, written in 1848, became popular in 1914 as the battle hymn that personified Germany's religious conviction in her superiority and invincibility. It was sung spontaneously in villages and cities throughout the country and was typical of the wartime German soldiers' songs which tended to be militant and determined in character. Their natural love of jollier music sometimes prevailed, however, and the verses of rousing marching songs were often printed in full on postcards. The Iron Cross was the symbol of German military achievement and valour which was represented on mugs, garters and brooches – on every conceivable article sold in the shops, particularly on postcards, and God and Justice were both implicitly believed to be in favour of the Central Powers.

The French were particularly successful at finding emotional slogans which were taken up quickly by *Poilus* (the familiar French name for her soldiers) and civilians alike. Later in the War, Verdun gave French propagandists the perfect vehicle. It symbolised the doorway to France where the German invaders would be forced to halt, and the bravery of the French soldier in ensuring that they would not pass. *On les aura* (We'll get them), was the *Poilu*'s determined and enthusiastic rallying cry, followed by *Nous les vaincrons* (We'll conquer them). The French military artist Georges Scott represented the slogan *On ne passe pas* in his famous portrait of a pugnacious *Poilu*. Like Bert Thomas's equally famous portrait of the British Tommy, *Arf a Mo Kaiser*, it captures the national spirit of the fighting soldier.

As Bert Thomas so aptly showed, the British attitude was humorous, good-natured and equally determined, which helped to put across the propaganda message in a way the Germans admired and failed totally to comprehend or reproduce. The popular Scottish football cry, 'Are we downhearted?' was taken up with gusto by the Tommies landing in France in August 1914. It was started by the kilted Argyll and Sutherlands, taken up and thrown back with a roar by each new battalion that landed in Boulogne: the Worcesters, the Royal Scots, and even by the excited townspeople. Songs were always popular with the British soldier. The Old Boer War song, *Soldiers of the Queen, my Lads* was also heard in Boulogne in those early days of the War, and *Goodbye Dolly, I must leave you*, but the great hit song of the War was first sung in France by the Connaught Rangers on 13 August, 1914.

From that day the song, *It's a long, long way to Tipperary*, caught the imagination of the fighting world, and became so incredibly popular that it was sung by all the Allied and Commonwealth troops (including Chinese working behind lines for the French), in the music halls back in Britain, and even by the German soldiers and the new American soldiers as they came over to fight three years later. The composer, Jack Judge, who worked a market stall, wrote the song for a bet and must have been overwhelmed by its instant success story.

Another extremely popular song, *Take me back to dear old Blighty*, ran *Tipperary* a close second. The word 'Blighty' is reputed to come from the British Army's days in India, a derivative from the Mohammedan word, 'bilayat' meaning 'own district'. Tommy added the final 'y' and eventually it emerged as 'Blighty', referring to the U.K. National Anthems were sung with emotion and enthusiasm on every possible occasion, civil and military, and the French and British sang each others' national songs with equal conviction. *Tipperary* became another British National Anthem to the French and Belgians and was played by them as an alternative to, or immediately after, *God Save the King*.

The need for a recruiting campaign was not necessary in Germany and France as conscription was an established way of life in each country, but the Kaiser appealed to his people on 31 July

L'UNION SACRÉE

130

130 Emile Dupuis represents the Sacred Alliance of the Allied flags. The message on the reverse reads, '*Just a simple card to wish you many happy returns of this day. When I get a home I will send you a silk one*'. The *Union Sacrèe* was an agreement between the French Government and the Trades Unions that there would not be any strikes during the war. Posted 27 March 1916. *French*.

131 America's entry in April 1917 produced a flood of patriotic cards, similar in vein to those produced in the Allied countries in 1914. America was barely 60 years away from its Civil War, when rallying to the flag was a widespread call. *American: (Pub. Merval Corp., N.Y.)*

132 Fine embossed and gilded card extolling the prompt contribution made by India using an extract from a speech made at the Guildhall in 1914 by Prime Minister Asquith – '*Two divisions of her magnificent Army are already on their way*'. British: *(Pub. Birn Bros.)*

131

132

E dire che sono quelli venuti ad insegnarci la civiltà!
Et dire qu'ils sont ceux qui nous ont appris la civilité!!

133

EIN SCHLAG!
und ihr steht im Hemd da!!

134

"WE ARE PROUD OF YOU
Lord Kitchener

BRITISH TO T

137

UNION DES SOCIÉTÉS POUR LA DÉFENSE NATIONALE

Belges êtes vous prêts?

Tous les Belges se doivent à la défense de la Patrie.
Ne comptons que sur nous mêmes pour nous défendre
et faisons les sacrifices nécessaires pour assurer notre
existence comme peuple libre et indépendant.

135

NOT SUCH
A BIG
HANDFUL
AFTER ALL!

ARMY
NAVY
AERO
MARINES
LABOR

136

ALTHOUGH FROM FRIE
I'M SAD AT BI
THIS VIEW WILL TE
IF ASKED "ARE

138

139

140

141

TAKE ME BACK TO DEAR OLD BLIGHTY. (1).

Jack Dunn, son of a gun, over in France to-day,
Keeps fit, doing his bit, up to his eyes in clay;
Each night, after a fight, to pass the time along,
He's got a little gramophone that plays this song.

BÔH DO KRIVDY HROMOM

A JUNÁK GUĽAMI

God's thunderbolts and heroes'
bullets to punish injustice!

142

OLD HOME. FAREWELL!

REINTHAL & NEWMAN, PUBS., N. Y.

143

"THE COMING STORM"

REINTHAL & NEWMAN, N. Y.   Painted by Philip Boileau

133 Racist propaganda card decrying the value of Allied Colonial Forces: *'And to think they are the ones who taught us civilisation'*. Presumably this card was made before April 1915 when the Italians finally decided to join the war – on the Allied side! *Italian.*

134 A German home propaganda card showing the Allies dreaming about getting to Berlin, which they have found on a map. The mighty German iron fist is about to hammer them and the caption says, *'One blow and they will stay at home.'* *German*: (*Pub. Wm Baron.*)

135 A rare Belgian card anticipating danger from Germany. *'Belgium, are you ready?'* Produced for the Union of Societies for National Defence by the publication *La Vie Illustrée*. Artist James Thiriar (1889–1965) was an illustrator and costume designer. During the First World War years he was stationed in Britain and produced sketches of the front for the *Illustrated London News*. Posted 26.11.1913.

136 Both the Allies and the Germans were very aware that the entry of America into the war and the arrival of US troops on the Western Front would be a deciding factor. The early American battles at the Marne and St Mihiel in 1918 demonstrated the Nation's formidable capabilities. *American.' Comical Kaiser Series'.*

137 'We are proud of you', a quotation from Kitchener on card by Artist J. L. Biggar. The words are probably a misquote from a message sent to Sir John French Commander of the BEF after the battle of Mons in 1914, which was *'Congratulate troops on their splendid work and we are all proud of them'*. *British: (Pub. Brown & Calder.)*

138 The *'Downhearted'* phrase was taken up enthusiastically by Tommy from the first landings of the B.E.F. at Boulogne in August 1914. Version by comic artist, 'AE'. Message on reverse reads, *'I think will offer for the fighting line when I go back'*. Posted 3 August 1917. *British: (Pub. Wildt & Kray.)*

139 Song Number Two on Tommy's wartime hit parade. This is No 1 of 4 cards, each carrying verses of this popular song. Bamforth and Co. of Holmfirth, Yorks started as lantern slide manufacturers in 1870. During the War they produced many series of illustrated songs and hymns, both patriotic and sentimental. *British: (Pub. Bamforth.)*

144

145

On les aura !

Souscrivez aux Bons de la Défense nationale

146

D'après l'Illustration   G.Scott

ON NE PASSE PAS !

147

140 Card No 1 of a gloriously exuberant set of cards designed to promote admiration for France's British, Belgian and Russian Allies. The priest is saying, *'Allies and friends, God will watch over our armies and he will break the swords of the savage hordes'*. Presumably he is also watching over the Germans. *French: (Pub. 'Hermine'.)*

141 Rare card issued by the Czechoslovakian Recruiting Office in New York. *'God's thunderbolts and heroes' bullets to punish injustice.'* The image is one of a number of posters drawn by Czech Artist Vojtech Preissig to encourage Czechs and Slovaks in America to join the Czech Legion. Preissig lived in the USA. *American.*

142, 143 Pair of cards by Philip Boileau, well known for his pre-war cards of typical American beauties, from a most attractive Patriotic Series, drawn just before America came in. Boileau died in January 1917, so did not see America's entry into the War. The majority of his cards were published by Reinthal and Newman, and many of them were printed and distributed in England. *American: (Pub. Reinthal & Newman, N.Y.)*

144 Stylish card by Artist A. Rubino (who prior to WW1 worked in Paris) probably published in October 1918 when the Italian armies finally stopped the enemy's advance at the battle of Vittorio Veneto and moved to recapture all the lands lost since 1917, kicking out the Austro-Hungarian double-headed eagle. *Italian: (Pub. G Ricordi, Milan.)*

145 *'Hail and Victory in the New Year'*. Card posted 30.12.14. *German.*

146 *'We'll get them'*. This well-known picture by Abel Faivre was drawn as a poster in 1916 appealing to the people to buy National War Bonds. On the reverse are details about the Bonds (with 5% interest) which may be purchased at banks, post offices, from lawyers, etc. *French: (Pub. Sevampez, Paris.)*

147 *'They will not pass'* (slogan attributed to Pétain). Georges Scott's immortal *Poilu* guards the frontier at Verdun and personifies the spirit of the French Army. The message on the reverse, written in December 1918 reads, *'I have been wanting to write to you for an eternity – since returning there's been the flu (I was the 58th person to catch it). Happily everyone*

*is on their feet again, but what work! And the Armistice
– you will be accusing me of forgetting you in the joy of
the radiant victory. This month of November has been
ideal – Paris's joy has been sweet and intense – these
Paris streets with their Flags, with their crowds were
beauty itself. Above all there are smiles with the tears
and like a great love in the atmosphere.'* A gem of a
card – marvellous picture by a great artist and the
written message a true social document recording
the tribulations and joys of those turbulent times.
French: (Pub. Galérie Patriotique.)

148 Handpainted. *'We will conquer them.'* As the
Bulldog symbolizes Britain's determined spirit, so
the Cockerel symbolizes France's proud *'élan'*. The
whole country was convinced that the superiority
of their famous quick-fire '75' gun would be a
significant and winning factor in the War. *French:
(Pub. Coquemer, Paris.)*

149 Morale-boosting Feld-Postkarte, posted
Berlin 25.11.14 with regimental postmark 'Garde-
Schutzen-Batl'. Fritz gives Ivan, the Poilu and John
Bull a whacking. *German.*

149A Anti-Russian propaganda showing
archetypical soldiers acting true to typecasting with
captured vodka! This was pretty close to the truth.
German.

148

1914 for support: 'This is a dark day and a dark hour … The sword is being forced into my hand
… This War will demand of us enormous sacrifice in life and money.' His prophetic words,
delivered with the self-deluded conviction of his unbalanced and flamboyant personality, drew
immediate response. The following day, in Berlin alone, 30,000 happy warriors flocked to report
in. In a few days five million had reported for service.

The mood in France was less euphoric, but with the subdued fervour of a religious crusade,
reservists poured from villages and towns, jamming the public transport systems. Four million
had soon reported to fight for *La Patrie* and *La Gloire*.

Britain however depended upon her very small professional army, her powerful navy and
volunteers. It soon became apparent that an intensive recruiting campaign was necessary after
the first delirious rush to the recruiting stations, when entire cricket and rugby teams, families
and groups of friends enlisted together as unthinkingly as lemmings hurling themselves over
clifftops. 100,000 enrolled in Kitchener's new Army in the first month. The Central London
Recruiting Office had to be temporarily closed until the necessary equipment and training
facilities were available.

The postcard proved an excellent propaganda tool in this campaign. The first posters appeared
on London walls on 6 August, but the postcards underlined and re-iterated their message in a
personal way the poster never could. The message could be encouraging or barbed, appealing to
the recipient's feelings of patriotism or sense of shame as appropriate.

149

149A

150 A very interesting card. It shows the British secret weapon, the tank, first used in September 1916. It is terrifying the Germans. Oddly it has the printed message, '*Passed by Censor, 5 January 1917*'. The card is not British and clearly not German so it is probably French and makes ironic fun of Germany's favourite slogan, '*God Punish England*'.

151 Artist Carrey shows the Allies saluting the soldiers of Verdun. General Joffre's message to them after three weeks of resisting the heaviest German bombardment of the War so far – in February/March 1916 – is congratulatory and encouraging, for he viewed the holding of Verdun as the symbol of French determination. But over 540,000 French casualties would fall at Verdun before the end of the campaign. *French: (Pub. Laureys.)*

152 Official War Office Red Cross card. Romantic images of soldiers at the front were not an Allied exclusive. Posted 14 September 1916. *German.*

153 Artist J L. Biggar represents Britain as a bulldog ready to honour the famous treaty (the 'Scrap of Paper') which brought her into the War. As she stands on the Paper, her pups from the Empire rush to join her. *British: (Pub. T. & C. Allan.)*

154 The newly-arrived American soldier sends the Kaiser packing back towards Berlin. September 1918. As the war ended the Kaiser went to Holland where it is said he asked for 'a cup of good English tea'. *Posted 26 February 1919. French.*

152

153

154

155 L. Ravenhill draws a demoralised Turkish soldier rushing away from Jerusalem and Baghdad to *'Any Old Place'* when abandoned by his German ally. It refers to the capture, on 9 December 1917, of Jerusalem by General Allenby who used railways to great effect, despite attempts by the Turks to stop him. *British.*

156 *'See our valiant battalions pushing back your oppressor'*. Alsace-Lorraine, taken from France after the Franco-Prussian War, being liberated by enthusiastic French troops and the German standard brought down – wishful thinking that became reality under the terms of the Armistice. *French.*

157 St. Clair War Series. No 5 of set by H. Canivet of the War's most popular song, *'It's a long, long way to Tipperary'*, believed to have been sung by the 2nd Battalion of the Connaught Rangers on 13 August 1914 as they disembarked in Boulogne. *British: (Pub. Dobson, Molle & Co., Edinburgh.)*

JOHNNIE TURK, whose German master has let him down.

155

156

157

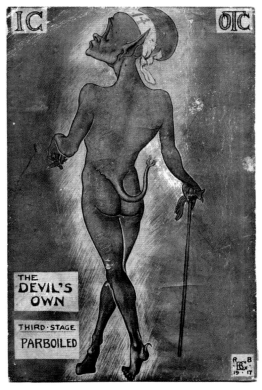

158

We'll be here to welcome you back!

160

DOWN TEXAS WAY (3)

I keep hearing a Southern tune,
Makes me feel like a crazy loon;
Want to dance 'neath a harvest moon,
The family's expecting me along home soon.

159

Die deutschen Barbaren!

161

158 In 1903 George III, when watching a military review, asked about a particular group of men and when told that they were all lawyers exclaimed, *'Call them the Devil's Own'*. He wasn't keen on lawyers! By 1914 the Territorial formation was known as 'The Inns of Court Officer Training Corps' (ICOTC) and a splendid set of cards depicts the progression of a volunteer from start to completion of training. This is the Third Stage – *'Parboiled'*. *British. 1917.*

159 This picture reflects the entry of America into the war but the song *'Down Texas Way'* was written by an Englishman, Arthur J. Mills, in 1917 and was most popular amongst Canadian troops. *British: (Pub. Bamforth.)*

160 *'Waiting Series'* No. 1198 by Artist Oscar Wilson. The sentimental postcard helped to reassure Tommy that his girl would still be his when he returned. Every soldier away from home feared a *'Dear John'* letter which was one saying that his loved one had found someone else. Card sent to a Belgian soldier in the Anglo-Belgian hospital at St. Aubin from his English sweetheart. *British: (Pub. Inter-Art Co.)*

161 Allied propaganda majored upon depicting the Germans as brutes and relentlessly accused them of atrocities during their conquest of *'Poor Little Belgium'*. This Feldpostkarte, showing a German soldier helping in a family kitchen with children all around, was probably an official attempt to counteract the bad effect on morale of the Allied propaganda. *German.*

162 Posted 6 November 1914. From the earliest days of the War, the Allied Governments promoted admiration of the other's valour and commitment. One way was to popularise the other's national anthem, hence the *Marseillaise* in English for the British market. *British: (Pub. C. W. Faulkner.)*

163 Card by Artist A. Hofer. As Britain had not been invaded, France tended to feel her suffering was less. The French Government launched a campaign to *'sell'* Britain to the French people. One way was to teach them her National Anthem. *French: (Pub. A. T. Paris.)*

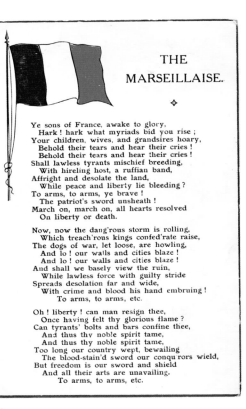

162

164 '*King George V, his Fleet and his Empire*'. In 1914 Nations and Causes were generally identified with the names of their leaders – the '*Men of the Moment*'. In Britain it was clearly the King (one fought for '*King and Country*') and the nation had lived on the reputation of the Navy as the best in the world as well as the Empire covering a large part of the globe – the days when the Phillips Atlas was mostly red. *British: (Pub. A&C Taylor.)*

165 'Tarteifle!' is an obscure exclamation or curse by the panicking Germans, provoked by the landing of the BEF at Boulogne and elsewhere. Sent from a French soldier to his parents. 9 November 1914. *French.*

166

167

166 'The class of asses. How can one teach them anything?... What a lot of donkeys they are!!' The Prussian General Staff Corps was a trained body that gave their armies a decided advantage over the Allies in the use of large armies. Here an arrogant Prussian lecturer thinks that he is superior to a class comprising Hannibal, Caesar, Alexander the Great, Frederick the Great and Napoleon. *Italian.*

167 'Michel', the national personification of Germany, loses his patience with the lying pack and gives the Allies – Russia, Belgian, Britain and France – a wake-up. German humour seems to involve a lot of bottom beating. *German: Feldpostkarte: (Pub. Hermann Lorch, Dortmund.)*

168 Artist Bela Jusko depicts the bravery of the Hungarian Hussars in typical Harry Payne style. The picture may owe something to the Hussars' (temporary) defeat of the Russians in December 1914 at Liminowa. *Hussar* means 'one in twenty' and comes from 15th Century Hungary where one man in twenty from every village was conscripted. *Hungarian: (Pub. Rotophot Budapest.)*

169 *'A good move by Uncle Sam'*, who gives bags of cash to the French and British. This is probably meant to be J. P. Morgan who through his banks lent $50 million to the French in 1915 enabling them to buy arms – hardly the act of a neutral. *French.*

170 Another aspect of Uncle Sam and a rare and complicated 1916 card from Artist Emile Dupuis (qv). Captioned 'In the shadow of Liberty' it shows Uncle Sam under the Statue of Liberty. He is weighing the cost in lives of the sinking of the Lusitania (in the top right hand corner, intently watched by a German, see No 220) against the money he had been lending to the Allies, especially France. French: (Pub Visé, Paris).

171 A drowning child in a *Lusitania* lifebelt cries, *'Mummy! Mummy! Why?'* Of the total of 1959 passengers aboard, 94 of the 129 children died. Artist Poulbot. *French: (Pub. Visé, Paris 'Petits Francais' Series.)*

168

169

172, 173 Military Artist A. Pearse gives his interpretation of the Allies' favourite song – which was even sung by the German soldiers – and often played by France and Belgium as the British National Anthem. The cards (first and last of series of 4) follow Tommy's optimistic progress from *'debarkation'* at Calais, through to occupation of Berlin. Posted 20 May 1915. *British: (Pub. B. Feldman & Co, London.)*

A l'ombre de la Liberté...
In the shadow of Liberty.

ÉTATS-UNIS

170

— Maman! maman! pourquoi?

171

"IT'S A LONG, LONG WAY FROM TIPPERARY."

THE DEBARKATION—CALAIS.

Up to mighty London came an Irishman one day,
    As the streets are paved with gold, sure ev'ryone was gay,
Singing songs of Piccadilly, Strand and Leicester Square,
    Till Paddy got excited, then he shouted to them there:—
    "It's a long way to Tipperary, it's a long way to go;
    It's a long way to Tipperary, to the sweetest girl I know!
    Good bye Piccadilly, farewell Leicester Square,
    It's a long, long way to Tipperary, but my heart's right there!"

By permission of B. Feldman & Co., 2 & 3 Arthur St., London, W.C.

172

"IT'S A LONG, LONG WAY FROM TIPPERARY."

MARCHING THROUGH BERLIN.—The Kaiser Wilhelm Strasse.

Paddy wrote a letter to his Irish Molly .O',
    Saying, " Should you not receive it, write and let me know!
If I make mistakes in 'spelling,' Molly, dear," said he,
    " Remember it's the pen that's bad, don't lay the blame on me."
" It's a long way to Tipperary, it's a long way to go;
    It's a long way to Tipperary, to the sweetest girl I know!
    Good bye Piccadilly, farewell Leicester Square,
    It's a long, long way to Tipperary, but my heart's right there!"

By permission of B. Feldman & Co., 2 & 3 Arthur St., London, W.C.

173

174

174 This huge figure of Hindenburg was made of wood. Modelled by Georg Marschall, it was 12m high and weighed 26 tons. Metal nails of gold, silver and iron were bought and hammered into the figure, the proceeds going to the families of war casualties. It was inaugurated with great pomp before a huge crowd by Crown Princess August Wilhelm in September 1915. Accounts vary but there are reports of 1.5 million marks being raised and others that state that all the donations were lost when the Lufthfarerbank went bankrupt. Postcards were also sold as fund-raisers. *German: (Pub. Hofbruckerei Hermann Bergmann, Berlin.)*

175 Popular military artist Emile Dupuis portrays Greece dithering, (*'with whom should I dance?'*), between the German *Pickelhaube* and the French *casquette*. It was not until July 1917 that Greece openly committed herself to the Allied side. *French.*

176 *'Reunited for the same Ideal.'* The French Zouave and the Italian Alpini became comrades when Italy joined the Allied side in May 1915. In 1859 the French fought for Italy in the Second War of Independence. *French: (Pub. Lévy Fils & Co, Paris.) 1915.*

Hellas!.. Hélas! avec lequel danser?   GRÈCE
Hellas! Alas! with which shall i dance?

175

1859 - 1915

RÉUNIS POUR LE MÊME IDÉAL

176

177 This exhortation to *'Wake Up!'* is captioned as an extract from a 'Patriotic film' produced by the *Daily Express*. The order is less aimed at the soldiers than the Nation and the drawing is probably a representation of troops after the defeat at Mons.

178 France prepares Revenge (*la Revanche*) for the losses in the Franco–Prussian War. The proud 'Lion of Belfort' proclaims, *'And to think I have been asleep for 44 years. France will become France once again.'* Artist Jan Mettrix. Posted 1914. *French: (Pub. Laclau, Toulouse.)*

179 *'Feste druff''* Let the Russians, French and English have it! In the early days of the war it was common to show all British (or English) soldiers wearing kilts! Posted 1.11.14. *German: Feldpostkarte.*

179

180 Krampus is the dark and scary beast who accompanies the benign St Nicholas on 6 December. Here he sprouts the multi heads of the Allies and is chastised by Germany and Austria. Artist K. Th. Zelger, 1914. Zelger was a well-known children's illustrator (often in the form of strip cartoons) and during WW1 he designed many propaganda postcards. *Austrian.*

180

181 Marvellous lampoon, in characteristic German chamber pot style, showing Nicholas of Russia, George V of England, and President Poincaré of France fleeing towards St Petersburg, London and Bordeaux. Poincaré beseeches, *'My God, don't leave me. I can see a spiked helmet.'* A mysterious skeletal hand lobs a bomb over Poincaré's protective umbrella. *German: 1914.*

181

Postcards comforted those left behind that their loved ones would soon be safely back, for everyone knew, of course, that the War would be won by Christmas. They reassured those on their way to the Front and those left holding the fort at home that volunteering was the right decision, that honour and duty made it so, and Tommy was persuaded that his girl would still be waiting for him when he came back. In America, once the decision to join the Allies had finally been taken by President Wilson, a similar campaign was mounted.

The theme of comrades in arms against the wicked foe was promulgated on all sides. In France it was particularly necessary to educate the public and the fighting forces about Britain's involvement and her valour in battle. The average Frenchman felt that Britain had never known what it was like to be invaded, whilst France had not known, in war after war, what it was like not to be invaded. France, therefore, must have more at stake and be suffering more. Series after series of emotional appeals to comradely feelings were posed, photographed, published on postcards and distributed to the troops in both armies. The stereotyped national characters depicted on these cards put them in the comic card category for modern viewers. In Britain the brave and unstinting efforts of the Commonwealth were much publicised on cards and the ability of the combined efforts of all the Allies to reduce the Kaiser to size was confidently believed in and portrayed with humorous and witty effect by many postcard artists.

Germany and Austria proclaimed combined strength and belief in their invincibility in many representations of victory over Britain, France, Russia, Montenegro and Serbia. The Allies were often shown in the form of their animal personifications, and usually display as national characteristics cowardice or perfidy. The widespread portrayal of the British as stupid and cowardly foes (which also appeared in wartime comic papers) incensed one German soldier whose personal experiences as a despatch runner taught him that the picture could not be further from the truth. He also knew that beating a cowardly enemy gave no great credit to the victor. His name was Adolph Hitler and he went on to become a pastmaster of lethally effective propaganda. Hitler came to believe that the British understood the psychology of propaganda far better than did the Germans, and admired the effect of leaflets dropped behind the German lines to demoralise the German troops.

Some alliances were a long time a-forming, as several nations hesitated and even changed sides. The Central Powers were as anxious to woo the U.S.A. to their side as were the Allies, but were irritated by President Wilson's tardiness in taking sides and by his unsuccessful attempts to conclude an early peace.

The attitude of Italy who actually changed sides, was viciously lampooned by a hurt Germany, who pictured Italy as a brigand, stabbing Germany in the back. The theme of a tug of war, with an indecisive referee or onlooker was used by Germany to illustrate Italy's changing allegiance, and Greece also came in for ridicule because of her lack of resolution.

Jingoistic patriotism worked admirably to keep up morale, provided things were going well. As the troops at the Front soon discovered, however, conditions were appalling, battles were not always won. Soon patriotism was not enough to keep up spirits, and stronger medicine was called for …

The Hatred

The second phase in the campaign to prolong war fever was the whipping up of hatred, a technique employed with heavy handed venom by Germany and with barbed humour and strong emotional impact by the Allies. A certain amount of artificial baring of teeth was necessary between Britain and Germany. The two nations saw themselves as temperamentally similar; the two Royal Houses were closely related and the Kaiser (since his rush to the bedside of his dying Grandmother, Queen Victoria, who expired in his arms) had cut quite a popular figure in England.

The 'atrocity' stories promulgated by both sides quickly remedied this undesirable state of affairs. Tales of cruelty, rape and pillage in Belgium and Serbia by the barbaric Hun and his disregard for the sanctity of international treaties appealed to the traditional British feeling of support for the underdog, and also roused strong feelings in neighbouring France. Even the still-dithering Italians were influenced by horrific images of the rape of Belgium. Towns and villages pillaged, orphans made homeless, women raped, pregnant women stabbed, babies used for bayonet practice, old people made homeless or killed, terrible weapons like gas or burning petrol: these were themes seized upon and magnified by the propagandists. The concept of German *Kultur* was applied to this atrocious behaviour, a theme taken up with immense effect by the most powerful propagandist artist to emerge from the War, Louis Raemakers. He was a Dutch cartoonist who gained international fame from the strength and sincerity of his cartoons. He moved to England in 1916, the more easily to supply the Allied Press. Many of his stark black and white drawings were reproduced in booklet form – some ironically entitled *Drawings of a Neutral,* which were sold to raise money for French and British wounded, or for the Red Cross. They first appeared in the newspaper, *Der Telegraaf* of Amsterdam. Serbia ran a close second to Belgium in gaining Allied sympathy, and German treatment of the countries she invaded made Britain more determined to preserve her centuries old record of successfully repelling invaders. Her attitude to the enemy, however, was still often expressed with typical British humour.

The greatest gift ever made to the propagandists was the shooting by a German firing squad of the English Matron of the Red Cross Hospital in Brussels, Edith Cavell. This unassuming daughter of a Norfolk Vicar became a legend and a martyr, and her death did more to stoke the fires of hatred against the Germans than any other incident in the War – in the Allied countries and in the as-yet-uncommitted U.S.A. Recalled on 1 August from leave in Norfolk, Edith Cavell was soon to see the full horrors of invasion all around her. 'I can only feel the deep and tender pity of a friend within the gates, and observe with sympathy and admiration the high courage and self control of a people enduring a long, terrible agony,' she wrote in the *Nursing Mirror,* with the Battle of Mons raging only 50 miles away.

Several hundred wounded Allied soldiers were helped by Edith Cavell and her underground group to reach the Belgian border and cross to safety (often to return, when healed, to the Front). The soldiers were sheltered in the hospital or in friendly Belgian homes, fed, provided with civilian clothes, papers and money and led to the border. Arrested in August 1915 with several others of her group, she was court-martialled, sentenced to death after a 'confession' and shot by firing squad at the *Tir National* on 12 October. There is no real evidence for the rumours

L'INGORDO
TROP DUR

182

AN AWFUL WARNING.

AUSTRIA (TO RUMANIA). "NOW, BE CAREFUL! REMEMBER WHAT I DID TO SERBIA!"

NO. 43. [*Reproduced by special permission of the Proprietors of "Punch."*]

183

THE LIMIT.

Scene: THE COAST OF BELGIUM.

THE KAISER: "'WHAT ARE THE WILD WAVES SAYING?'"
WILD WAVES: "WE WERE JUST SAYING, 'THUS FAR, AND NO FARTHER!,'"

NO. 36. [*Reproduced by special permission of the Proprietors of "Punch."*]

184

185

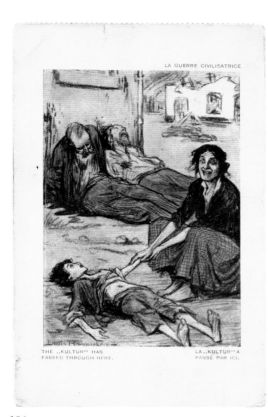

186

182 The Kaiser finds the world too hard a bite. On the reverse a father with Ambulance No 246 writes a charming message to his children, describing the weather and the scenery as he finds a quiet moment to take a walk along the river. Posted 21 June 1916 from Breteuil. *French: (Pub Arca.) Sent 21 June 1916.*

183 A *Punch* cartoon. The Austrian eagle threatens Rumania while a slightly chastened Serbia looks on (nevertheless with one of the eagle's feathers in its mouth). Rumania remained neutral as the beginning of the war but eventually joined the Allies. The message on the back reads, '*I understand they have heard from Lloyd at home – but I haven't had my word yet! Hope he comes through alright – though those brutes of Germans are doing their foulest.*' *British: (Pub. Jarrold & Sons.) Posted 14 May 1915.*

184 A *Punch* cartoon. The Kaiser listens to the waves telling him, '*Thus far and no farther*', as he stands on the shores of Belgium looking longingly at Britain. By the time that this card was posted all ideas of invading Britain were well and truly dead. *Posted 22 April 1916. British. (Pub. Jarrold & Sons.)*

185 The Kaiser gives a lecture on dastardly international strategy. '*Without worrying about our treaties, we will traitorously invade Belgium.*' This may be a piece of 'Black Propaganda' circulated in Belgium before the war as an attempt to stir up disquiet in the German army. *Belgian: (Pub. A. V et M. Brussels.)*

186 Profits of sale to French Red Cross. Louis Raemakers, the Dutch artist whose biting comments on the War were the most powerful Allied propaganda weapon, portrays the '*Civilising War*' and the effects of German '*Kultur*'. The caption says '*Kultur has passed by here*'. *French.*

187 Profits of sale to French Red Cross. Artist Louis Raemakers. Belgian orphans look for their parents' graves. Many of Raemakers' cartoons were first published in the Amsterdam newspaper, '*Der Telegraaf*' and were reprinted as postcards in booklet form. Some booklets were sold in aid of the Amsterdam Fund for wounded soldiers which was under the supervision of the French Consul in Amsterdam. The caption says '*Kreuzland, Kreuzland, Uber Alles*'. *French.*

188 The Belgian Lion, *'Wounded but not dead.'* Artist Hirlemann. In 1870 the city of Belfort was under siege by the Prussians but never fell and a splendid lion sculpture was made to commemorate the achievement. It is so dramatic that its form is often used, as here, to represent stubborn resistance. Card for distribution in all Allied Countries by the *Belgian Committee. Posted 3 July 1915. French: (Pub. L V. Co.).*

189 Card with French caption, published in Italy. The martyr Serbia is stabbed in the back by Bulgaria and attacked by Austria and Germany. Greece holds Judas money and tramples a treaty underfoot. *Italian.*

190 German *'Michel'* (John Bull's counterpart) occupies Belgium, but his position is threatened by English, Belgian and French troops. The card represents the battles of the Yser and was sent by a Belgian, probably in Holland, to a Belgian lady, probably a refugee, in England. Sent in an envelope, 24 March 1916. *Probably Dutch.*

188

189

190

DANZA MACABRA EUROPEA 28

GUGLIELMO IL SANGUINARIO
GUILLAUME LE SANGUINAIRE

LIT. LONGO · TREVISO

191

192

191 In 1914 Italian Artist Alberto Martini produced a powerful series of 36 propaganda cards, now very rare, under the title *Danza Macabra Europea* attacking Germany for its brutality and the Austro-Hungarian Empire for its attacks on ethnic Italians in such provinces as Trieste and Trento. This, No 28, is captioned *'William the Bloodthirsty'*. Some of his pictures were exhibited in Leicester in 1916. *Italian: (Pub. Treviso.)*

192 A rare, bitter and detailed anti-war tirade from the humorous artist, '*Cynicus*' (Martin Anderson, 1854–1932). Lust and mammon are blamed for all the evils of the war – the gagging of parliament, the press and the truth, for profiteering, militarism, the plight of widows… *British*.

LA TURPINITE : POUDRE INSECTICIDE FRANÇAISE.

Pierre CHATillon 1915

193

194

193 *'Turpinite: French insectiside powder'*. 'Turpinite' was the name given to a poison gas invented in the 1980s by French chemist Eugene Turpin (see card No 261). It was said to act invisibly with widespread lethal consequences, leaving victims unmarked. So terrifying was this prospect that the word was used colloquially as 'Secret Weapon'. Some accounts even suggested that the German casualties supposedly caused by the Angels of Mons were due to 'Turpinite'. Here the French Secret Weapon will kill the German lice. Artist Pierre Chatillon, 1915. *French: (Pub. Edition Grellinger, Paris.)*

194 Edith Cavell's grave at the Brussels *Tir National*. The wreath marked *'Elisabeth'* is from the Queen of the Belgians. The death by German firing squad on 12 October 1915 was a propaganda gift to the Allies and she attained 'martyr' status. Nurse Cavell had reportedly helped over 1,000 Allied troops over the frontier of occupied Belgium. After the announcement of her death sentence, recruiting doubled for eight successive weeks (jumping from 5,000 to 10,000 per week). *Belgian: (Pub. Em. Thill, Brussels.)*

195

195A

196

195 Artist T. Cartiel perpetuates the 'cowardly murder' story. Caption on reverse reads, '*Condemned by a military tribunal in Belgium, under the charge of having favoured the evasion of British soldiers, Miss Edith Cavell, of Norwich, a voluntary nurse, is taken to the execution ground on the 12th October at daybreak. She faints: the German officer gives his soldiers the order to fire: they hesitate to shoot on the prostrate body of a woman. The fiend takes his revolver and leaning upon his victim, blows her brains out.*' Pure fiction! *French: (Pub. Laureys, Paris.)*

195A An extremely rare and valuable woven silk card of Nurse Cavell. Versions also exist showing her with two dogs (which appear easier to find). *French.*

196 Belgian memorial to Miss Cavell which was unveiled on 20 November 1918. Note the incorrect month in the caption – it should read 12 OCTOBER, not August, 1915. *Belgian.*

197 A Flame-thrower in action. More than any other artist during the War, Louis Raemakers captures the stark horror of war and man's inhumanity to man. The flame-thrower was first used by the Germans at Hooge, near Ypres in Belgium. *French.*

198 'The Triumph of the Victim', part of a rare 1917 series inspired by Nurse Cavell by Artist Tito Corbella, better known for his Art Deco-style glamour girls (see Card No 649). *British: (Pub. Inter-Art Co.)*

199 'The Murder of Miss Cavell inspires German "Kultur"', part of the same powerful series by Corbella. *British: (Pub. Inter-Art Co.)*

and elaborations on the basic tale; of the 'fiendish' German officer who, as Edith Cavell fainted, shot her in the head when his firing squad hesitated. The truth was enough, and her death released a tidal wave of outraged fury. 'There are thousands of such women, but a year ago we did not know it', commented Asquith on this symbol of the new, liberated woman. But the most famous words are her own, told to the English chaplain, Stirling Cahan, the night before her death: 'I realise that patriotism is not enough. I must have no hatred or bitterness towards anyone.' The rest of the world hated bitterly for her and the Germans were soon to realise what a momentous blunder they had made. A huge recruiting campaign was launched in Britain after her death with prodigious success. In September 1915 only 71,617 men enlisted as the rush to the recruiting offices waned. In the following month, when Edith Cavell was executed, the figure rose to 113,285 and reached its peak in November 1915, with 121,793 recruits.

Germany's answer was to refute the atrocity stories as lies and to represent the so-called barbaric German soldiers as kind and children-loving in enemy territory. Scathing attacks on German *kultur* were countered by atrocity stories of Russian (and in particular, Cossack) culture or English barbarism. Stories were spread of whole English families industriously converting normal bullets into dum dum bullets around the kitchen table. Hatred became a way of life (c.f. The *Gott Strafe England* campaign) as the British Naval blockade really began to bite and civilians starved, and Lissauer's *Hymn of Hate* was sung everywhere. 'Hate Sermons' and 'Hate Lectures' were given: a University Professor in Munich taught: 'We must hate the very essence of everything English. We must hate the very soul of England'. The public were kept in extreme ignorance of the real events of the War. Defeats on the Somme and at Verdun were reported as tactical retreats and no news of the Battle of the Marne was officially given. But stories of Britain's perfidy on the High Seas were reported in detail. A practice reputedly recommended by Britain's then First Lord of the Admiralty, Winston Churchill, was the running up of the appropriate friendly colours to lure enemy shipping into range and then to fire on them. Merchant ships, known as Q ships were equipped with concealed weapons which could quickly be activated.

In France the hatred, known as *La Haine Sacrée*, was fundamental, intense and almost religious in nature. No need here for artificial arousal of a people who were fighting a war of revenge: revenge for 1870, revenge for

197

198

THE MURDER OF MISS CAVELL
INSPIRES GERMAN "KULTUR„

199

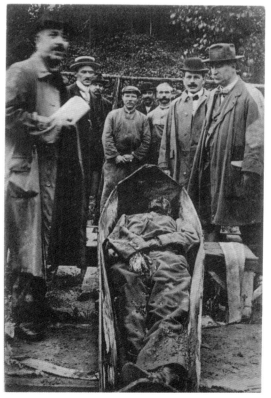

200

200 The text on the back says, '*Rammler, a German soldier, shot (without trial) at the same time as Baucq and Miss Cavell for refusing to fire on this nurse (Edith Cavell). His coffin was found between these two patriots.*' Philippe Baucq and another member of the escape-route team were arrested on 31 July 1915. Edith was arrested on 5 August. *Belgian: (Pub R. Ringoet, Louvain.)*

201–206 'Composite' Series (placed together they form the head of the Kaiser) showing German atrocities. *French: (Pub. Ch Fontaine.'Guerre Européenne de 1914-1915. Edition Patriotique'.)*

201 The Germans pillaging in Belgium and Northern France.

202 The assassins throw bombs, explosives and incendiaries.

203 The traitors abusing the white flag.

204 The bandits rape women and massacre children.

205 The pirates torpedo innocent neutral civilians.

206 The cowards use poisoned gas and burning petrol.

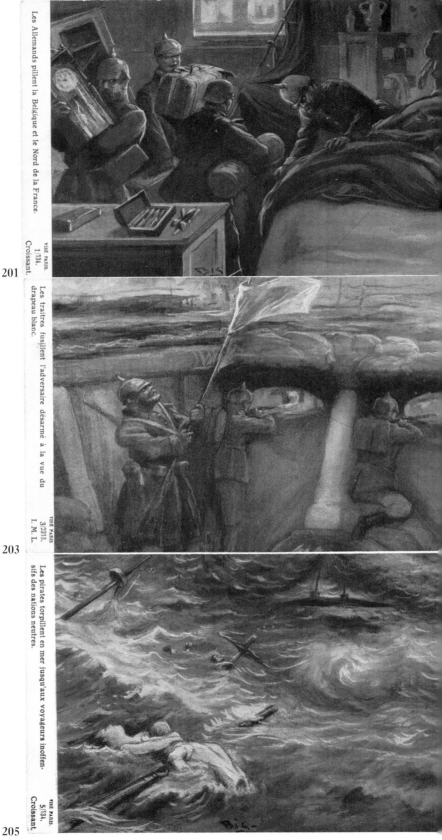

201

203

205

Les Allemands pillent la Belgique et le Nord de la France.

VISÉ PARIS. 1/134. Croissant.

Les traitres fusillent l'adversaire désarmé à la vue du drapeau blanc.

VISÉ PARIS 3/2313. I. M. L.

Les pirates torpillent en mer jusqu'aux voyageurs inoffensifs des nations neutres.

VISÉ PARIS. 5/134. Croissant.

VISÉ PARIS,
2/2313.

Les assassins jettent des bombes explosives et incendiaires

202

VISÉ PARIS
4/2313.
I. M. L.

Les bandits violent les femmes et massacrent les enfants.

204

VISÉ PARIS
6/2313.
I. M. L.

Et les lâches emploient les gaz asphyxiants et le pétrole
enflammé contre nos soldats.

206

207 By Georges Scott, published in August 1914.
Alsace votes to reunite joyfully with France.
Alsace-Lorraine was taken from the French by the
Germans after the Franco-Prussian War of 1870
and declared 'Imperial Territory'. The recovery of
the confiscated territory became the obsessive focus
of France's hatred for Germany. *French.*

208 By Joe English, German to weeping figure of
Belgium, '*I have always loved you*'. Series '*Drawings
from the Trenches. Yzer 1915. Joe E, 55 Transport
Coy*'. English, who was a Flemish anti-Walloon
(French-speaking Belgians) Artist, died in August
1918 from appendicitis and has 'Martyr' status in
the Ijzer Tower, Dixsmuide, where he is buried in
the Crypt under one of the headstones he designed
for Flemish soldiers bearing the letters '*AVV-VVK*'
(*All for Flanders – Flanders for Christ.*) *Belgian.*

207

208

209

209 Jean–Jacques Waltz, better known as '*Hansi*', was Alsace's most popular anti-German artist. Just prior to WW1 he was imprisoned several times, escaping in 1914 to join the French Army's Propaganda Department. He suffered more persecution by the Nazis during WW2 and died in his native Colmar in 1951. The nose is rather naughty. *French: (Pub. P. et J. Gallais, Paris.)*

210 'The Good Lord of the Germans' (figure with pickelhaube point on his head being crucified) as his French guardian stands by. *'Oh. If I could assuage my thirst with blood?'*. Artist O'Géry. October 1914. *French.*

211 Official card for the widows and orphans of the Austro-Hungarian Imperial Mountain Infantry. The card shows a medic of the regiment shot in the back by a wounded Alpini. Artist H. Bertle. 9.6.1915. *Austrian: (Pub. Ministry of National Defence.)*

210

211

212 *'The lessons of Aesop adapted to our times: The tortoise and the eagle. A tortoise asked an eagle to teach him the secrets of flying. When the eagle hoisted him up in the air, the bird was soon forced to let him go and the tortoise fell downwards like a rock and was smashed. In the same manner, Bulgaria, after it has been lured by Germany into the war, one day will have to pay heavily for its untamed ambition'.* Unusual Tuck card with Dutch description on reverse. *British.*

213 'The War – Creil'. In September 1914 the German 1st Army under von Kluck had reached the area of Creil on the Oise in what became known as the First Battle of the Marne. Creil, roughly 50 km north of Paris, had important marshalling yards and though the German advance was stopped, the bridge over the river was destroyed. A French soldier writes in February 1919 to his young cousin, stating that he is about to be sent *'I know not where.'* He explains that the beautiful bridge had been destroyed by *'les boches'* but that German prisoners rebuilt it. *'French: (Pub. L'H, Paris.)*

212

La Guerre — CREIL - Les Allemands incendiant l'Ile   L'H. Paris

213

214

214 Artist Georges d'Ostoya (who drew for the satirical magazine *'L'Assiette au Beurre'* pre-WW1) lampoons the German Royal Family. The Kaiser invites son Oscar to embrace him. *'Yes papa,'* he replies, *'but let me change my trousers first.'* The implication may be that Oscar is a coward. The fifth son of the Kaiser, he had won the Iron Cross in 1914 but shortly afterwards he collapsed and spent several months excused front line duties. *French.*

215 *'The War. The abuse of the white flag'.* British propaganda on a French card, reinforcing the image of the enemy as barbarians. German soldiers fire on wounded British soldiers brandishing a white flag. Copyright *'The Sphere'* but with a French reverse.

216 In 1914 when food became scarce In Germany, they produced 'K bread' (*Kriegsbrot*) which substituted potatoes for wheat. The French made many satirical anti-German plays on words using 'K' (synonymous with the childish French word for pooh, 'kaka (or 'caca'). *French.*

217 4 August 1914. Heroic Belgium, having suffered the horrors of the German invasion and occupation, now demands reparation. This is propaganda, following the Armistice and in anticipation of the Peace Conference at Versailles. Artist A. Pageot, Oct 1918. *Belgian: (Pub. M. Vanderoost, Brussels.)*

215

216

217

218

219

220

218 A poignant card by Poulbot, '*It was there, our house.*' *French: (Pub. A. Ternois.)*

219 Artist Raoul Arus shows a village pillaged by the enemy. Allied propaganda maintained a relentless promotion of the 'Barbarian' image of the Germans. *French: (Pub. A. N., Paris.)*

220 Here are the bare facts of the sinking of the *Lusitania* posted 3 June 1915, a month after the tragedy. The sinking of this neutral ship, with its many American passengers, was one of the major factors in America's decision finally to enter the War. The Germans had warned America of the resumption of unrestricted U-Boat warfare, but the ship sailed in spite of the risk. Although denied by the Allies, it has since been suggested by witnesses on board that the *Lusitania* was both armed and carrying ammunitions. *British: (Pub. Millar & Lang.)*

Alsace-Lorraine, for humiliations and hardships still vivid in the race memory. On 9 August 1914 General Joffre, the French Commander in Chief, exhorted : 'Children of Alsace! After 44 years of sad waiting, French soldiers are treading once more the soil of your noble country. They are the first workers in the great work of revenge. What emotion and what pride for them! To complete this work they are ready to sacrifice their life.' Like the British, the French propagandists concentrated on stories of German cruelty and inhumanity to engender hatred. But a French political commentator, H. D. Davray, wrote in 1916: 'The English are fighting for their honour, for the defence of their existence, and the security of the British Empire, but they do not know as we do the passionate wrath and bitterness of hate.' Much of the hatred was concentrated on that Arch Villain, the Kaiser and his whole family was reviled. Postcards were issued with the Soldiers' Ten Commandments, the first being *Thou Shalt Always Kill*. The bayonet was feted and represented on postcards as a maiden, Rosalie, 'a fount of charms'.

The U.S.A. was assiduously wooed by each side. Much publicity was given by the Central Powers to the U Boat *Deutschland* (the largest in the world) when she arrived in the U.S.A. Her Commander, Captain Koenig, ran the gauntlet of the British blockade to bring a cargo full of freight to Baltimore to preserve the trading links between Germany and the U.S.A. despite determined efforts by the British Fleet to find and sink her.

The sinking of the *Lusitania* vied with the execution of Edith Cavell as a tool for enflaming Allied and neutral (specifically U.S.A.) feelings against Germany. The bare facts of the story are that the 32,000 ton passenger liner, commanded by Captain Turner, returning to Liverpool from New York, was sunk off the Old Head at Kinsale, at 2.28pm on 7 May 1915 in thick fog. She was torpedoed by the German U Boat 20 commanded by Captain Schweiger and took only 18 minutes to sink completely, with the loss of over 1200 men, women and children. More than 1 in 10 were U.S. citizens. It was publicised by the Allies as an inhuman German atrocity on an unarmed passenger liner, carrying innocent, neutral civilians. It is very probable, however, that the *Lusitania* was heavily armed. She was also carrying a cargo over which great pains had been taken to conceal the exact nature. From the way two massive explosions occurred in different parts of the vessel, the cargo seems to have been of a highly explosive character. Her safety was jeopardised by the alteration in balance caused by her heavy cargo – which she was not built to carry – and by the inefficiency of her life boat launching system. The *Lusitania* sailed on her final voyage despite repeated and public warnings by anxious German businessmen in the New *York Press* of the danger civilians would run in sailing on her. The Admiralty were only too aware, from the sinking of the *Centurion* and the *Candidate* on the previous day off the Irish coast, of U Boat activity on the direct path of the *Lusitania*. Could the sinking have been averted? Was the Admiralty even indirectly responsible? Did Britain (and her First Lord of the Admiralty in particular) welcome the traumatic experience which would bring the horrors of war directly to America's door in the hopes of engineering her entry into the War?

Whatever the truth, the Allies certainly derived far more benefit than the Central Powers from the tragedy. Encouraged by fierce propaganda, the civilised world was outraged, and the official verdict was 'wilful and wholesale murder'.

Germany's counter to the successful atrocity campaign was a flood of cartoons in a very basic strain of ponderous comic jibes. As the War began, feelings were mutually wary, but respectful. The German attitude soon changed to a scathing view of the national characteristics of the Allies, who were seen as predominantly cowardly. Natural bodily functions were gleefully depicted, as were puns on the *laus* (louse) part of Nicolaus of Russia's name and the de-lousing process was soon applied to the whole idea of despatching the Central Powers' enemies.

The mixed nationalities and colours of Britain's fighting force and her Allies also came in for ridicule. The French were quite capable of replying in kind to counter the basic German insult and satirical cards of this nature certainly provided light relief to the soldiers fighting, on both sides, in what were probably the grimmest conditions man has ever endured.

More than any of the wartime postcards, those with a propaganda message seem to capture the mood and style of a bygone age, whose spirit could never be regained. Would the hearty British songs, the sentimental French photographs or the German lavatory jokes jolly us into engaging in war now? Only the stark reality of Raemakers' literally shocking drawings seem relevant and, sadly, even topical in many parts of the world today. For he has crystallised the terrible truth of man's perennial inhumanity to man.

The Reality

The Men   The Machines   The War at Sea   The War in the Air

The Men

Reality was the crash and roar of unbearable sound, the sweet sickly stench of rotting flesh. Reality was death and sweat and fear that made men defaecate in their clothes. Reality was burying arms and legs, heads and torsos, that had once been companions. Reality was to live in mud and filth. Yet many of those who survived whole, would do it all again, to recapture the sharpness of the senses that comes with imminent death and to share once more the intense comradeship of the trenches. None of the men who fought this terrible War is still alive today [Harry Patch, the last British veteran, died in July 2009, aged 111]. However their postcards remain to chronicle their progress from the jingoism at home to the devastation at the Front. The men left home marching to cheers. When they arrived in France they were also cheered. As they marched to the trenches the local band would play them on their way. The first time that they went, they probably cheered back. After that, their innocence gone, they knew that there was nothing to cheer about. As they marched forward they would pass columns of pitiful refugees, pushing handcarts, barrows, bicycles laden with their belongings.

Postcards were produced showing the plight of the refugees to stimulate recruiting by the desire to revenge 'Poor Belgium.' Many too are the cards showing Regiments of all countries 'Cheering when ordered to the trenches'. Cynics say the cheering men have just come *out* of the trenches, or that they are cheering for some other reason than going to the trenches.

Death soon became a constant companion. The walls of the trenches were often made of sandbags and bodies, and in the torrential rain that seemed endlessly to cover the battlefield the walls would collapse, pouring the green slime of human remains on to those below. Men would be ordered to repair the walls and to spread chloride of lime to disinfect and clear the awful smell. Those scenes were not recorded on picture postcards – not officially anyway. Sometimes neutral states, like Holland, were able to obtain pictures of battle casualties and enterprising local publishers would produce cards for home consumption to show the neutral civilians. Such cards are almost impossible to find today, and never circulated freely in the combatant countries. The trenches even had their own diseases like trench mouth and trench foot in addition to those carried by the millions of rats which ran everywhere.

Movement above ground was literally impossible due to the command of the battlefield made possible by the machine gun, and by the prolific use of barbed wire. It was natural, therefore, that opposing sides would tunnel towards each other, hoping either to place mines under the other's trenches or to make a surprise attack to take a prisoner. These tunnels, dug by sappers and known as saps by the Tommies, were sometimes up to a mile in length and took months to dig. Listening posts were set up in the trenches with men pressing their ears to the ground straining to hear the noise of picks and shovels. Occasionally, opposing tunnels would suddenly burst into each other and intensive close combat with machine guns and flame throwers would take place many feet underground. The force of the explosives would frequently collapse the tunnels and bury men of both sides alive.

Once the front line settled down in Europe, following the checking of the German advance on the Marne and the subsequent limited withdrawal of the German forces, there was very

INFANTRY MARCHING TO SOMME TRENCHES

221

221 *'French Infantry marching to Somme Trenches.'* On the left of the picture are soldiers with trumpets and a couple of interested locals. Actions in the *Département* of the Somme are usually associated with the British. From material supplied by French Official Photographers. *British: (Pub. Newspaper Illustrations Ltd.)*

72. A BRITISH SENTRY IN FLANDERS.

OFFICIAL PHOTOGRAPH. CROWN COPYRIGHT RESERVED.

222

222 Caption on reverse reads. *'Lonesome sentry duty as well as the comradeship of the trenches falls to Tommy's lot on the drear landscapes of Flanders.'* The Daily Mail published a series of Battle Postcards, the first of which were issued on 6 September 1916. Twenty two series of sets of 8 were printed in all and can still be found today. To complete a collection of the whole series is a fascinating challenge that is well worth taking up. The most difficult cards to find are those of the later series. *British: (Pub. Daily Mail. Series IX.)*

MARINES LANDING AT OSTEND.

223

223 Ostend was raided in the middle of August 1914 by German Uhlans (Cavalry) who fought with the local gendarmes. Britain sent these marines to protect the town and Winston Churchill announced on 27 August 1914, '... a *strong force of British Marines has been sent to Ostend and has occupied the town and surroundings without delay.'* But by October the Germans had taken Ostend. Note the naval 'no peaks' hats. *British: (Pub. War Photogravure Publications.)*

224 'The War 1914–1917. American soldiers in France.' The Doughboy was clearly as attractive to the locals as his successor the 'G.I.' was to prove in WW2. Though the card says '1914–1917' the Americans did not land in Europe until 1917. *French: (Pub. Neurdin et Cie, Paris.)*

224A 'Mail for the Folks at Home'. A YMCA card. The Young Men's Christian Association was founded in London in 1844 and it and other organisations such as the Expeditionary Force Canteens provided mail and canteen services behind the lines. *American: (Pub. Illustrated Postal Card and Nov Co, N.Y.)*

225 *'Belgian refugees. Victims of the Kaiser's Lords.'* Many refugees went to Holland and many to Britain often working in war factories. In all over 1 million Belgians fled the country, *'No such problems in Britain'* – the message reads, '*… have dinner with me somewhere and go to a play*'. *British.*

Guerre 1914-1917. — LES AMERICAINS EN FRANCE. — AMERICAN SOLDIERS IN FRANCE.
On fait vite connaissance. — A french girl forming acquaintance with a soldier.

224

Mail for the Folks at Home.

224A

"WHITHER SHALL WE GO?"
(BELGIAN REFUGEES) VICTIMS OF THE KAISER'S LORDS.

225

20. Выселеніе изъ Дальняго.

226

226 A similar pathetic scene in Russia. *Russian: (Pub. M. Pikowsky, Odessa.)*

227 Fine photographic card of the 29th Div Cycle Company in Ragley. Such photographic cards are enthusiastically sought by Collectors. The 29th was formed early in 1915 and saw its first action in Gallipoli, though it probably left the bicycles in the UK. *British.*

228 Starkly realistic depiction of the horrors of War. Notice that the dead men's boots (in the middle of the picture) have been removed to be used again. *Dutch.*

227

little movement for the next three years. The maze of trenches on each side stretched 600 miles from the North Sea to Switzerland and grew increasingly complex. There were front line trenches, second line trenches, reserve trenches, communication trenches – but only one trench really terrified the soldiers – the assault trench. It was from there, usually at dawn when the human spirit is supposedly at its lowest ebb, that they would 'go over the top'. Usually they were fortified by alcohol to give them courage. The British got a double ration of rum and the association of going over the top with the issue of rum became so strong that rumours of rum being brought forward worried the Tommies, who could guess the next step. As attacks were generally made at first light, and the rum issued in the dark, men would often rejoin the queue unseen for a second or third issue from the 'jar'.

The soldiers were encouraged to be unthinking automatons, obediently moving on the command of their officers, up the side of the trench and over the top to advance on the enemy,

229 '"Tommy"' at home in captured German dugouts. Even by 1916 the general public rarely saw pictures that showed the true state of life on the battlefields. Bruce Bairnsfather the cartoonist got into hot water for showing too much reality in his drawings. *British: (Pub. Daily Mail. Series IV.)*

'TOMMY' AT HOME IN GERMAN DUG-OUTS

229

230 Caption on reverse reads, *'Every British trench is its own post-office, with telephone and telegraph wires. A wiring party is here going forward to its special-work.' British: (Pub. Daily Mail. Series XVII.)*

135   Crown Copyright reserved   A WIRING PARTY GOING TO THE TRENCHES   "Daily Mail" Official Photograph

230

sometimes marching, sometimes singing, crawling, falling and dying. One German company runner wrote, after the War, of his experiences at the first battle of Ypres in October 1914, when movement was still relatively free. He describes the company's advance into their very first battle: 'And then came a damp, cold night in Flanders, through which we marched in silence, and when the day began to emerge from the mists, suddenly an iron greeting came whizzing at us over our heads, and with a sharp report sent the little pellets flying between our ranks, ripping up the wet ground; but even before the little cloud had passed, from two hundred throats the first hurrah rose to meet the first messenger of death. Then a crackling and a roaring, a singing and a howling began, and with feverish eyes each one of us was drawn forward, faster and faster, until suddenly past turnip fields and hedges the fight began, the fight of man against man. And from the distance the strains of a song reached our ears, coming closer and closer, leaping from company to company, and just as Death plunged a busy hand into our ranks, the

231 'A brawny Maori Butcher'. 'ANZACS' (Australian and New Zealand Army Corps) was the acronym applied to soldiers of those nations as they assembled in Egypt before the landings in Gallipoli. In the first years of the war the Maoris served in the 'Native Contingent' but in 1916 it became the 'New Zealand Pioneer Battalion'. *British: (Pub. Daily Mail. Series XX.)*

232 Russian dead on and around electrified wire. *Dutch.*

233 Burnt out wreckage of aeroplane and dead pilot. Postcards showing real photographs of wrecks and crashes are much sought-after by collectors. *British.*

234 Posted in France on 17 February 1918. The message reads, '*... my health is still flourishing despite my long stay in the trenches ... I'm beginning to get fed up in the first line. As grenadiers, it is we who are always the furthest forward... and often we have to fight with grenades, battles which cost human lives, and so it needs brave men and the brave are found among the Bretons.*' The picture is meant to represent underground warfare at Verdun. *French: (Pub. E.L.D., Paris.)*

235 Types of Allied Armies, Series II, Australians. Caption on reverse reads, '*Splendid Australia! Immediately on the outbreak of war, the Commonwealth placed the Royal Australian Navy under control of the Admiralty and offered to send 20,000 troops to the United Kingdom. In addition Australia is now sending an Infantry Brigade and a complete Field Hospital.*' *British: (Pub. Tuck.)*

236 A card from a *Daily Mirror* sponsored series known as 'The Canadian Official.' Not at all like the real thing! *British: (Pub. Pictorial Newspaper Co.)*

233

LA BATAILLE SOUS VERDUN, 1916
Les Allemands ayant envahi un souterrain 20 volontaires français, avec une mitrailleuse les en chassèrent malgré la projection de liqui-des enflammés.

THE BATTLE AROUND VERDUN 1916
The Germans having invaded an underground, 20 volunteers drive them away with a maxim-gun in spite of the projection of flaming liquids.
Visé, Paris

234

AN AUSTRALIAN CONTINGENT.

235

A CANADIAN BULLDOG

236

237 A good meal in the trenches. The card was posted in Belgium on 20 August 1916 and part of the message reads, '*O yes I should like to return again to my dear old Antwerp. Will it be this year?*' We can answer the sender – 'No'. *French: (Pub. Baudinière.)*

238 Mobile German field kitchen in Douai during the occupation. Probably published after hostilities. Note lorry with trailer in the background. *French: (Pub. Levy Fits, Paris.)*

905. La Grande Guerre 1914-15-16 Front Belge - Un bon repas dans les tranchées.

« PHOT-EXPRESS »   Visé Paris 905

IMP. BAUDINIÈRE, NANTERRE

237

Visé Paris n° 3581   E. Baron, phot., Douai
16   LA GRANDE GUERRE 1914-18. — *Douai pendant l'occupation.* — *Cuisine roulante allemande.*

238

song reached us too and we passed it along : *Deutschland, Deutschland, Über Alles. Über Alles in Der Welt!* That company runner was Adolph Hitler.

The great armies of the War brought together more men in one place than had ever been assembled before. Their letters had to be delivered and collected, their weapons repaired, their ammunition replenished. All the stores of war had to be provided; picks and shovels, barbed wire, coffins, blankets, water bottles, helmets and on and on into many thousands of items. A system of staged supply was established to do all these things and the immense casualties forced the development of an efficient aid and evacuation system. The injured man would first be treated by his pals, who would put on a simple bandage if possible, then stretcher bearers would take him and others to the First Aid Post nearest to the spot; then to the Regimental Aid Post farther back; then out of Regimental hands into the Advanced Field Ambulance and slowly back. The worse the wound, the further back they went. If it was a Blighty one, they

239 'The Soldiers' Toilet.' From official French sources. The absence of any substantial earthworks suggests that this is nowhere near the front line and the striped shirt of the man in the middle might indicate that this is a Breton unit (it's a long shot). *British: (Pub. Newspaper Illustrations Ltd.)*

240 *'Dream of yesterday (15 August)'*. The Germans toast their capture of Paris. *'Reality of tomorrow (Up to the neck!!!)'*. The Kaiser in a barrel of mollases. *French.*

239

240

went home. The great armies depended upon their administration. Now the tail began to wag the dog, there were more suppliers than fighters and the methods created and developed to keep the armies afield were to be used again in the next war, and have changed little today, except in sophistication. The rear areas were usually based on villages and existing small towns. The soldiers taking a rest from the trenches were able to shop, make love – usually for a price – go to a cinema and buy picture postcards.

But those vast bodies of men were also targets for those other than enemies. The British forces in France were a huge captive market to enterprising business firms, who realised that fighting formed a very small part of a soldier's life. It was mostly waiting, and while he was waiting, Tommy needed something to do. So why not improve himself. Pelmanism, a mind training course to improve general knowledge, health, observation, memory, and almost every human faculty, was one of the most aggressively marketed courses. The course, known by the Tommies as Helpmanism, took

241 *'USA Sammies find the French climate appetising'.* Issued by the 'YMCA Hut Fund to provide Comforts, Shelter and Recreation for our Soldiers.' Series of 312 cards. *American.*

242 *'Canadian Kitchens at Havre.'* Retailer's name overprinted on the reverse – Quin & Axtens Ltd. SW9. *American: (Pub. Y.M.C.A. Hut Fund.)*

241

242

many weeks to complete and in 1917 the Pelman Institute claimed that 41 Generals, 8 Admirals and 10,000 officers and men were Pelman trained and that the Government were thinking about nationalizing the Institute so that everyone would take the course and the War would soon be won. The British press carried advertisements for postal degree courses available to the troops and for those with 'nerves' in the fighting areas, there were patent medicines, such as Sanatogen and Bynogen, available to relieve them. Budding artists would be asked in advertisements, *Can you Sketch?* and invited to send in a sample of their work. Newspapers and magazines enthusiastically sought regular orders from the fighting forces and offered various enticements to get them. *The Daily Mail* offered £10,000 free life insurance to the men in the trenches, but the newspaper risked little, since the cover was only for death caused by Zeppelins! It was another world, quite different to that at home, but Tommy had something to provide stability. He had his Bible. But it was not primarily for reading, it was for carrying in the breast pocket. Almost everyone knew of someone whose life had been saved when his Bible stopped a bullet.

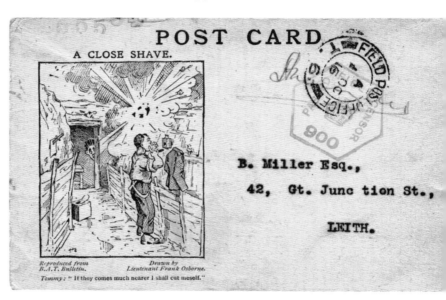

243

243A

TO THE GIRL HE LEFT BEHIND HIM.

R.A.O.B. SECOND MOTOR AMBULANCE.

140. Guerre 1914-15. — OFFÉMONT. Convoi de ravitaillement.   " Ed. Pays de France"

243, 243A Cartoon by Lt Frank Osborne, posted from the front on 1 October 1916. Part of the message reads,"... *and so Jimmy F is still dodging it...*' Conscription had been introduced in Britain in January 1916 so Jimmy F was having a good run. Posted 1 October 1916. Passed by Censor 900. *British.*

244 Types of Allied Armies Series II. '*The last letter to the Girl he left Behind Him*'. A group of Belgian Guards Officers early in 1914. The card was posted on 17 December 1914 and the message reads, '*... just done a twenty mile route march. Germans very near today.*' *British: (Pub. Tuck.)*

245 Superb photo of the R.A.O.B. (Royal Antidiluvian Order of Buffalos) Charity's 2nd Motor Ambulance 1915. These were manned by volunteers and after the war became the basis for the first civilian ambulance service. The vehicle here is probably a Sunbeam. *British.*

246 A supply waggon apparently with few supplies. Two of the men seem to be wearing aprons so perhaps they are about to cut meat unless of course they were about to eat the horses! The caption says '*Guerre 1914-15*' so it was still early days. *French: (Pub. Vaugirard, Paris.)*

247 In early October 1915 the Central Powers invaded Serbia and on 5 October the Allies landed at Salonika in Greece in a fruitless attempt to help. Serbs, Italians, Russians, French, Greek, Chinese and British all worked together, but for 12 months were contained within the 'Bird Cage', a defensive concentration camp area around Salonika where malaria caused many deaths. This 1916 Xmas card was sent to England on 5/3/17 and was passed by the Censor whose mark is unclear. *British: (Pub. Photochrom Co. Ltd.)*

247

248 This is an unusually scruffy lot of German soldiers. Perhaps they are on fatigues and on a 'smoking break'. However the sender is probably pictured in the group and the card was addressed to 'Frau' so it may have been to a wife or a mother. *Feldpostbrief 25.8.15. German.*

249 '*British infantry under shelter behind a wall.*' Written by a French soldier on 29 October 1914. The message ends by saying the recipient must have heard of the deaths of three soldiers of the A.S.F., one of whose brothers was wounded, and that another was taken prisoner. On 1 September the British retreat from Mons had reached Néry and fighting took place around the local cemetery. Is it too fanciful to guess that this is a scene in that cemetery? *French: (Pub. Le Deley, Paris.)*

250 A Frenchman's vision of Alsace and Lorraine. The British had their Angels of Mons (qv). *French: (Pub. A. Noyer, Paris.) Artist F. Petit-Gérard.*

248

249

50

51

52

251 One of a series of twenty patriotic cards covering many aspects of the War seen rose-tinted from the U.S.A. *American: (Pub. Merval Corp., N.Y.)*

252 Comradeship was something that hundreds of thousands of men would find for the first time with the help of the YMCA and the huts gave them somewhere to sit down and to write home, as this soldier is doing. *American: (Pub. Merval Corp. N.Y.)*

253 The caption describes the picture as '*The American journalists' mission*'. Whoever the American journalists were, they were no more truthful about the reality of the War in their reports than their European counterparts. *French: (Pub. Levy Fils, Paris.)*

254 Message on reverse, '*Souvenir of 2 French prisoner of war comrades to their English comrade, Swayne. Munster 20 May 1917.*' There were four P.O.W camps at Munster, one of which was solely for Russian prisoners. This is obviously part of a concert party act, an activity that featured in most camps. Camp photo.

255 German soldiers in the Vosges trenches. Note the solidly constructed wooden walls and benches. It all looks too clean and ordered to be anywhere near the front line. *German: (Pub. Colour photographers, Stuttgart.)*

256 'The World War 1914/15. '*The German Territorials are coming.*' Unlike the Americans pictured in Card 251 the Germans are dressed for battle and weather – somewhere very cold. Russia, perhaps. *German: (Pub. Karl Schmidt, Dresden.)*

253

254

255

256

The Machines

The War in the West became a titanic struggle between millions of men living in a line of trenches 600 miles long from the Channel to Switzerland. That line of trenches would hardly move throughout the whole War and would dictate the tactics of both sides. And the reason was the machine gun.

The Germans treated the machine gun as an infantry weapon, and equipped their infantry battalions with them, sometimes two guns per battalion. The British, French and Belgians regarded the machine gun more as a light artillery weapon and issued few to the infantry. The result was that the Germans possessed overwhelming fire-power well forward that gave them control of the battlefield. The Allies reacted by also adopting the tactics of using their machine guns with interlocking arcs of fire, well forward and from protected positions. The ground between the opposing armies became a No–Mans Land. Thus the War became a stalemate with the machine gun proving to be a defensive weapon neither side could defeat. Attempts to break the deadlock included poison gas and tanks.

The Germans were the first to use gas. On 22 April 1915 on the Ypres sector they attacked, using chlorine, which was released from cylinders and blown by the wind towards the French lines. The effect was dramatic and immediate: taken entirely by surprise, the French, with their Colonial Turco troops, ran, spluttering with pain, away from the green cloud. Strangely, the Germans seemed to have no reserves ready to exploit the gap which had opened in the Allied

257 A famous and much-reproduced image (also on prints and more recently on mugs), usually mis-captioned as 'French soldiers'. In fact they are Belgian Chasseurs attacked by the Germans on their retreat from Malines. It shows machine-gunners in a forward position and, behind, the typical Belgian dog carts that transported them. Another image in the same series shows 17 Belgian Chasseurs holed up in a house, surrounded by Prussians, who refused to surrender and who were all killed. The incident was mentioned in the May 1915, 'Bryce Report', on German atrocities (much discredited post-war for exaggeration). *Belgian: (Pub. on Rue Ma Campagne, Brussels.)*

258 German soldiers wearing gas masks. August 1917. The first major use of lethal poison gas was that of Chlorine at Ypres by the Germans on 22 April 1915. *French: (Pub. Friends of the Army Museum, Paris.)*

259 From Official French sources. The weapon could be a French 2.58 trench mortar. Note how many men were needed to move one weapon! *British: (Pub. Newspaper Illustrations Ltd.)*

12 Les Masques Allemands Août 1917   *Collection F. Flameng*

258

REMOVING A TRENCH GRENADE GUN TO POSITION

259

lines. Furious fighting followed, and the day was saved by Canadian troops who quickly moved up to fill the breach. Within a few days the Allies issued an elementary form of respirator which consisted of a cotton wool pad, dipped in a chemical solution that was tied with tapes over the nose and mouth to give protection against the fumes. Another German innovation was 'stink gas'. A foul-smelling gas was mixed with the poison, which encouraged the soldiers to take off their helmets to clear the smell, only to fall prey to the poison. The soldier whose health had been destroyed by gas was one of the most pitiful sights after the War.

260 Although the men have their heads protected, their hands are bare and susceptible to attacks by blister gases, such as mustard gas. This probably means that the picture was taken before blister gases were introduced by the Germans in the summer of 1917. The man in the foreground might have been fooled by stink-gas into removing his helmet. *British.*

261 The caption reads, '*Turpin the great French chemist, inventor of melinite and other explosives which assure the superiority of our 75.*' The '75' was the quick firing field gun. *French.*

262 Another French Army photograph. The gun has lifting handles on top and is clearly a very heavy weapon – perhaps a naval gun. It is captioned as being on the Somme but it would be quite a way back from the front line. *British: (Pub. Newspaper Illustrations.)*

3—Attacking Front Line Trenches.

260

LA GUERRE de 1914 — TURPIN, le grand Chimiste Français, inventeur de la Mélinite et autres explosifs qui assurent la supériorité de notre canon de 75   A. R.

261

A WELL-SCREENED GUN ON THE SOMME FRONT

262

263 Telephone and telegraph line communications were the major means of passing information during the War on land but keeping the wires intact under shellfire was both difficult and dangerous. Radio was very unreliable and the airways liable to eavesdropping by the enemy. *French. 1914.*

CAMPAGNE DE 1914
ARMEE FRANÇAISE. — *La Téléphonie militaire*   *ND Phot*
70

263

264 Signalling over long distances in Africa was possible using a heliograph. Wireless was insufficiently developed to equip all small mobile parties. The heliograph is an instrument which consists of two mirrors so arranged that sunlight can be beamed in any chosen direction. The beam is interrupted by a key operated shutter and Morse code signals can be sent to an observer who watches from afar using a telescope. *German: (Pub. H. Rathjen, Hamburg.)*

Heliographen-Station   D.-S.-W.-Afrika

264

The tank was created out of the need to break the trench warefare stalemate by crossing both No-Mans Land and the enemy's trenches, and it owed its existence to determined and far-sighted men like William Tritton, Ernest Swinton and Winston Churchill. Tanks were first used during the Battle of the Somme on 15 September 1916 and Haig has been accused of employing them before they were ready in a vain attempt to snatch victory from disaster.

Modifications and improvements followed rapidly upon the first action. 'Male' tanks had two ex-naval six pounder guns, one in a sponson each side, plus four machine guns, Female' tanks had six machine guns. The Mark 1s had a maximum speed of 3.5 mph, no springs and no soundproofing. The noisy, smoky engine and grinding gearbox took up most of the crew compartment, rapidly bringing the temperature inside up to 90°F and filling the space with choking fumes. The crew of eight had great difficulty in keeping their balance as the tank

265 This is a British tank which had been captured by the Germans and then used by them. Note the German cross on the side. The caption says that it was destroyed by a shell near la Pompelle, one of a string of French forts defending Reims. There is now a fine museum in the old fort. *French.*

266 '*French Infantry in Occupation of Hun Trenches.*' Note the efficient German metal shelter, reminiscent of the French Maginot Line forts. From an official photo by the photographic section of the French Army. *British: (Pub Newspaper Illustrations, London.)*

267 Recruiting Procession, Croydon. The crowds turn out to see the armoured vehicles, (possibly Austins), and doubtless there was a band somewhere. The whole affair was meant to encourage men to sign up. The card is dated 'Oct 2nd 1915' and so we were still relying upon volunteers for our armed forces. *British: (Pub. Harrison Price Studios.)*

142. LA POMPELLE — Attaque allemande du 15 juillet 1918
Tank allemand Liesel blessé à mort par un obus français s'écroule dans la tranchée française de première ligne — Broken down tank in a trench.

265

FRENCH INFANTRY IN OCCUPATION OF HUN TRENCHES

266

Recruiting Procession Croydon.
Oct 2nd 1915

267

268 Hand-coloured 'Field Sketch' of Maubeuge burning on 5 September 1914 after fire by German heavy artillery. Two days later the Belgian fort fell having been under siege since the 24th of August. Unusually, an advert card for Kalichlord Toothpaste. *German.*

269 Photograph of bridge-building exercise by 139 Field Co., RE supervised by the officer in the mac on the right. Sent from Buxton by Sapper, 'hubby Will', to his dear wife on 13.7.15. *British.*

270 'French Tanks' [Renault F17, with the first independent rotating turret] 'gloriously' in Strasbourg, 9 Dec 1918. Alsace had been annexed to France on 5 December (after having lost it to the Germans in the Franco–Prussian War of 1870) to great celebration. 'Le Tigre' was the nickname of Georges Clemenceau. *French.*

271 Captioned 'Whippet Tanks in action', these tanks look more like Renaults – also known as 'Mosquitos'. Card issued for the War Bond Campaign by the National War Savings Committee. Tanks were often used for fund-raising purposes in the UK. *British: (Pub. A.M. Davis & Co.)*

271

272 Hand-painted tribute to the French 75mm field gun, the best of the War. It was one of the first field guns to feature a system of recuperation which virtually eliminated recoil when the gun was fired, hence doing away with the need to re-aim after each round. *French.*

273 'Searchlights which lit up the Zeppelin till its fall, 21 February 1916.' Two Zeppelins are listed as being brought down by 'enemy fire' on this date – LZ47, at Verdun and LZ65 at Vitry-le-Francois. *French: (Pub. E. Le Deley, Paris.)*

272

273

274 'The little German maid.' Artist Albert Beerts. Spy scares and rumours swept the front line and the home fronts and many innocent people were no doubt summarily executed as spies. *French: (Pub. A. Noyer, Paris.)*

275 A German prisoner being questioned. A card after the painting by French artist Georges Scott. The original sold for 6,950 fr. in 1948. The *Musee de L'Armée* in Paris exhibits many of his pictures. Allied soldiers were taught not to answer questions, the Germans were not, and consequently gave away more information under interrogation. *French.*

274

275

lurched along, pitching and rolling. Communication was impossible, except by hand signals because of the noise. As the only light had to enter through the narrow observation slits, it was often too dark even for hand signals, and generally only the commander and driver had any idea of where they were and what was happening. External communication was achieved by stopping and getting out, although pigeons were sometimes carried. However the exhausted and hungry crews frequently found the temptation of a fresh meal too great and ate their communications.

  The British produced an armoured fighting vehicle capable of crossing trenches, the French a self-propelled gun with little armour. Their tank, the Schneider, was first used on 16 April 1917 and was a failure. Its development was abandoned and later Renault produced a small light two man tank, the M17. This tank was copied by the Americans, whose own tank-building programme was in difficulties, and known as the 6 ton tank. It wasn't until some British tanks

276 *'Taken!'* German prisoners of the French. Cards with a prisoner of war theme are much collected, and those bearing postmarks of the camp, whether Allied or Central Powers, are particularly valuable. *French: (Pub. I. Lapina. Paris.)*

276

277 Artist's impression of a damaged British ambulance at Verdun, a card published by the 'British ambulances for French wounded' (it claims to have '120 at the French front'). The distinguished committee included the Duke of Portland and Admiral the Right Hon Lord Beresford. *British.*

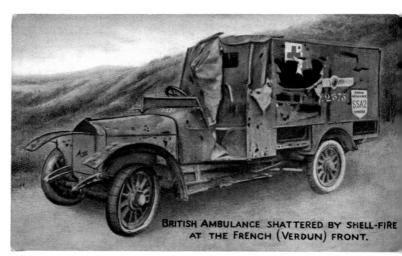

BRITISH AMBULANCE SHATTERED BY SHELL-FIRE AT THE FRENCH (VERDUN) FRONT.

277

were captured at Cambrai in November 1917 that the Germans had many armoured vehicles. They designed and produced a massive vehicle 24 ft long, 10 ft wide and 11 ft high, known as the A7V Sturmpanzerwagen. It carried one six pounder gun, six machine guns and a crew of 18! It was never produced in quantity and only saw action half a dozen times before the Armistice.

   The First World War was the first truly mechanized war, the first war in which technology became so significant a factor that special staffs had to be trained to understand and evaluate its proper uses. The introduction of the tank meant the need for anti-tank weapons, and the Germans were not slow in using the 'K' rifle bullet, whose tungsten carbide core enabled it to penetrate the armour of the British Mark 1! They went on to produce the Mauser T rifle to cope with the British Mark IV tank, whose armour stopped the 'K' bullet. The French, in an attempt to increase the effectiveness of their aerial bombing against infantry, introduced the *fléchette*

278

278 Written note identifies-marching men as '*German prisoners passing thru' Frimley.*' Careful examination reveals that many of the men are smiling. They were doubtless glad to be safe until the end of the war. *British.*

279 An innovative use of a searchlight to enable work to be carried out at night – the illumination was nicknamed 'artificial moonlight'. *British.*

279

or little arrow. The Germans first produced the *flammenwerfer* or flamethrower and used it at Hooge on 30 July 1915. The earliest models, carried by one man, worked by gas pressure and threw a jet of burning oil about twenty yards.

Trench warfare meant the development of short range and hand to hand weapons. These ranged from clubs with barbed wire wrapped around the business end, through an endless

280 At the Front Series 1. Commanders quickly realized the value of the motor car as a reconnaissance vehicle. This was to be the first truly mechanized war. Marching troops did not always appreciate Generals rushing past them in cars. *British: (Pub. Tuck.)*

281 Typical piece of picturesque French propaganda, with troops charging through poison gas without gas masks. Probably a reflection upon the fact that French troops came under limited artillery fire with gas shells at Nieuport in March 1915. *French* (Pub. *E. Le Deley, Paris.)*

282 'Belgian 222m mortar in action In Flanders.' These heavy mortars had limited elevation and no rotation other than moving the whole weapon, which is what the soldiers are trying to do with the long pole. *British: (Pub. Y.M.C.A. Hut Fund.)*

283 *'The Brigadier's Side Car'.* Frankly we doubt that a Brigadier would have got in one, however, it is further evidence of the mechanisation of war that characterised the fighting. At the Front Series 1. *British: (Pub. Tuck.)*

284 Legend reads, '*The taking of St. Georges by the Belgians, December 1914*'. Artist Albert Beerts. The message on the back says, '*An Affectionate good morning from the trenches of the Belgian front. Your devoted friend. All my passionate kisses.*' Now known as St Joris, the small town is immediately east of Nieuwpoort. Posted 3 December 1915. *French: (Pub. A. H. Kati, Paris.)*

THE GENERAL'S OBSERVATION CAR.

280

1914-15.. Nos Soldats chargent courageusement à travers les fumées asphixiantes.

1914-15.. Our Soldiers charge courageously through the asphixing fumes

281

THE BELGIAN ARMY IN FLANDERS – A 222 M.M. MORTAR IN ACTION

282

THE BRIGADIER'S SIDE CAR.

283

284

variety of knives and daggers to grenades and mortars. Since opposing trenches were generally further apart than a grenade could be thrown by hand, mortars and rifles were adapted to shoot grenades, thus enabling forward infantry to have their own close support artillery which they could use from the safety of their own trenches.

The bicycle was a very important engine of war, and used by all combatants to move men behind the front lines or to patrol areas of possible infiltration. The Italian Bersaglieri, or Sharpshooter Regiments, with whom Benito Mussolini, the future Fascist dictator' served as a private, had an attached bicycle battalion. Their bicycles were collapsible and folded small enough to be carried on a man's back. The British had several Cycle Corps, as had the Germans. Training included not only riding the machine – the 'learning to ride by numbers' was based on horse drill and was still being taught in the same way in the 1950s – but also how to build barricades and obstacles with them. Perhaps the most dramatic innovations of the War on the ground came in the areas of movement and communications. The railways had been used for strategic and tactical movement of troops and supplies as early as the Crimea, but the first 'railway war' was the American Civil War. In Europe the Germans had the advantage of having their internal lines of railway communication, while the French had some disruption due to the German occupation. The use of the railways divided into two broad functions: the reinforcement and supply of large static armies and the provision of mobility to a small force to enable it to garrison a large area. Before the advent of radio, long distance communication was achieved by telegraph or in sunny climates, such as Africa, by heliograph. In Europe the major medium and long range communication

Il generale Cadorna stringe cordialmente la mano al Maresciallo Haig.
La Lega Italo-Britannica, in nome del popolo inglese, invia
saluti fraterni ai valorosi soldati italiani combattenti sulle
Alpi, sull' Isonzo e sul Carso.

285   286

system at the beginning of the War was the
field telephone. The British had used the field
telephone in the Boer War and their signals
organization was well-established. Repair units
known as Advanced Signal Stations were on
hand to repair the constant damage to cables
resulting from the shelling. In 1914 most of
the combatant armies had radio, although
it was unreliable and the sets were only just
movable. One early British field radio, together
with its batteries, needed a squad of nine men
just to carry it! The continual damage to cable
communications from the guns accelerated the
development of radio, but there were so few
channels that the airways became jammed, and
one side was easily able to listen to the other.
This naturally prompted the development
of codes, yet another hazard in the accurate
transmission of messages. Radio was of major
significance at sea, while field telephone and
telegraph continued in greater use on land.

285 *'1st Automobile Centre'*. Based in Turin,
the vehicles operated in the typically dangerous
mountainous roads of the North Italy campaign.
The caption equates to the American WW2 *'Hell on
Wheels'* convoys, which acted with speed and spirit.
A compelling image but sadly the artist's signature
in the bottom right hand corner is indecipherable.
Italian: (Pub. V.E, Boeri, Rome.)

286 A supposed meeting between Haig and General
Cadorna. Cadorna was Chief of Staff of the Italian
army for the first 3 years of the War. After the major
defeat of the Italians at Caporetto, General Cadorna
was relieved of his post. The card was posted on
3 January 1918 and the message says, '*I hope that
the War will finish this year. There is still no signs of
I (sic) getting leave worse luck. Joe, I.E. [Italian
Expeditionary] Force.*' Italian.

14. YPRES, 1916.
Téléphone de Campagne.
A field Telephon.

287 British field telephone, Ypres 1916. Phone wires could either be left to trail over the ground or raised on poles. The latter method was clearly rarely possible in the front line, the former method used an 'earth return' system which left communications susceptible to German tapping. *Belgian: (Pub. Marco Marcovici, Brussels.)*

288 Trench warfare, and the immediate hail of bullets that a head over the parapet produced, accelerated the development of these periscopes. Commercial versions were available in portable form. *French: (Pub. Laureys, Paris.)*

289 British soldier searching for a German spy in Belgium. During the retreat from Mons there were many spy scares. As the Germans advanced they feared spies amongst the populations that they had captured. *French: (Pub. ELD. Paris.)*

287

Visé Paris N° 526
LA VIE SUR LE FRONT. OBSERVATION PAR LE PÉRISCOPE
Life on the front. Observing through the periscope

288

1914... EN BELGIQUE — Soldats Anglais
cherchant un espion Allemand
1914. IN BELGIUM — British soldiers
looking for a german spy

289

BRABANT-LE-ROI (Meuse) — Un engin des assassins Boches
Descendu le 21 Février 1916, à 20 h. 47, par la Section des Anti-Canons de Revigny

Vieux Paris (E D)

10.00

290

Cliché Chusseau-Flaviens

1914. Blessés Anglais a la défense d'Anvers
16me Série 1914.. English wounded from Attwerps defense (E D)

291

Meanwhile the British pigeon service had
grown to 20,000 birds with 380 handlers by 1918, and found employment in both intelligence and
combat roles. In a growing policy of centralizing functions, the Director of Signals took over the
central control of pigeons in June 1915.

The internal combustion engine revolutionized the conduct of war. It was not just in the armoured
cars or tanks and aeroplanes that it made an impact. It turned electric generators, pumped water
out of trenches, powered despatch riders' motorcycles, gave commanders a vehicle in which to visit
their troops and reconnoitre the battleground and, in the shape of Paris taxis and London buses,
carried troops to the trenches. It also began to take over the only remaining task that horses had,
now that the horse cavalry was finished : the task of moving supply trains and field guns.

The French looked upon their field gun the '75', with almost religious fervour. It was feted
throughout France in every conceivable way and postcards in their millions were produced
offering *Gloire à Notre 75*. The gun was the best medium field piece owned by any of the armies;
its value lying in its lightness, which made it extremely useful in the Dardanelles operation,
and its recoil system which eliminated backward travel of the carriage during firing. This latter
characteristic together with developed breech mechanism and gun laying devices allowed a
very high rate of fire. Ammunition expenditure, however, was grossly underestimated by all the
combatants, a situation which was aggravated by the consumption of the quick firing guns. The
so–called 'Shell Scandal' in Britain in June 1916, in which politicians blamed the War Office for
shortages of shells, was one of the key factors in bringing down the Liberal Government. *To this
day no other Liberal Government has been returned to power.*

The Germans made effective tactical and propaganda use of their 420 mm howitzers, known

THE PRISONERS

RAEMAEKERS' WAR CARTOONS

292

290 Another Zeppelin, LV77, brought down by the French at 2047 hours on 21 February 1916 at Brabant-le Roi by the Revigny (about 30 miles south west of Verdun) anti-aircraft guns, though it reportedly took over 20 shots (see Card 342.) Interestingly the gun is mounted directly onto a motor vehicle making it easy to move. *French: (Pub: E.L.D., Paris.)*

291 *'English wounded from the Attwerp's [sic] defense.'* Winston Churchill instigated a gallant attack on the Port of Antwerp (which the Belgians, after a desperate defence, had ceded to the Germans on 9 October 1914). It was made by his newly formed Royal Naval Division (amongst them an excited Rupert Brooke). It was not a success, and the RND, who had left Dover on the 4th, returned to it on the 9th with their wounded. *French: (Pub. E. Le Deley, Paris.)*

292 A cartoon by the well-known Dutch artist, Raemakers, who captures the disheartened mood of these French soldiers. Posted from Sutton Veny Camp, 3 Aug 1916. It was at this camp that Bruce Bairnsfather drew his famous *'Better 'Ole'* cartoon. *British: (Pub. C. Pulman & Sons Ltd.)*

as Big Berthas, supposedly named after Bertha von Bohlen, head of the Krupp family. Later, when the Germans began to shell Paris in March 1918, the high velocity gun used, which threw a 260lb shell 76 miles from the forest of Courcy, was nicknamed Big Bertha as well. Its barrel was 110 feet long and the gun weighed 142 tons. The effectiveness of the guns was matched by an improvement in the type and range of ammunition used. British field guns had started the War equipped only with shrapnel ammunition but by the battle of Loos were able to fire high explosive, and by 1916 most light guns of both sides could fire smoke shells. The explosive charges used in shells were based on picric acid. Chemical control of picric acid to enable it to be packed into the shell cases had first been established by the French who applied the name Melinite to the mixture. The British used the same compound and called it Lyddite.

Early on in the War the French were very secretive about their ammunition and their 75 and were sensitive to spy scares. In the retreat from Mons there were virulent rumours about flashing lights and mysterious cyclists pedalling furiously towards the Germans. Anyone in unfamiliar dress was likely to be taken prisoner and if not shot, at least interrogated – a continual hazard for prisoners.

Although some prisoners, like Charles de Gaulle, who was disabled and captured at Verdun in March 1916, spent many years in prisoner of war camps and were thus available for interrogation over a period, the best time to obtain information by interrogation was found to be immediately after capture. This was not just because the information would be more up to date, but the prisoner, relieved at being alive and out of the War, was more likely to talk. The British had created an Intelligence Corps at the start of the War. Their policy was to send an officer forward to 'examine' prisoners as soon as possible. Their technique was based on being friendly towards the enemy and they found that most prisoners were willing to answer questions. The ease with

293 *'The Tank Bank, After Business Hours'*. (See card No. 271.) The concept of 'National Savings' was created during the war in order to raise funds from the general public. One of the ways of doing this was to have half a dozen tanks tour the country in concert with speeches and the sale of War Bonds. Many millions of pounds were raised this way. This tank looks like a Mark V. *British.*

293

294 *'English machine guns in action, Northern France'*, a rather posed-looking shot. On the reverse is a somewhat desperate message from soldier Maurice to his parents, written on 29 June 1918: *'Poor Clauvet didn't have a chance but that's the fate that awaits us all at every second. We are bombarded night and day* [by aeroplanes] *and I assure you these alerts are serious. Your son who will never forget you.'* French.

294

which the British Intelligence Officers obtained information led to a simple form of training being introduced into the British Army. The soldiers were told that if they were captured and questioned they were only to give their Number, Rank and Name and no other information of any sort. This proved effective for at the end of the War the German General Staff were to complain that 'British prisoners were a great disappointment to interrogators'. The British interrogation system was based on a series of 'cages' in which prisoners were collected. At Divisional level the cages would be sited near the Field Ambulances so that wounded prisoners could also be quickly interviewed for tactical information and selected for further interrogation at Corps and Army cages. Much use was made of stool pigeons who mixed with the prisoners, picking up information by eavesdropping. After the interrogation process, prisoners were kept far away from the combat areas and had to settle down and accept captivity. Life in the prisoner of war camps was infinitely preferable to life at the Front and prisoners were able to write home, to receive Red Cross parcels and to relax in the knowledge that they would survive the War. Their letters were censored, of course, but unlike the official postcard that soldiers in the front

295 This card, posted on 30 December 1914, forecasts things to come – combined operations with the German Fleet and the air support of airships and aeroplanes. *German.*

296 Longmoor Station. The importance of railways in war was well established in the American Civil War and a 'Military Training Railway' was established at Longmoor in Hampshire. Standard and various narrow gauges lines were set up and in 1916 railway companies were formed. The branch line to Bordon Camp was still running in the 1950s – one of the authors travelled on it! *British.*

297 Girls pose in their factory for this rare photograph while making wings for RAF planes. *British.*

298 Girls making shells in the Cammell Laird factory, Sheffield. Here they seem to be machining the cases rather than filling the shells with explosive chemicals. In the latter process the girls' skins often turned yellow, earning them the nickname of 'The Canary Girls'. Part of a series by Artist E.F. Skinner. Card 'Passed by the Censor. 21/12/16'. *British.*

Luftflotte begleitet Kriegsschiffe

295

Longmoor Station.

296

297

SHELL WORKERS.   CAMMELL LAIRD. SHEFFIELD.

298

Salvation Army making Doughnuts under bombardment of German Guns, Front Line-France.

299

A.F.A. 2042.
114 Gen.No./5248.

FIELD SERVICE

POST CARD.

The address only to be written on this side. If anything else is added the post card will be destroyed.

[Crown Copyright Reserved.]

300

SCHLOSS FRICOURT

Erinnerung an den

Feldzug 1914/15

Im Felde gez. Nov 1914 S

301

line had to use, they did not leave the recipient wondering if the sender was still alive. The pre-printed Field Post Cards of the warring armies say little, but speak volumes: 'I have received no letter from you for a long time' is an essay that needs only a little imagination to complete.

The picture postcard depicted the type of war the nation concerned wished its people to see. In Britain the most comprehensive and probably the most popular series of cards ever produced in the history of the postcard was the *Daily Mail* 'Battle Series'. In 1916 the Press Bureau asked for tenders for the exclusive right to reproduce as postcards, pictures taken by official photographers of the fighting on the Western Front. The *Daily Mail* tender was accepted, half the net profits to go to military charities, with a minimum payment of £5,000. The issue of the cards and the excitement they caused were recorded by the *Daily Mail*: '8 August 1916: First Forty Official Pictures. Four of the largest and most eminent firms in the postcard printing trade are already engaged'..... and.. 'Yesterday one important organization sent a first order for 250,000 cards. All tastes are suited in the production of the cards. They will be in three styles, photogravure, three-colour and silver print style (photographic facsimile). Some are printed in the two styles and some in all three. For the convenience of collectors every card is numbered ...' Seven sets of cards, numbered IV to X, were put on sale on 6 September. The *Daily Mail* told the story the following day: '7 September 1916. Amazing demand for *Daily Mail* Battle Postcards. At 11 o'clock yesterday morning the *Daily Mail* branch offices were an astonishing spectacle of high-tide work. The wholesale dealers had already been cleaned out by the retailers, the retailers were bombarding the wholesalers with repeat orders and for their own repeat orders the wholesalers were sending not only vans, but carts of all kinds, motor cars of all kinds, trucks of all kinds, hand barrows, box cycles, cyclists with sacks and even boys who went away bent under emergency parcels almost as big as themselves. The routine of ordinary business had to be abandoned ... There were other searchers too, among the show sets of the war postcards. They were the buyers who looked for the face of their own man. The reality was that many tens of thousands would never ever see the face of their own man again.'

302

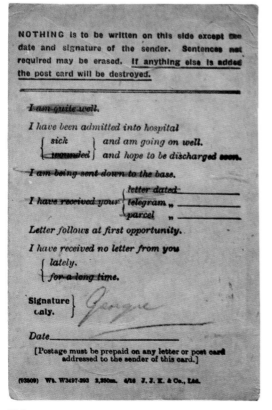

303

299 Salvation Army girls making doughnuts in their field kitchen 'under bombardment of German guns, Front Line – France.' American: *(Pub. The Chicago Daily News.)*

300 Front side of official field postcard. At the beginning of the War the official cards were normal size, but those produced from 1917 onward were much smaller, presumably to save paper. *British.*

301 Official field postcard showing more imagination than the plain British card. Fricourt Chateau, November 1914. Fricourt is a small village on the Somme that was occupied by the Germans in 1914. *German.*

302 The card commemorates exactly what it says. The message on the reverse says, '*... there is some talk of the boys going home for six months so I might be amongst that lot. The names on this card are where we were the* first 1000 days *... your Blighty Nephew?*' The figure is holding the Australian flag and the shoulder flash is probably that of the 2nd/17th Battalion of the Royal New South Wales Regiment. *Australian.*

303 Standard army postcard with alternative messages. The sad part is that though the sender is sick he has '*received no letter from you lately*'. Army Form A2042. *British.*

The War at Sea

Just as the new armies in Europe were to live and fight underground, so the new navies were to fight underwater. The battle under the seas was the key to the outcome of the War and had Germany been less timid in the initial use of her *Unterseeboots* she might have been the victor and not the loser.

The British public, confident in the knowledge that their Grand Fleet had almost complete command of the sea in 1914, were expecting a major battle between the opposing surface fleets in which the enemy would be destroyed. Since the turn of the century naval development in most powerful nations had concentrated on the all big gun armoured battleship, championed in Britain by Admiral John (Jacky) Arbuthnot Fisher, who re-organized the Navy during his six years as First Sea Lord from 1904. The type was known as 'Dreadnoughts' after the first British vessel, and in 1914 Britain had 29 of them and Germany 18.

Unlike Britain, however, the Germans, under the direction of Admiral von Tirpitz, had appreciated the potential of the submarine. Tirpitz did not rush into building U-boats as France had done around 1900, but waited to see what mistakes would be made in their development. Following secret trials in the North Sea in 1912 and the emergence of the concept of diesel power for surface movement and electric batteries for underwater movement, Germany put maximum effort into submarine production. Thus by 1914 she had twice as many submarines building or in commission as had Britain, although Britain had more afloat.

The Kaiser was determined to keep his High Seas Fleet intact by avoiding a direct confrontation with the British Home Fleet. Thus German policy was based on maintaining a threat of a naval action sufficient to tie the Home Fleet to the North Sea, but only to venture out from time to time in order to prove that the battle threat was a real one. The surface war at sea therefore became a series of isolated incidents, like Heligoland, the Falkland Islands and Jutland. Thus in collecting the picture postcards of the naval war it is possible to concentrate upon clearly defined actions and to build up a representation of both sides involved, just as is possible with opposing generals in set piece battles.

The picture cards of ships are scarce. Firstly there are many collectors, and as a result 'undiscovered' cards are hard to find. Secondly the Germans very quickly imposed censorship upon the picture postcard and prevented their vessels being photographed. The British were slower and postcards showing H.M. Ships were still being sent to neutral countries in 1916. However, on 6 June 1916, further postcards picturing H.M. Ships were forbidden and although there were some Admiralty authorized exceptions, such as the Photochrom Series published in June 1916 showing scenes from *Britain Prepared,* the official film of the Fleet, very few later cards can be found today. The British cards, therefore, tend to chronicle the early actions of the War, and the German cards are all preoccupied with the U-boat and its more significant exploits.

Surface actions began off Heligoland in the same month that War broke out. The British with a force of battle cruisers, light cruisers, destroyers and submarines raided German patrols off Heligoland on 28 August 1914 hoping to entice their capital ships out from their lair at

304

305

304 *'The sinking of the German Cruiser Mainz off Heligoland, August 28 1914.'* News card that would have been produced very soon after the event, the first naval battle of the war and a British victory for Admiral Beatty. *British*: *(Pub. C. Cozens, Portsmouth.)*

305 *H.M.S. Queen Mary* was involved in the sinking of the *Mainz* and was sunk herself at Jutland. Strangely, postcards depicting warships are often less valuable than those showing aeroplanes or motor transport. Since the issue of ship cards during the War was strictly controlled by the Censor, these cards must inevitably become much more valuable as demand begins to overtake the limited supply. *British*.

306 *H.M.S. Queen Elizabeth* took part in the Naval bombardment during the Dardanelles campaign from March 1915, firing from anchor in the Aegean and across the Peninsula. One of her unexploded shells can still be seen in the wall of the fort at Cannakale. She was then the most powerful Superdreadnought afloat with 8 x 15" guns. *British*.

306

307 'The Anglo-French fleet under fire from the Dardanelles Forts.' (February–March 1915.) From a painting by Paul Teschinsky. The Dardanelles Channel shrinks to less than a mile at the Narrows and the Germans, the Turks' allies, helped to set up the shore guns. *German: (Pub. Philipp Reclam Jnr, Leipzig.)*

307

307A In June 1918 HMS *D6* was sunk north of Inishtrahull Island, off the west coast of Ireland, by *UB73*. Some accounts describe two of her crew as being taken prisoners, the rest perished. Message on reverse, '*Dear Dad, I have left my ship as I have a poisoned finger and my nose is also bad. Florrie & Baby are fine and everything else A.1. So buck up Dad.*' Diving expeditions were mounted in 2005 and 2007 to reach her but no positive results appear to have succeeded. Posted 1915. *British: (Pub: Gale & Polden, Portsmouth.)*

307A

308 H.M.A.S. *Sydney* sometimes pretended to be S.M.S. *Emden*. It has been suggested that when the *Sydney* and the *Emden* met, each was pretending to be the other! They fought in the Battle of the Cocos Islands on 9th November 1914 – the Sydney won. *British: (Pub. Beagles.)*

309 The *Emden* had been shelling Coco Island's radio station when the *Sydney* caught her. 9 Nov 1914. *British.*

H.M.A.S. SYDNEY
WHICH SUCCEEDED IN DESTROYING THE NOTORIOUS GERMAN
CRUISER EMDEN AT COCOS KEELING ISLAND ON 9TH NOVEMBER 1914

308

The German Cruiser "Emden" after the Battleship "Sydney" had finished with her. Cocos Island, November 9th, 1914.

COPYRIGHT

309

310

311

310 Reproduction of painting by Prof. Hans Bohrdt, recording the defeat of von Spee's squadron at the Falkland Islands on 8 December 1914. The reverse carries a poem entitled '*The Last Man.*' The defiant sailor is waving the flag of the Imperial German Navy. *German.*

311 Reproduction of painting by Prof. Hans Bohrdt. The message on the back is in English and the card may have been taken unused from a German prisoner. The message reads, '*Some picture. How they like to gloat over it all. I asked one prisoner when the War would finish. He said "never in our time because Germany will never give in".*' *German.*

312 An extraordinary story – of German U-boat *UC-5* (pictured). Between July 1915–April 1916 she sank 32 vessels, including the hospital ship *Anglia*, with the loss of 129 casualties and crew. While on mine-laying duties she was forced to surface on 27 April because of the number of Allied ships nearby and ran aground on a sandbank. German Captain Mohrbutter's message for help was intercepted and HMS *Firedrake* soon arrived on the scene. The ship was scuttled and the Captain was captured with his crew of 17. *U5* was then raised, towed to the Thames and there stayed for 3 weeks, raising money for sailors' funds (over 200,000 visitors paid to see her.) *British.*

312

313

314

313 *'On the command turret of a U-Boat'*. Artist Prof Willy Stower. Card in aid of the U-Boat Fund. Posted 12.11.17. *German: (Pub. J.J. Weber, Leipzig.)*

314 A remarkable card showing the sinkings by U-boat of British ships from February 1917 to January 1918. It confirms British records that the worst-ever month was April 1917. *German: (Pub. Otto Eisner, Berlin.)*

315 Admiral Jellicoe was responsible for organizing anti-U-boat measures in 1916/17. It is unlikely that he would have approved of the method said to have been tried out by the British early in the War, which relied upon training seagulls to aim their droppings on U-boat periscopes, thus blinding them and leaving them vulnerable to attack. (Jellicoe commanded the Grand Fleet at Jutland.) *British: (Pub. F. W. Woolworth.)*

316 Admiral Fisher introduced the *Dreadnought* battleship to the Royal Navy. He was said to have corresponded with von Tirpitz during the War and to have commented to the German regarding the *Lusitania* sinking *'In your place I would have done the same.'* *British: (Pub. Photochrom.)*

317 Admiral Beatty commanded the force which led the German High Seas Fleet on to Jellicoe's battleships at Jutland. When the Germans escaped, Beatty-versus-Jellicoe arguments raged throughout Britain. *British: (Pub. Tuck.)*

318 Vice Admiral de Robeck commanded the Fleet operations at Gallipoli in both the assault and evacuation phases. Portrait by Francis Dodd. *Dutch.*

315

ADMIRAL SIR JOHN R. JELLICOE.

ADMIRAL JACKY FISHER.
First Sea Lord.

316

ADMIRAL SIR DAVID BEATTY.

317

ADMIRALER I DEN BRITISKE FLAADE.   *Portrætter ved Francis Dodd.*
Viceadmiral SIR JOHN M. DE ROBECK,
havde Befalingen over den britiske Østmiddelhavsflaade ved Dardanel-
strædet i de første Maaneder af 1915, da Landgangshæren blev overført
til Gallipolihalvøen ; han befalede o..saa over den Flaadestyrke, som
førte Hæren tilbage.

318

Wilhelmshaven. The presence of the cruisers and submarines was concealed, the Germans being led into believing that only destroyers were involved. The S.M.S. *Strassburg* and S.M.S. *Mainz* were among the first German arrivals and the British decoy destroyers were subjected to a heavy battering, particularly from the *Mainz*. Accordingly the battle cruisers were called up and five of them, including the *Queen Mary* under the command of Admiral Beatty, came to the rescue. The *Mainz* and two other German cruisers were sunk and many of the other German ships would have suffered the same fate had not a heavy mist allowed them to escape.

On 1 November, off the coast of Chile at the battle of Coronel, the Germans had their revenge, and Britain suffered her first major naval defeat for over 100 years. When the War began a large number of German warships were scattered around the Pacific area. Their commander, Vice-Admiral Graf von Spee, collected them together intending to raid the Allied trade routes before setting sail to Germany. A hastily assembled squadron under Rear-Admiral Sir Christopher Craddock was despatched to meet the Germans, but its outdated cruisers, *Good Hope* and *Monmouth* were no match for modern German ships and were sunk. The two other British ships, *Glasgow* and *Otranto* were badly damaged, while von Spee's force suffered very little. But retribution was at hand!

The S.M.S. *Emden*, also one of von Spee's ships, had decided not to assemble with the main party in August, but to continue as a lone commerce raider, and during September and October she captured 19 British merchant ships and sank a Russian cruiser and a French destroyer. The Emden was aided in her role by being very similar in construction to the H.M.A.S. *Sydney*, and carried a dummy funnel which could be put up to convert her from her own three funnels to the Sydney's four, thus enabling her to deceive Allied vessels. The *Sydney* meanwhile was also aware of her similarity to the Emden and determined to use that fact if she met any of von Spee's force. By the long arm of coincidence the *Emden* and the *Sydney* met at the Cocos Keeling Islands, south of Sumatra on 9 November 1914, and in the resultant action the *Emden* was forced ashore with the loss of 111 men. Which of the two captains had been the more surprised at seeing the other's ship would be fascinating to know.

The Germans made considerable use of lone raiders, some being outright warships and some being converted merchantmen. One of the most spectacular of these raiders was the *Wolf*. Originally it had been a merchant ship named *Wachtfels* and it was converted to carry a light aeroplane, *Wolfchen*, and fitted with seven 5.9"guns. Painted black, looking perfectly peaceable and carrying a variety of flags to be run up as appropriate, the *Wolf* and her crew sailed a distance equal to three journeys around the world. Under Captain Nierger, she was at sea for 14 months from December 1916, sank 300,000 tons of Allied shipping and captured stores worth 40 million marks. During the whole of her voyage she had no communication with home and may have been the last true independent pirate command, but although she returned home safely things were not so good with the regular German Navy.

Before the first year of the War was out, the Germans suffered a major defeat at the battle of the Falkland Islands and von Spee was killed. After this the High Seas Fleet remained in hiding in its home base at Jade Bay in Wilhelmshaven and took no direct part in hostilities until the biggest naval battle the world had ever seen – Jutland.

On 31 May 1916 the British Home Fleet under Admiral Jellicoe met the German High Seas Fleet under Admiral Scheer in the North Sea. The battle, known to the Germans as Skagerrak and to the British as Jutland, was the only time that the two fleets met, and left the British undisputed masters of the German surface ships. Scheer had not intended to have an encounter with the whole British Fleet, but had hoped to lure a part of it out into the North Sea where he could then destroy it by superior force. As it was, when the enemies did meet, the Germans had 100 ships and the British 150 and Scheer himself had been led by Beatty into Jellicoe's battleships. Mist and darkness saved Scheer and he slipped away from Jellicoe during the night. The British lost 14 ships, three of them battle cruisers, and 6,784 men. The Germans lost 11 ships and 3,039 men. Tactically the victory was Germany's and she celebrated it as one, but strategically she was unable to replace her losses and was never seriously to challenge the British Fleet again. It was the end of the War on the top of the sea. The War underneath still had a long way to go.

The U-boat was an on-off affair. Both Britain and Germany depended upon imports and both set out to blockade the other. Britain, with control of the sea's surface, announced in March 1915 that she would seize all goods on the high seas that were bound for Germany. America, still trading with Germany, protested vehemently, but to no avail. The Germans meanwhile had declared that they would sink all merchant ships in Allied waters and warned that that could include neutral vessels. This unrestricted submarine warfare was firmly advocated by Tirpitz and the naval commanders, but the Kaiser and his advisers felt that it could alienate America and other neutral countries upon whose trade they relied. The on-off aspect of the U-boat campaign relates to whether it was restricted, i.e. to establish the identity of a vessel first, and then if found to be an enemy to sink or capture it, or unrestricted, i.e. to sink on sight – the Germans were to vacillate from one to the other and back again.

The detection of submarines in 1914 was impossible unless they exposed a periscope or conning tower. The main danger to a submarine was in being found on the surface when it could be shelled or rammed. During the first U-boat sweep of the War in August 1914, when

319 In 1914 U-boats could only be detected while on the surface and the best way of sinking them was by ramming. This shows H.M.S. *Ariel* sinking *U-12* off the east coast of Scotland. *British: (Pub. Abrahams & Sons. Devonport.)*

320 H.M.S. *Iron Duke* was Jellicoe's flagship at Jutland on 31 May 1916. Posted on 10 December 1914, the message reads '...*another big boat for you, I saw quite a lot of these from the Forth Bridge yesterday.*' Careless talk like that gave the German spy, J. C. Silber, the chance to solve the secret of the 'Q' ships. *British: (Pub. Rotary Photo Co.)*

321 The *Seydlitz* on fire at Jutland having been hit 21 times. The *Seydlitz* got away in the dark, survived the war and was eventually confined at Scapa Flow. Picture probably obtained from German sources through Holland. *British.*

322 '*In the submerged torpedo flat of a battleship. Interior of the chamber from which the torpedoes are fired. The torpedo in the foreground is partly engaged in the tube through which it will be fired.*' By Artist Muirhead Bone. *British: (Britain at War. The Grand Fleet Series.)*

323 Portrait by P. Reith of Captain-lieutenant Otto Weddigen, commander of the victorious *U-9* which sank three British cruisers on 22 September 1914. Posted 1.8.16. *German: (Pub. Knorr & Hirth, Munich.)*

A "BLOCKADER" RAMMED: THE SINKING OF A GERMAN PIRATE SUBMARINE BY A BRITISH DESTROYER.

319

H.M.S. IRON DUKE
FLAGSHIP OF ADMIRAL SIR JOHN R. JELLICOE IN SUPREME COMMAND OF BRITAIN'S FLEETS

320

SEYDLITZ. ON. FIRE. AT. JUTLAND.

321

IN THE SUBMERGED TORPEDO FLAT OF A BATTLESHIP
By MUIRHEAD BONE.

Interior of the Chamber from which the torpedoes are fired. The torpedo in the foreground is partly engaged in the tube through which it will be fired. To the right is seen the exterior of another tube. The men are lowering, for stowage in safety, a trial torpedo which has been fired for a practice run and then re-captured.

BRITAIN AT WAR · THE GRAND FLEET

322

P. RIETH   KAPITÄNLEUTNANT WEDDIGEN

NOS HÉROS

FUSILIER MARIN 1915

323   324

WITH THE AMERICAN FLEET. KEEN AS MUSTARD IN THE U-BOAT HUNT.

325

"CORKED UP"

Изъ Киля его дредноты
Черчиль выкурить собрался
Головѣ меньше заботы,
Безъ портовъ Кайзеръ остался.

326   327

Mammoth Scrap Book of American newspaper cuttings regarding voyage of "Deutschland." Presented by German-Americans to the Royal Library. Berlin.

328

Torpedo Room shewing torpedo tubes, operating gear, firing gear, electric motor for capstan, etc.,

329

ten U–boats set out to look for the Home Fleet, one was caught and rammed by the cruiser *Birmingham*. Defence against submarines consisted of elaborate mining, which increased to gigantic proportions as the War progressed, and patrolling. In order to protect Britain's shores, the Admiralty formed a coastal yacht and motor boat patrol charged with looking for U–boats. As only about one in ten of the patrol was armed and then only with a rifle, imagination was needed to decide what to do should a U–boat be found. The problem was solved by training two-man teams of swimmers, one team in each motor launch. The idea was that the motor launch would draw in as close as possible to the U–boat and then the two men would plunge into the sea. One man carried a black bag. The other carried a hammer. The technique would be to place the hood over the periscope, blind the submarine and

324 *Fusilier Marin* 1915. Card offered free by the newspaper *Le Matin*. The French Marines played a major role in the early fighting on the Yser around Nieupoort and Diksmuide in October/ November 1914 under Admiral Ronarc'h. *French: (Pub. Visé Paris, Nos Héros.)*

325 *'With the American Fleet. Keen as mustard in the U-boat hunt.'* One of a series of 312 cards sold to raise funds for Y.M.C.A. huts. The Americans joined the War in April 1917 and their Navy became active at that time. Because of the US late entry into the war few naval battles were fought, few ships lost and few of the enemy's sunk. *American.*

326 The cork represents the British Home Fleet whose flagship was H.M.S. *Iron Duke* and the bottle the Jade Bay anchorage behind Wilhelmshaven in which the German High Seas Fleet hid for safety. *British: (Pub. Valentine.)*

327 At the end of June 1914 the Kaiser invited the British Navy to Kiel for the opening of the Kiel Canal. The Russian text of this card explains the picture of a dismayed Kaiser as how he must have felt when 8 of Churchill's Dreadnoughts arrived. Perhaps this contributed to the German policy of doing their best to avoid a naval battle. *'War in Caricature Series'.* Passed by Censor 8 October 1914. *Russian: (Pub: P.S. Bubentsov, Moscow.)*

328 Scrapbook compiled in America by pro-German sympathizers, to commemorate the visit of the German submarine *Deutschland* to Baltimore in 1916 with a cargo of dye stuffs. The *Deutschland* ran the gauntlet of an intensive British Blockade and her arrival stirred American anti-British feelings. *British: (Pub. Odhams.)*

then the glass would be smashed by the man with the hammer! U-boat U-21 drew the first blood in September 1914 by sinking H.M.S. *Pathfinder* off St. Abb's Head. Thus 50 years had elapsed between the first ever recorded sinking by a submarine – the sinking of the *Housatonic* in Charleston Harbour on 17 February 1864 by a Confederate hand-propelled vessel – and what was probably the second. It was to be the first of thousands and before the War ended the U-boats would have sunk one quarter of the world's total tonnage.

On 22 September 1914, Captain Otto Weddigen, commanding U-9 was to win a notable victory that caused rejoicing in Germany and the issue of thousands of jubilant propaganda postcards. Captain Weddigen had sailed for the Flanders Bight with the task of preventing British landings on the Belgian coast during the battle of the Marne. On the voyage he had trouble with his batteries, which delayed him, and he surfaced to recharge them. He then saw three armoured cruisers, the *Aboukir*, the *Hogue* and the *Cressy*, steaming at ten knots in line abreast, about two miles apart. He dived, unseen by the British ships, and fired one torpedo at the *Aboukir* from 500 yards. It was a direct hit and the *Aboukir* began to sink. The captain of the *Aboukir* thought that he had struck a mine and signalled to the other two cruisers to pick up survivors. Weddigen fired five more torpedoes at a range of 300 yards, with four of them scoring hits and sinking both of the cruisers. The U-9 only carried six torpedoes and with these she had sunk three cruisers in less than 60 minutes.

On 7 May 1915, U-boat U-20 torpedoed the British Liner *Lusitania* off the Irish Coast. She sank with the loss of over 1200 lives, 124 being American. The United States reacted violently, and public opinion began to move against the German cause, the 'atrocity' of the sinking adding fuel to the atrocity stories spread in Europe by Allied propaganda. Although the Germans alone among the belligerents had given American war correspondents free access to their front line in the hope of proving the falsity of the atrocity stories, the *Lusitania* sinking did the German cause great harm. There were many German sympathizers in America and many people of German origin. Considerable money and effort went into promoting the German cause and German fears of further upsetting the Americans led to the calling off of the unrestricted submarine warfare in April 1916.

Germany was very concerned to maintain her trading links with America, for she realized that if America came in to the War on the side of the Allies, all would be lost. By maintaining her trade she hoped to continue to be treated as a friend by the United States. Her surface ships were severely blockaded by the British Navy, so she laid down six enormous commercial submarines, the first of their kind ever produced. The first of these was the *Deutschland*, 213 feet long, displacing 1512 tons on the surface and with a complement of 56. In June 1916 the *Deutschland* made a journey to the United States and returned with a cargo of nickel, tin and rubber. The trip was a great success, despite the efforts of the British Navy to find and sink the *Deutschland*, and in America bands and cheering crowds met the submarine. The German-American organizations collected hundreds of newspaper cuttings about the voyage and entered them into a giant scrap book which they presented to the Berlin Library. Despite all the excitement however, in less than a year America would be at war with Germany and American ships would go submarine hunting in the Atlantic, and in part that situation was due to a secret weapon and a secret agent.

The secret weapon was British. It was called the Q, or mystery ship. Like the raider *Wolf*, Q ships were merchantmen carrying concealed guns and the first ship converted was the *Victoria* in November 1914. Restricted warfare U-boat tactics against solo unarmed merchantmen were to surface, interrogate the vessel and sink it by gunfire. The Q ship would wait until the U-boat had closed to and then bring its concealed weapons into action. The first sinking of a U–boat by a Q ship was by the *Prince Charles* on 24 July 1915. Since no Germans escaped to tell the tale, the secret remained safe until a German spy, Jules Silber, in Britain found out about it. He had obtained a position in the British Postal Censorship Department and was responsible for censoring mail going in and out of Britain to Southern Holland. Holland was a neutral in the War and became a clearing house for all espionage activities on both sides. Silber, using his 'Passed by the Censor' stamp, was able to communicate with his German superiors by post without fear of exposure. One day he noticed a letter from a young woman to a friend in Holland in which she mentioned the refitting of old merchant ships, and that her brother, a gunnery officer, had something to do with it. Silber investigated the woman and discovered the truth about the Q ships. Within a few days the German authorities had the information and U–boats no longer surfaced to deal with lone merchantmen. It was another factor which, combined with the chronic shortages of food and material at home, would lead to the re-introduction of unrestricted submarine warfare in February 1917.

In 1917 the Germans reasoned that their only chance of winning the War was to bring Britain to its knees quickly by an all out submarine campaign. They accepted the fact that America would almost certainly enter the War following a declaration of unrestricted warfare, but believed that it would be at least a year before America could make a significant contribution on the ground in Europe. However the U–boat campaign had an immediate and dramatic effect and April 1917 saw the peak of sinkings with 373 Allied ships going down during the month. One in four of the merchant vessels leaving British ports would never return. In Britain there was consternation, and arrangements for rationing were prepared. Lloyd George the Prime Minister was convinced that the convoy system would help to combat the submarine menace and introduced it in May 1917 against considerable opposition from the Admiralty. It was an instant success and merchant sinkings decreased. America finally came to war during the same month and immediately seized all the German merchant fleet vessels then in American ports, using these in due course to carry her soldiers to Europe without a single loss. The major naval commitment was in convoy work, laying minefields and in anti-submarine work. It was the beginning of the end for Germany and the effectiveness of her submarine campaign gradually decreased until in March 1918, for the first time, the Allies shipping replacements exceeded their losses. It was a close run thing. During the period of restricted submarine warfare from April 1916 to April 1917, Britain managed to keep her Home Front adequately supplied. Germany did not, and suffered the consequences of lowered morale, internal unrest and, finally, on 29 October 1918, mutiny. Her sailors had had enough and refused to fight any more. Had she not relaxed for that vital year, then who knows what the result might have been? Some indication might be deduced from the fact that even including that year, for every U–boat sunk by the Allies, the Germans sank 32 ships in return.

330

331

332

329 Showing the interior of the German 'Super Submarine', *Deutschland*, supposedly a commercial submarine, yet here seen to possess torpedo tubes probably fitted after she was taken over by the German Navy in February 1917. *British: (Pub. Odhams. 'Exhibited under the auspices of "John Bull".)*

330, 331, 332, 333, 334, 335 The War at sea was largely a conflict between the British and the Germans and the picture postcards show virtually no other ships than theirs. The French did make a contribution, however, in sets of humorous postcards which were available to our sailors through the auspices of the Fleet Newspaper Committee. One such set, exhibiting a truly British-style sense of humour, is that of 20 cards by H. Gervèse. *French: (Pub. in Toulon by Raffaelli.)*

333

334

335

The War in the Air

The Aeroplanes

The Royal Flying Corps was founded in Britain in 1912 with a Naval Wing (the Royal Naval Air Service) and a Military Wing. At the outbreak of war, Major-General Sir David Henderson left his post at the War Office to command the Royal Flying Corps on the Western Front. Similarly all the main combatant nations had a nucleus force of reconnaissance and/or fighter planes which could also be used to drop offensive missiles. Of the Allies, France was the best equipped, with 21 general duty squadrons set up.

Firstly, Britain relied heavily on French products to supplement her home grown squadrons of B.E.2.s (Bleriot Experimentals) which were produced at the Royal Aircraft Factory at Farnborough, along with F.E.s (Farman Experimentals). The famous Sopwith Pups, Triplanes and Camels, the Handley Page bombers, de Havillands and Airco Scouts were to come into their own as the War, and the importance of aerial strength, developed.

Belgium's small Air Force was almost exclusively composed of Farman bi-planes. Italy's own force of Ansaldo reconnaissance planes and Caproni bombers was reinforced by French Hanriots when she made her late entry on the Allied side in May 1915. Russia's Air Force also depended upon French planes and replacements.

Japan's small contribution to the Allied effort included some aerial scuffles. Her small Air Force comprised of Taubes bought from the Rumpler plant. When the U.S.A. joined the Allies in April 1917, the American Expeditionary Forces Air Arm had no U.S.-made planes. They were soon equipped with British, French and Italian planes, their strength increased to 11 squadrons in their first three months, and they made a significant contribution to the War in the Air on the Western Front.

On the Central Power's side, Germany was the best prepared and equipped of all the fighting nations, with well over 40 squadrons formed at the outbreak of hostilities. They were mostly equipped with Austrian designed Taubes. A series of devastatingly effective aeroplanes were soon rushed from the drawing board into production for the brilliant German pilots – the Albatross reconnaissance/fighter, the Gotha, a highly successful bomber, and several versions of the feared Fokker.

Austria, as well as being the home of the Taube, also produced the Lohner seaplane, which was very effective as a bomber.

These amazing new war birds and their achievements became a source of great fascination and excitement to the civilians and ground troops of both sides. Postcards were soon in the shops in all countries showing aeroplanes performing every conceivable manoeuvre and feat. 'Artists' impressions' often resulted in slightly weird and wonderful machines for two reasons – the somewhat erratic censorship system discouraged the clear reproduction of accurate designs for obvious security reasons, and enthusiasm for the subject, divorced from any technical knowledge, accounted for many inaccuracies. Photographs of action scenes were often 'improved' by the skilful drawing in of activity in the air as well! Aeroplanes were also incorporated in the design of patriotic and sentimental cards.

336

336 Photograph by R. Dabbs & R. Ottway of H.M.S. *Iron Duke,* showing the salvaging of a stranded seaplane. *British.*

337 Anzacs in France. Series XX. The caption says 'New Zealand Premier's Visit' and on the reverse reads. '*The Rt Hon. W. F. Massey and Sir Joseph Ward at the front. They are seen beside a war plane talking about its capabilities.'* Massey was Prime Minister between 1912 and 1919. *British: (Pub. Daily Mail.)*

338 German anti-aircraft gun, probably the Krupp L30 (extended barrel) version of the 77mm field gun. *French: (Pub. E. Le Dely, Paris.)*

337

338

339 *'British Battle-plane ascends (sic) at night.'* This is probably an impression of the DH2, prototypes of which saw service in July 1915. Artist Algernon Black. Passed for publication by Press Bureau, 27 Oct 1917. *British: (Pub. Photochrom.)*

340 By artist Prof. Hans Rudolf Schulze. Posted 25 February 1915, it shows German seaplanes flying over the English Fleet. In the early stages of the war aeroplanes were mostly used for observation purposes which was particularly useful at sea. *Posted 25.2.15. German.*

341 Camp Photographer's card. An extremely rare photograph of the Royal Flying Corps – spud-bashing! Some new recruits have not been issued yet with their uniforms. *British.*

339

340

341

The Techniques of Air Warfare

It soon became apparent that there were three distinct and vital uses for this new weapon. Firstly as reconnoissance scouts; secondly, as aerial reconnoissance became a significant factor, attempts had then to be made to hinder and destroy them and the concept of the 'Fighter' was born. With no radio or television and only poorly reproduced newspaper pictures for information, the postcard was invaluable in showing these fascinating details of the development of weaponry and aeroplanes. The third function of the aeroplane was as a bomber. The first bomb attack of the War is credited to French Voisins, which bombed targets on the Rhine. German targets for bombing from aeroplanes in Britain were London and the East Anglian and Kentish coastal belts. Occasional forays were made as far inland as Birmingham and as far North as Newcastle. British casualties were in the thousands as the weight and efficiency of the bombs grew. Air raids were first mounted during the day as targets were obviously easier to locate, but as English defences improved, the raids switched to night time on 3 September 1917. For the first time since the Civil War, the civilian populace was involved in and subjected to the dangers of war. Paris was also a target for German bombers, the first raid on the French capital being on 29 August 1914. When other French cities were also bombed, the French instituted a series of 'reprisal' raids on German towns rather than on military targets. In Britain, public outcry was so great at the loss of human life and injury and damage to property and strategic targets, that it was a considerable factor in the formation of a fighting force to protect her shores. The outcome was the setting up of the Royal Air Force on 1 April 1918. Its most famous airman was Prince Albert (later to become King George VI) who transferred to the R.A.F. The postcard served as an effective vehicle to publicize successes in bombing targets and thus in reassuring the public that measures were being strongly taken.

Those Magnificent Men

The most glamorous, romantic and exciting heroes of the entire War in the eyes of the civilian populace were the Pilots or 'Aces' as they were known. In reality their existence was terrifying and often short-lived. The most immediate danger was from their own anti-aircraft guns. The gun crews, confused by the growing volume of traffic in the skies and by hard to distinguish markings, fired indiscriminately at anything that flew too close to them, often bringing down their own planes.

The French invented the title 'As', previously applied to sporting heroes, for the gallant pilots. The very first pilot to see his opponent's plane being brought down after an aerial combat was Joseph Frantz, whose observer Quenault hit a German Aviatik on 5 October 1914. Garros, the instigator of the deflector plate system, was the first to qualify as an 'As' between 1 April 1915 and his capture behind German lines three weeks later. Guynemer, second in the French league of scores with 54 hits, was their most popular Ace.

The German High Command encouraged the hero cult of the brave pilot, with much publicity about their daring deeds in the press and many commemorative souvenirs commercially available. Favourite souvenirs were, of course, postcards. Every aspect of the War in the Air is recorded on postcards and among the most interesting and valuable are those showing the glamorous Aces.

The first, and possibly the greatest, aerial genius to emerge was Oswald Boelcke. He developed and perfected the fighting techniques, manoeuvres, tactics, formations and the first manual of aerial combat. Boelcke was adored and respected by his pilots and especially by a certain young cavalry officer from the Uhlans. With tremendous persistence he was transferred to the flying service, at first as in observer. He passed his flying tests with considerable difficulty

342 Close up of engine of wreckage of a Zeppelin brought down by a machine gun at Revigny (see also Card No 290). The use of machine guns for anti–aircraft and aircraft fire prompted a rapid development of different ammunition types. In particular, tracer cartridges that gave out light or smoke were developed in order to help the machine gunner adjust his aim. To a lesser extent the burning chemical in the tracer also helped to set fire to the target on impact. *French: (Pub. Baudinière, Paris.)*

342

343 *'The Victor's Salute'.* The chivalry between pilots of both sides was legendary. A British Pilot honours his fallen German opponents. At the start of aerial warfare pilots shot at each other with pistols and usually missed but things changed dramatically once machine guns were fitted to aeroplanes. From a picture by A. Galland, *'Page of Glory'. French: (Pub. A.N. Paris.)*

343

344 Belgian anti–aircraft guns on the Flanders front. A major challenge for the gunners was to make a good aim at the moving target which was almost impossible to hit with a single shell. High explosive proximity shells spread the killing zone of gunfire and by bunching guns together a 'cloud' of fire could be created. *British: (Pub. YMCA Hut Fund.)*

345 Aviator Vedrines preparing his Maxim gun. Jules Charles Vedrines was a flamboyant and somewhat controversial pilot who performed a number of 'firsts' including flying faster than 100 mph. In 1912 he won the Gordon Bennett Cup in Chicago. He had a distinguished WW1 record, mainly on special missions. He was killed on 21 April 1919 on a flight to Rome when he crash-landed near Lyon. *French: (Pub. E. Le Deley, Paris.)*

344

GUERRE AÉRIENNE — L'Aviateur Vedrines
apprêtant sa mitrailleuse

AERIAL WAR – The Aviator Vedrines
preparing his maxim gun

Visé, Paris

345

Not free or unmolested shall the
      foeman's Aircraft roam
   With the vigilant R.N.A.S.
To guard the Hearth and Home,
   Not alone doth length of record
      Fame and Glory bring;
Then for brave deeds done
      and Glory won –
   Let the world
      their praises ring.

FROM ONE OF THE
R.N.A.S.

346

347

348

349

346 RNAS card with handsome gold crest. Message on reverse, '*My dear little wifie. Just another card to cheer you up. Am now waiting to cross. All my fondest love & kisses, your faithful Hubby, Bert.*' Posted in Dover 27 February 1917. *British: (Pub B.B. London.)*

347 Anthony Herman Gerard Fokker was a Dutch pioneer aviator who went on to design and manufacture the famous Fokker WW1 warplane for the Germans from his factory in Schweringen, Germany. So effective was it that the Allies feared '*The Fokker Scourge*'. *German: (Pub. W. Sanke, Berlin.)*

348 '*The European War Series 1914. Notabilities.*' The caption on the reverse reads, '... *Sir John French spoke highly in Despatches of the admirable work done by the Royal Flying Corps under Sir David Henderson. Their skill, energy and perseverance have been beyond all praise.*' *British: (Pub. Tuck.)*

Nos As
LIEUTENANT MADON

350

349 Oberleutenant Göring. Hermann Göring won the *'Pour le Mérite'* in June 1918). He finished a distinguished WW1 career with 22 victories. He went on to become a senior member of the Nazi Party and head of the Luftwaffe in the Second World War. *German: (Pub. W. Sanke, Berlin.)*

350 The French invented the word *'Ace'* and cultivated the exploits of their crack squadrons like the *Cigognes* (Storks), the *'Sportifs'* and the *'Escadrille Americaine'*, rather like a flying Foreign Legion of dare-devil American volunteers. Georges Felix Madon, born in Tunisia, was France's 4th ranked Ace with 41 official victories (unofficially 64.) *French: (Pub. A. Foye.)*

351 Boelcke. The 'Father' of the tactics and lore of aerial battle, revered by his airmen and respected by his enemies, Boelcke scored 40 victories and won the coveted Blue Max (*Pour le Mérite*). A fine portrait. *German: (Pub. Stengel & Co, Dresden.)*

352 *'The Red Baron'*. With a total score of 80 victories, Richthofen was the undoubted Ace of Aces. His personal score of 21 in April 1917 (4 in one day) contributed to the month being called *'Bloody April'* for the R.F.C., who lost 5 planes for every one lost by von Richthofen. He was shot down on 21 April 1918 and precisely where and how that happened, as well as where his body was finally buried, remain uncertain even today. *German: (Pub. W. Sanke, Berlin.)*

353 Immelman, Boelcke's great friend and rival, inventor of a famous manoeuvre known as the 'Immelman Turn', which incorporated a half turn at the top of a loop, was another winner of The Blue Max. Most aviators seem to have had a pet dog. Richthofen had a great dane called *Moritz*. Immelman was killed in June 1916 with 15 victories scored. *German: (Pub. W. Sanke, Berlin.)*

Boelcke

351

Rittmeister Manfred Frhr. von Richthofen

Leutnant Immelmann

352   353

after an initial failure: his name was the Baron Manfred von Richthofen. Von Richthofen was a ruthless hunter and a legend in his own time. His exploits live on, in the myths and fables of the Bloody Red Baron. He was Germany's greatest propaganda weapon, fêted by the Royal family, winning all his country's top military awards, including the coveted *Pour le Mérite* (the Blue Max) on 6 January 1917 after his sixteenth victory. He eventually became the War's top 'scorer' with 80 kills, Boelcke died in an unfortunate collision with his friend and fellow pilot, Erwin Boehme, on 28 October 1916, with a total of 40 enemy victories. With Immelman (inventor of the 'Immelman Turn', winner of the Blue Max, with a score of 15 hits and Boelcke's natural 'heir') also dead, the leader's mantle fell naturally on Richthofen's shoulders. Promoted to Rittmeister (a Cavalry rank, because of his Uhlan origins, equivalent to Captain) he was given his own Squadron, Jagdstaffel 11, and was finally chosen on 26 June 1917 by the German High Command to lead an élite unit, comprising four squadrons, known officially as a Jagdeschwader. The world christened it The Flying Circus. The brightly coloured aeroplanes favoured by the pilots, with Richthofen's vivid red Fokker in the lead, added to the 'circus' image. Udet, the Number 2 German scorer, with 62 victories, was chosen by Richthofen to take over his No. 11 Squadron, which formed part of The Flying Circus.

On 6 July 1917 the Baron was badly wounded in the head. Despite his swift return to action on 26 July, he never fully recovered from the injury and was more aware of his own vulnerability, as well as being constantly worried about his rasher young brother, Lothar. Lothar, however, survived the War (with 40 victories to his credit) while Manfred's fears for his own survival were fully justified.

The fateful day was 21 April 1918, the exact cause a disputed mystery which is still not officially resolved. Before take off, Richthofen scorned to observe a widely held flying man's superstition. After signing a postcard of himself for his mechanic's son, he then allowed the same mechanic to photograph him, despite the fact that Boelcke among others had been photographed minutes before their last flight. The photograph, showing the Baron with a huge dog, Moritz, still exists today, but the postcard is still to be unearthed, and presents a treasure trail for postcard collectors to follow.

While himself pursuing a raw young Canadian pilot, Wilfred May, the Red Baron was pursued by another Canadian, Captain A. Roy Brown. Brown, extremely ill with dysentry and convinced that he had scored a hit and that he even saw the pilot slump, returning to camp. He was officially credited with the kill by the R.A.F., newly formed, and looking for good publicity. May's own report shows that Richthofen continued to chase him after Brown had disappeared and credit for bringing down Richthofen is claimed by Australian Lewis Gunners who were providing anti-aircraft fire from the ground.

The British shunned the individual personality cult, or even the crack squadron cult, and glorified the achievements of the flying arm as a whole, it was impossible, however, to suppress public interest in such heroes as Hawker, Ball, Mannock and McCudden, although postcards of them are comparatively rare.

Hawker had the ultimate accolade of being defeated only by the master himself – Richthofen. Richthofen regretted his death and would have been content to bring down his opponent's machine. Hawker had won the V.C for shooting down three armed enemy planes with only a carbine in his Bristol Scout.

Ball's death was claimed by Richthofen's brother, Lothar. Also a V.C, Ball, with 44 victories, was a great tactician and invented some individual manoeuvres. He was also highly respected by his German opponents who sent back the contents of his pockets after his death, including a £1 note and a pen knife.

Major Edward Mannock, V.C, an Irishman, was the top British scorer, with 73 victories attributed to him. He was a great hero within the R.F.C. and a tremendous inspiration to novice pilots. He was killed on 26 July 1918 by groundfire.

Major James Thomas Byford McCudden, with 57 victories, was one of the most decorated of British Aces. He had the V.C, D.S.O. and bar, M.C. and bar, M.M. and the *Croix de Guerre*.

Although late to enter the War, the American pilots soon built a fine reputation and popular heroes like Luke, 17 victories, Lufbery, also 17 and Rickenbacker, 26 victories, put up a creditable score during 1918 alone.

If Britain chose not to play up the achievements of her individual pilots in their battles with other enemy pilots, great prominence was given to the 'Zep Slayers', individuals who brought down the dreaded Zeppelins, as the German air ships were indiscriminately called. The Germans deliberately used these sinister, ghostly machines of death to inspire terror in the civilians of France and Britain and to intensify anti-British hatred in the Fatherland. Postcards were on sale showing Zeppelins bombing English towns, with the British people fleeing in hysterical panic from their trail. German children sang '*Fly Zeppelin, fly to England. England shall be destroyed with fire.*' Although supremely effective as psychological weapons, the air ships also inflicted much loss of life, casualties and damage. From their bases at Fuhlsbuttel and Nordholz Zeppelins first raided Norfolk on 19 January 1915. Two airships killed four people and injured 16. The reign of terror had begun. London's first raid was on 31 May 1915 and seven people were killed and 35 injured. The biggest raid was on 2 September 1918 when 14 German airships (Zeppelins and Shutte–Lanz's) crossed the British coastline. Only four civilians were killed,

Climbing.

354

RUSSIAN BATTLE BIPLANE (SIKORSKI)

356

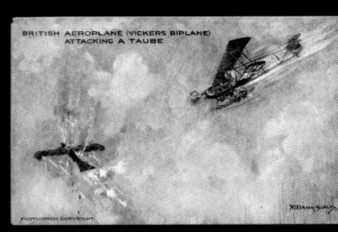

BRITISH AEROPLANE (VICKERS BIPLANE)
ATTACKING A TAUBE

PHOTOCHROM COPYRIGHT

357

Diving
with engine running.

355

BELGIAN BIPLANE (BROUCKÈRE)

358

ITALIAN SCOUTING MONOPLANE

359

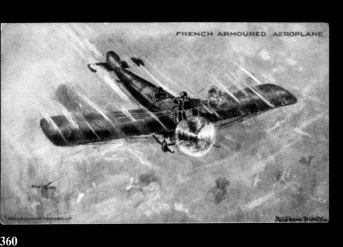

FRENCH ARMOURED AEROPLANE

360

BRITISH ARMOURED SEAPLANE

361

Der Earl of Denbigh im englischen Parlament sagte:
„Systematisch müssen wir die Rheinbrücken zerstören."

362

Zeppelin kommt!

363

THE END OF THE "BABY-KILLER."

364

Behold the end of a raiding "Gotha."
A prey to Kentish fire.
Our boys at the guns have finished the Huns
And lit their funeral pyre.

A Stirring Episode in the Raid of 22nd Aug., 1917.

365

366

354 '*In the Air Series*' by Artist G.T. Clarkson. Posted 5 November 1918. Type of plane not stated for censorship reasons. On the reverse, a husband on active service writes to his wife, hoping she has '*kept free from the flu.*' The great Spanish flu epidemic was starting: 21 million would die in it worldwide. *British: (Pub. Tuck.)*

355 '*In the Air Series*' by Artist G. T. Clarkson. Posted 15 November 1918, just after the Armistice. A father writes to his son, '*I expect you had a good time when the good news was made known – did they close the schools at all?*' *British: (Pub. Tuck.)*

356, 357, 358, 359, 360, 361 Set of 6 cards by Artist Algernon Black showing planes of the Allies. *British: (Pub. Photochrom)*

362 Artist's impression of English planes bombing the Rhine Bridges, following an exhortation by the Earl of Denbigh in 1915, in Parliament, to do so (according to the caption). He repeated the call in a lecture to the London Chamber of Commerce saying that he wanted to make '*...life for the enemy impossible.*' *German: (Pub. Bayer, Berlin.)*

Les vainqueurs d'un combat aérien.   1860.
The conquerors of an aerial fight.
Победители воздушной битвы.   D'Après l'Illustration.
   Le sergent aviateur Frantz.   Le soldat mecanicien Quenault.

367

368

Die Trümmer eines frz. Flugzeuges

369

370

however, and the great spectacle of the night was the destruction of SL11 at Cuffley by Lt. William Leefe-Robinson. The monstrous airship was nearly 200 yards long with a crew of 16 and Leefe-Robinson was awarded the V.C. (the first for action at home) for his extremely hazardous accomplishment.

On 5 April 1917, Lt. William Leefe-Robinson was engaged in flying duties on the Western Front. He was forced down with three other Bristols by Richthofen's Squadron, All four pilots set their machines on fire, but were then captured. Leefe-Robinson died in the great flu epidemic of 1919, but he and his fellow 'Zep-Slayers' became national heroes.

The end of the War left Germany without an Air Force according to the terms of the Armistice, while the Allies finished the War with the efficient production of progressive

363 Posted 7 December 1916. This card shows the hysterical panic the Germans hoped to cause with the Zeppelins. On the reverse is a printed song of encouragement to destroy London and the incongruous written message sent fond birthday wishes to a mother from her son! The card is one of a series. Artist Arthur Thiele. *German: (Pub. Gebrüder Dietrich. Leipzig.)*

364 German airship in British searchlights. The first successful rigid airship was built by Count Zeppelin in 1900. Over the years he developed and improved his invention and in 1914 the airship was a viable weapon of war. The Germans used these sinister, ghostly machines of death to inspire terror in the civilians of France and Britain and to whip up anti-British hatred in the Fatherland. Postcards were on sale showing Zeppelins bombing English towns, with the British people fleeing in pandemonium from their trail. Its psychological value was used to the utmost by the Germans. *British: (Pub. Valentine.)*

365 The 22nd August 1917 was the last day of the eight daytime Gotha bombing raids on England which had begun in the Spring. Twelve civilians were killed in this attack and 3 bombers were brought down out of the 15 employed. As Britain's defences improved to become more efficient, the Germans then switched to night-time raids. *British: (Pub. Lane & Gentry, Margate.)*

366 *'THE FOURTH!!!!'* Zeppelin L31 was shot down at Potters Bar on 1 October 1916 by (then) Lt. W.J. Tempest. The commander of the airship was Lt. Heinrich Mathy, at that time the pilot of the most raids over Britain. The event was a widely publicised feat and a large variety of postcards commemorating it can be found. *British: (Pub. Geo. Pulman.)*

367 A rare card of the pair, Sgt Aviator Joseph Frantz and Corporal Mechanic Louis Quenault, who brought down the very first enemy plane of the War in aerial combat – a German Aviatik – on 5 October 1914 over Rheims. *French: (Pub. L. Lapina, Paris.)*

368 Artist's impression of German airships in combat with British planes over the English Channel. The unlikely scenario is that the Zeppelins are getting the better of the aeroplanes. In fact it was soon realised that Zeppelins were vulnerable to attack in the air and for long range raids their

place was increasingly taken by the Gotha bomber. Written 25.6.16. *German.*

369 Remains of French aeroplane viewed by German soldiers, including a *'Medic'* who arrived too late on the scene, if the shape to the bottom left corner really is the charred remains of the pilot, as it would appear. Feld-Postkarte. Posted 16.1.17. *German.*

370 On the night of 2 September 1916 a reported 16 German airships crossed the British coastline in what would be the largest such air raid of the war. The great spectacle of the night was the destruction of *SL11* at Cuffley by Lt. William Leefe-Robinson, for which feat he was awarded the V.C., the first for action at home. This propellor blade from *SL11* was found the following day by Sgt F, Whiteman of the ASC who is in the picture. *British: (Pub. McCara & Whiteman, London.)*

371 A handwritten message on reverse reads, *'These are the men [Robinson VC, Tempest DSO and Sowrey DSO] who brought the 3 Zepps down by burning. Sowrey flew so low over our houses one day he nearly touched the chimney pots'.* Sowrey's first kill was *L32* which he shot down near Billericay on 23 September 1916 and for which he was awarded the DSO. *British: (Pub. C. W. Faulkner.)*

THE ZEPP SLAYERS

Lieut. Robinson V.C.   Lieut. W. Tempest D.S.O.   Lieut. F. Sowrey, D.S.O.

371

and reliable fighter and bomber planes well under way in England and France. Production of the fine American Liberty engine was also well advanced. The Allied countries were all set for the exciting inter-war era of aerial speed and distance records – with stars like Lindbergh and Amy Johnson.

4 Humour & Sentiment

Humour

In the hunt for picture postcards of the First World War, the category which is most easily found is the humorous one. The cards are normally inexpensive, a reflection upon their ready availability. Many picture cards were sent in envelopes or bought to collect, not to post. This is not generally the case with the humorous cards, since it is the thought of sharing the joke which prompted the sender to buy the card. Thus in the sharing of humour, there is a communication between individuals that binds them together, especially when laughing at a common hardship or adversity. The British, more than any other nation, have a sense of humour firmly ingrained as a national characteristic and the part that sense of humour played in maintaining the morale of British troops has never been fully recognized.

No one nation has a monopoly of any particular type of humour, yet in the main the British war humour is good natured and simple, while the French and German has an underlying vindictiveness. Broadly there are two themes into which most cards fit. One is humour against oneself and one's own situation, and the other is humour directed against the enemy.

Laughing at Oneself

One of the most prolific humorous British postcard artists active in the War was Donald McGill. He began drawing cards in 1904 after sketching a humorous picture on the back of a plain card to cheer up a nephew in hospital. He went on to design over 3,000 cards and one of those designs sold more than 3,000,000 copies. His early pre-war postcards are now highly valued, but his 1914-19 cards can still be obtained at a reasonable price and would form a magnificent collection representative of the war humour. The humour is simple, almost childlike, and can rarely be considered as wit. Wit, it is said, comes from the head, humour from the heart.

Tommy's humour was no different to the humour of his civilian counterpart, but there was more of it as it grew out of the greater adversities of the soldiers' life. He carried with him into the battle zone the cockney rhyming slang and adopted it for his own specialized use. The Commander of the German First Army, General von Kluck, became 'Old One o'Clock', and German heavy shells whose cloud burst formed thick black smoke were known as 'coal boxes' or 'Jack Johnsons' after the black boxer, Jack Johnson. The soldier's language, like the schoolboy's, was full of nicknames, many being legacies from earlier wars. 'Posee', 'rooty' and 'pawnee', meaning jam, bread and water, were derived from Hindustani words. So too was 'cushy', a term still in use today and meaning an easy or comfortable situation. *Kushi* in Hindustani means happy. Tommy was quick to pick up the Germans' word, *strafe*, used by the Germans as a daily greeting in *Got Strafe England* (God Punish England) and thence in the more general term for a military bombardment. Tommy found it highly amusing to 'strafe' anything with which he was displeased, from plum and apple jam to barbed wire.

The British artist most firmly associated with the War, and whose cards capture the full range of the British soldier's ability to laugh at his predicament is Bruce Bairnsfather, creator of Old Bill. Bairnsfather, who drew for the *Bystander* went to France in 1914 and for two years lived through the horrors of trench warfare. While he was there he sketched his impressions of life as he saw it and his cartoons were later collected and published as *Fragments from France*. The

372 *'Camp Silhouette Series'* Card No. 16. Tommy picked up the expression *'strafe'* (meaning 'punish' from the popular German phrase, *'Gott Strafe England'*, and used it to curse all the discomforts of life – from barbed wire to lice to plum and apple jam. *British: (Pub. Photochrom.)*

373 *'American Silhouette Series'* Card No. 38. A similar problem, only worse, would arise in the 1940s. The attraction of the American soldier lay not only in his better rate of pay, but also because he was the representative of a faraway culture, popularly considered to be the *'Land of Opportunity'. British: (Pub. Photochrom.)*

374 *'Goodbye and Thank you.'* Italy thumbs his nose at Germany being left high and dry, cheered on by the Allies. Italy, despite being allied with Germany, eventually decided to join the other side. Dated Paris 15 October 1915. *French: (Pub. M. Goré, Paris.)*

375 One of a set of six. The free translation is, *'Trench warfare. Morning coffee with added fat.'* The Germans reportedly tried to get industrial fat from rats and mice and this is a nice example of trench humour. *Written 1916. German: (Pub. Trau & Schwab, Dresden.)*.

376 *'German Thrashing'* of the Allies, another 'bottom walloping' card by well-known Artist H. Zahl. The Italians, French, Russians and British are warned not to come back – or else! Zahl later drew many postcards, some featuring small children in the style of Twelvetrees. *German.*

372

373

374

Im Schützengraben!
Morgenkaffee mit Fettoogen!

375

Deutsche Keile!

Nur nich drängeln,
's kommt noch jeder
dran.

376

"BYSTANDER" COPYRIGHT.

So Obvious.

The Young and Talkative One : "Who made that 'ole ?"
The Fed-up One : "Mice."

377

Bystander copyright.

"WHERE DID THAT ONE GO TO ?"

378

377 Bruce Bairnsfather became the most popular of all war humorists and created the character '*Old Bill*'. The Germans reckoned that Tommy's humour was a major asset which contributed to his high morale in the trenches. A story goes that the Germans tried to build in to their own soldiers a similar sense of humour. This Bairnsfather cartoon was used to illustrate a German manual on humour and in order to make sure that the message got across, the Germans added as a note to the caption, '*It was not mice, it was a shell.*' British: (Pub. The Bystander.)

378 This is Bruce Bairnsfather's first published cartoon, drawn in November 1914 in the area known as '*Plugstreet*' Wood. Bairnsfather was a 2nd Lieutenant in the 1st Warwickshire Regiment, and when he began his drawings had no inkling of what an archetype he was creating in his main character, '*Old Bill*'. The authors have placed a commemorative plaque on the site where this incident took place. *British: (Pub. The Bystander.)*

Bystander published many of his cartoons as postcards and Old Bill was the name by which the central character in the drawings became known. Unlike the majority of British humorous cards. Bairnsfather's were not coloured. They were printed entirely in dull brown mud colour, no doubt reminiscent of the way the front line itself appeared. His humour typifies the attitude of the Tommy and Bairnsfather himself recorded how he came to do his drawings: 'The first of my war drawings materialized during November 1914, in the neighbourhood known as 'Plugstreet Wood' and this same section was the inspiration for many more to follow. I happened to be a Second-Lieutenant in the First Royal Warwickshire Regiment at the time, and the battalion alternated with the Dublin Fusiliers in the honour of defending and maintaining a series of waterlogged slots in the flat ground, in front of the little shattered village of St. Yvon. On starting to draw, I had no deliberate idea of making sketches through the war, and had not the faintest idea of their coming popularity. They began by being trench-scribbled efforts which I found an irresistible urge to put down. The basic forces prompting these efforts were to me the satire in men ever finding themselves in such a macabre and pathetic predicament, the tragic mutilated landscapes, the primitive life in the mud, the ceaseless wearing drudgery for the soldiers with ever-present danger as the final nuisance. The morose yet stolid humour and relentless endurance of the men under these conditions appealed to me with such force that the drawings emerged as my only means of being articulate about what I felt. It was here during the latter part of November that I drew the sketch entitled, *Where did that one go to?* Possibly the drear conditions we all encountered in 1915 whilst in the trenches before Messines, were more inspiring to me than any. It was here that I thought of the ideas for a great number of sketches, among them, *Who made that 'ole? Mice*, the well known, *If yer knows a better 'ole, go to it* [it was actually drawn in October 1915 when BB was stationed at Sutton Veney and was published in the *Bystander*'s Christmas issue], was of much later vintage, belonging to the early Somme era, and this drawing more than perhaps any other, brought Old Bill to world-wide fame.'

In technique of presentation and quality of printing, the German cards of the War were initially by far the best. Since 1900 the Germans had had a lead in quality printing, and most British postcard publishers had their cards printed in Germany. The War gave a great boost to British printing

Our Billets at COLCHESTER
I don't think !

379

ACTIVE SERVICE.

FACING POWDER.

380

Well, by gum! the war'll s
be over now, Bill, if tha's
to do with it !—I nivver
thee stop at one job t

384

THE 'GENERAL' ISN'T PLEASED
WITH THE RESULT OF THE
MILITARY MANŒUVRES !

381

ACTIVE SERVICE.

THE RETREAT.

382

Until
They

An' pas

385

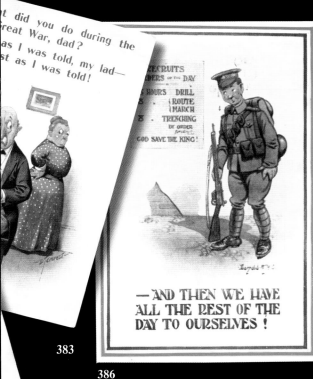

t did you do during the
reat War, dad?
as I was told, my lad—
st as I was told!

383

— AND THEN WE HAVE
ALL THE REST OF THE
DAY TO OURSELVES !

386

"POOR FELLOW—— WERE YOU
WOUNDED IN THE GREAT PUSH?"
"NO MUM! IN THE LITTLE MARY."

387

Let not Invasion scares or Bombs
from Zeppelins drive you balmy—
There's naught can harm old Britain now
for I have joined the Army!

ey hopped
me here
ey hopped
me there
almy
an' told
'Cough!'
e Army.

388

GERMAN
SALLY
REPULSED
BY
BRITISH
TROOPS
News 6.30

So I should think, the Hussy !
They ought to intern her !!
Je pense bien !—On aurait dû l'interner!

389

THE INQUISITIVE ONE – "Have you been wounded Sir?"

THE OTHER ONE – "No mi lady. I was cleaning the canarys cage out. an' the little beggar flew at me."

390

WHICH IS THE QUICKEST WAY TO THE HOSPITAL MY BOY?

STAND IN THE ROAD AND SHOUT "THREE CHEERS FOR THE KAISER". SIR.

391

379 A typical card by Reg Carter who had a natural talent for cartooning and by his teens was a commercial artist. His drawings, though funny, were not generally sophisticated in style. He drew strip cartoons for magazines and for the comic *The Beano. Posted April 29, 1915. British: (Pub. E. Mack.)*

380 'Facing Powder' in military parlance means facing the enemy in battle. National Series Card by Artist Glanville. No. 1020. *British: (Pub. Millar & Lang.)*

381 A laugh at a problem that became serious in Britain, France and Germany – and pretty well everywhere where soldiers were stationed. Posted 25 September 1914 from Shorncliffe Camp. The message says that '...*we have orders to parade on Thursday night...*' Perhaps the sender was a Territorial soldier on annual training at Shorncliffe from which he could easily have been sent straight overseas. *British.*

382 This sketch employs two puns – the barmaid has pulled the beer while the fatter older officer has 'pulled rank' to monopolise the maid, thus forcing the younger one to retreat. National Series Card No. 1021. *Artist Glanville. British: (Pub. Millar & Lang.)*

383 A good music hall joke converted to wartime. '*Comic Series*' Card No. 397 by Artist D. Tempest. *Posted 3 June 1917. British: (Pub. Bamforth).*

384 The postcard was a perfect vehicle for old one-liners! Witty '*Comic Series*' Card No. 419 by Artist D. Tempest. *Posted 7 Jan 1917. British: (Pub. Bamforth, Holmfirth.)*

385 One of the authors, though not of this vintage (!) clearly remembers standing in a long line of naked men as the Medical Officer held a delicate part of one's anatomy and commanded each in turn to 'Cough!' and then passed us all as fit to join the army. '*Comique Series*' Card No. 1786. *Posted 1918. British: (Pub. Inter-Art Co.)*

386 '*Recruits Series*' Card No. 923. Postcard artist supreme Donald McGill produced over 3,000 different designs during a career that lasted 58 years. British army policy decreed that soldiers should never be idle. *British. (Pub. Inter-Art Co.)*

HOW I FELT BEFORE THE TRIBUNAL.

392

What did we do in the war, my lads?
What did we do in the war?
Ask of the empty cans that lie
In millions on the shore.

393

387 *'Regent Series'* Card No. 2632 by Artist Reg Maurice. The soldier wears the convalescent's blue uniform and red tie. A well worked idea. Donald McGill's version was, *'Were you wounded at the front'*, to which the reply from a soldier with his hand on his bottom is, *'No ma'am, at the rear'*. *British: (Pub. Regent Pub. Co.)*

388 Artist A.E. Message on reverse, *'This is not my photo.'* Posted 21.2.16. from Hut 49 Westham Camp. The message from the sender to Miss Buttress suggests that he, *'… may not be here in a week's time.'* The battle of the Somme would begin in four months' time. *British.*

389 *'Comique Series'* Card No. 1476 by McGill. *Posted from a Camp Post Office. British: (Pub. Inter-Art Co.).*

390 The card was posted on 26 November 1915. Surprisingly it was still possible for civilians to travel to Europe despite the War. Part of the message reads, *'… it is a pity that you do not learn French as I could then take you to Paris.' British: (Pub. I. Salmon, Sevenoaks.)*

391 By Artist Reg Carter. *British: (Pub. E. Mack.)*

392 Military Tribunals were held for those applying for exemption from military service. There was a variety of reasons – e.g. moral (conscientious objectors), economic (preserving a business), family (looking after dependents), medical (disability). The Middlesex Appeal Tribunal heard 11,000 cases between 1916 and 1918. *Artist F. Gilson. British.*

393 A comment on the almost exclusive use of plum and apple to make the jam for Tommy's rations. Tommy spent a great deal of his time looking for strawberry jam, a situation depicted in one of Bairnsfather's cartoons which has the caption, 'When the 'ell is it going to be strawberry?'. *British.*

HE DIDN'T KNOW IT WAS LOADED

394

396

Coming back from the war.   — Retour de guerre.

395

"DEAR MOTHER: I'VE GOT A JOB
AT THE BASE!"

397

394 Germany gets more opposition than expected when invading Belgium, particularly from the forts. Posted in Canada and franked 'International Exhibition Toronto, Aug 28 1915.' As is often the case the comic card makes a more telling comment on the war than is immediately obvious. This is a very special card as it was drawn by Alfred Leete who drew the famous Kitchener poster. *British: (Pub. Lawrence & Jellicoe 'London Opinion' Postcards).*

395 *'Coming back from the War. Come my son, let's leave this inhospitable land'.* The Kaiser, dragging his army behind him, retreats from France through Alsace-Lorraine, over the Rhine, where the Russians await him beyond Berlin. This complex form of humour is more of the 'boosting-morale-propaganda-style' comment, quite likely to have been officially inspired. Artist. *E. Muller. French.*

396 An unusual card by Artist G.E. Shepheard. The reverse describes it as *'Some Tank'.* On the front is the pun *'Somme Tank!'.* It is a reference to the fact that the first use of the new secret armed and armoured weapon, prompted by Col Ernest Swinton and Winston Churchill, that could cross the barrier of the trenches, took place on the Somme. It was near Trones Wood when 18 of the monsters attacked. The effect was sensational, the Germans were stunned and terrified. The effect was short lived, however, and Haig was accused of squandering their use in 'penny packets. *British: (Pub. Tuck.)*

397 Often British cards make fun of the soldiers making fun of themselves – as here. So many young men away from home for the first time had to learn to darn, to iron, to remain clean and tidy and to peel potatoes. *'Comique Series'* Card No.1774. Artist Dudley Buxton. *Posted 25 April 1917. British: (Pub. Inter-Art Co.)*

houses, since the supply of German cards was abruptly cut off in August 1914, although some publishers were left with German stock in hand. Since cards printed in Germany were generally thought to be the best, such cards bore the legend 'Printed in Germany' and publishers needed to move their stock quickly before that information became a hindrance rather than a help. A popular gambit used by printers was to overprint the offending card with a suitable anti-German comment, which is well illustrated by the humorous card captioned, *I'm keeping things afloat* (Card No 406). The card, No. 406, was printed in Germany and it says so on the back. The second line of the caption was added in Britain.

In some instances there is remarkable similarity between British and German cards which illustrate the same idea. The cards depicting the rush to the cookhouse are extraordinarily alike, even to the soldier

Agitated retreat. — Retraite mouvementée.

398

Come to the cook-house door, Boys!

399

Camp Life at BARNARDS GREEN --- I DON'T think !

400

In Memo

401

THE GERMAN NAVY TAKING ROOT!

STIKPHASTZ

" AND THE GREEN GR

403

402

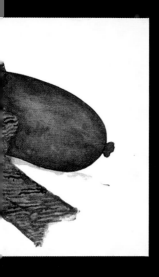

404

405

407

408

Guillaume pleure   Joffre rit

409

398 Pelted with tomatoes by the Allies, the Kaiser beats a hasty retreat complaining about the '*pigs…*'. Continental cards tend to be better printed with finer detail than the home produced ones. This card is no exception. Artist E. Muller. French.

399 'Come to the cookhouse door boys'. At one time bugle calls were an essential means of communication on the battlefield and dozens of different calls existed. A bugler once told one of the authors that the only way that he could remember them all was to connect their rhythms to bawdy verses. '*Celesque Series*', No Number. Artist A.R. Cattley. *British: (Pub. Photochrom.)*

400 Life at Barnards Green, at the foot of the Malvern Hills, seems to have been just the way the card shows, for the message reads, '*…I had a fine time last night, got off with a nice girl. What ho we do see life.*' *British: (Pub. J. Salmon.)*

401 '*In Memoriam for the German sausage*'. A fine piece of anticipatory propaganda as the card was posted on the 8th November 1914. Not only would Germany lose the war but very soon their beloved sausages would be very short of meat. The sender asks '*…what do you think of the German sausage the other side…?*' *British: (Pub. E. Mack.)*

402 The uninvited guest is a large louse on the dinner plate! They were going to see many more of those in the trenches. '*Celesque Series.*' *British: (Pub. Photochrom.)*

403 The German battleship is called '*Stikphastz*' a referral to the Kaiser's policy of avoiding a direct confrontation in force with the Royal Navy. *British: (Pub. H.B., Aldersgate.)*

404 A splendidly triumphant Italian Alpini ejects Austro-Hungarian Emperor Frans-Josef from the disputed territories of Trento and Trieste. On the reverse is an advert for a film at the Vittoria Cinema, Turin showing a film of the heroic episode, '*authorised by the Supreme Commander*'. Italian.

405 Puns and alliteration were popular forms during and after the war. Bruce Bairnsfather called one of his books '*Bullets and Billets*'. The sailor's hatband shows that his ship was called 'Itard'. *British: (Pub. E. Mack.)*

410

« I feel that I am a nice present to get soon ! »

411

Offert par le PHOSCAO

S.M. Dum-dum Ier
Signalement · Néron, tête carrée

412

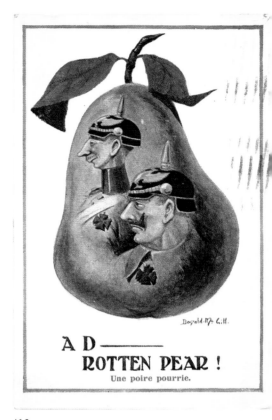

A D——
ROTTEN PEAR !
Une poire pourrie.

413

406 The card was printed in Germany, which is ironic. Most quality cards were before 1914. The cards would be printed in colour and then shipped to customers who would add their own punch lines. *British/German: (Pub. JayEmJay.)*

407 The Kaiser as a pig's head. The German word, '*Schweinhund*', actually best translated as 'Rat', is popularly translated as 'pigdog' and the Germans described the British thus. The Kaiser is getting a taste of his own medicine. *French.*

408 Series '*Our Enemy.*' Tsar Nicholas is depicted as a manufacturer of vodka with the trademark '*Palm of Peace!* This is a comment upon the popularly-held view that the Russians were drunkards – a conception fostered by German propaganda. The Tsar was strongly influenced by his wife who in turn was under the hypnotic influence of Rasputin – hence the Rasputin cap badge. *German.*

409 Caption says, '*Wilhelm cries, Joffre laughs.*' Artist Albert Beerts. Written 2 October 1915. This is simple propaganda for the public. While Joffre may smile at being made French Commander in Chief, German submarines sank over 1,000,000 tons of British shipping in the year. *French: (Pub. A. H. Katz, Paris.)*

410 Caricature of Franz-Joseph. The caption reads, '*Meditating!! Piemonte 1859. Serbia 1914.*' It is difficult to grasp what the Italians are getting at here. The year 1859 saw the formation of a movement to support Victor Emmanuel as King of Italy but it was also the year in which the Kaiser was born. Perhaps Franz-Joseph saw that as fatal to his Empire as the assassination of Archduke Franz Ferdinand in 1914.

411 Proof that not only the British have this sort of humour. It's all great fun! Artist F. Mackain. *French: (Pub. C. Savigny, Paris.)*

412 *'His Majesty Dum Dum the 1st. Description: square-headed Nero.'* In fact it was reported that Wilhelm sent a telegram to U.S. President Wilson on 7 September 1914 complaining of the illegal use of Dum-Dum bullets (expanding bullets) by the Belgians against his soldiers. He used this as an excuse for destroying Louvain *'for the protection of my troops.' French: (Advert card for Phoscao drinking chocolate.)*

413 *'Two-Eight-One Series'* Card No. 287. *'Pear and pair! The Kaiser and the Crown Prince'*. Artist Donald McGill in untypical style. *Posted 19 October 1916. British: (Pub. Inter-Art Co.)*

414 'The German Barbarians'. The Germans attempt to dispel Allied propaganda that German Kultur is barbaric by showing their soldiers playing with children. Written 19 January 1916. *German Feldpostkarte.*

415 En route to Paris the voracious, pillaging Germans take a 5-minute ration break by living off the land – incompetently. The soldier asleep has a hole in his shoe and by the end of the war much German personal equipment was made from cardboard. *Artist E. Muller. French.*

Die deutschen Barbaren!

414

On the way towards Paris, five minutes to go to the bar. —— Sur la route de Paris, cinq minutes d'arrêt-Buffet.

413

falling over on the way. American cards of the period are generally poor in quality and difficult to obtain in Europe, while French cards in which the *Poilus* laugh at themselves are few and far between. To the French the War was sacred, almost religious, particularly at the beginning and perhaps religion was too serious a thing to laugh at. By 1917 when it was apparent that death and destruction were hardly sacred, there was little laughter left in France.

Laughing at the Enemy

In the second category of laughing at the enemy, the fundamental difference between French and German attitudes, and British, becomes clear. The British retain an amused tolerance, a beautiful sense of the ridiculous, while the others employ caricature and vitriol. The Germans had a penchant for chamber pots and showed them being used by most of the Allies for everything from their normal function to hats. In many cards they attempted both to amuse and to make a propaganda point by showing Allied soldiers suffering from an excess of the problems that were currently affecting German soldiers.

This duality of approach is also seen in the German cards caricaturing Allied leaders and personalities. The Russians are depicted as drunkards and the Tsar as a manufacturer of Vodka. Rasputin, the strange mystical monk who held power over the Tsarina, was insinuated to be in control of the Tsar also, and hence of all Russia – presumably in the hope of upsetting the Russians and causing internal strife as well as amusing the Germans. Rasputin was eventually assassinated, by being poisoned, stabbed and drowned but not as a direct result of propaganda cards. In contrast to the generally colourful British cards, the German cards are frequently black and white, but with finely drawn illustrations. The absence of colour may be due to the lack of coloured inks resulting from the War, but there is no doubt that the biting points that they are making come over more strongly in the stark black and white. In another approach (and it does almost appear as if the Germans had 'policy themes' to follow for their humorous cards) the Allies and their leaders are shown as frightened of, often running away from, the superior German soldiers. This tack was not appreciated by the German soldiers themselves who had fought against the Allies and knew from bitter experience that they were not cowards. The British rarely tried to make political propaganda out of their humour, but were content just to laugh, even at their enemies. The French, however, were more like the Germans and poured scorn on their enemies' people and leaders, frequently bringing in the atrocity theme and passing comment on German *Kultur*.

By standing back over 60 years [now 100 years] and viewing the War as a whole, historians and soldiers have all come up with their ideas of what were the vital factors that decided its outcome. Some say the entry of America, others say the blockade of Germany, others the effects of the Russian Revolutions. Alone among the major armies engaged in battle in 1914, the British remained true to their leaders, kept their heads and maintained their morale. A major reason for the steadfast morale of the British troops was their sense of humour, and the picture postcards which the soldiers used in their millions portray that humour in a way no other medium can.

416 The Kaiser, apparently rabid, has smashed Reims cathedral and the attendant, who has come from the Berlin Lunatic Asylum, is asking if he would now like to smash Soissons cathedral too. In the lavatory pot are *'Haricots de Soissons'* (for use with an enema for which the attendant has a hose pipe) and on the tray is an anti-rabies serum. Artist E. Muller. *French.*

417 Fairground game of *'The Massacre of the Bandits'* (the Kaiser and Austro-Hungarian Emperor). The weapons are K K Bread (see also Card No. 216) and shells. A French soldier of the 42nd Battery of the 54th Artillery comments to his girlfriend on the reverse, *'My card isn't pretty, but here one can find nothing.'* Posted 28 December 1915. *French.*

418 Conversation between Italian and Rumanian soldiers about neutrality. Both countries were inclined towards the Central Powers before the War but after a period of neutrality each joined the Allies – Rumania in August 1916 and Italy in May 1916. *Rumanian.*

Third great german victory. — Troisieme grande victoire allemande.

416

POUR LES ETRENNES DE GUILLAUME

JEUX DE MASSACRE DES BANDITS

417

«Нейтралитетъ» или «Бѣгъ на мѣстѣ» (Изъ „Вампуки").

Итальянецъ, Долой Австрію! Румынъ. Долой! Итальянецъ. Объявимъ ей войну! Румынъ. Объявимъ! Итальянецъ. Спѣшимъ! Румынъ. Бѣжимъ! Итальянецъ. Бѣжимъ! Румынъ. Спѣшимъ! (Остаются на мѣстѣ).

418

419 The British people had total faith in the superiority of their Navy. It had been the mainstay of British power for over a hundred years. Here this gentle propaganda card illustrates how ridiculous the Kaiser is if he thinks he can take on our sailors, epitomised by Nelson. *British.*

420 Startled German complains that while last time it was '70' (i.e. Franco-Prussian War of 1870) this time it's '75'. The '75 was the superb quick firing French field gun. *French: (Pub. E. Le Deley, Paris.)*

421 Artist. Reg Carter. Posted 28 April '16 by a Grenadier Guard stationed in Chelsea Barracks. *British: (Pub. I. Salmon.)*

422 *'An Episode in the Humorous War Series'* 1914. The Kaiser asks, *'How have you come back to me in such a state, Marshal?'* Reply, *'Majesty they didn't want to let me leave without fitting me up with a cork… from Liège!!!'* (he has one in place of his nose). The famous oak bark corks of French Liège (in the Var – a Province in the south-east) are particularly strong. Sent by a soldier of the 7th Bn, *Chasseurs à Pied* stationed in the Var. Posted 24 April 1919. *French.*

423 *'The Hero'.* The Italian wounded and decorated soldier cries for help to shield him from the forbidding Red Cross Nurse and whatever is in the bowl. The Italians can laugh at themselves too. On the bed sheet is the Italian Gold Medal of Valor. *Italian.*

424 The Belgian mouse stops the German cat. A reference to the stout resistance the Belgian forts put up against the German invader. Sadly, the last of the forts at Namur fell just before the card was posted – on 27.8.14. *Belgian.*

425 *'Forbidden Fruit'* or *'Caught!'* Skyving takes place in all armies. Card sold for widows and orphans fund. *Printed in Vienna.*

419

420

421

422

423

424

425

Sentiment

The Great War separated many husbands and wives, sweethearts, parents and children, who had never been apart before. For the first time there was a need to communicate in writing by people who had little skill or experience in translating their feelings into words and in putting those words down on paper. The written messages on the reverse of the card, the 'personal' section of the postcard as it were, were often totally impersonal. They were full of meaningless clichés, refusing to recognize the homesickness, the love-sickness and the terror of not returning home or of being bereaved. And so the picture postcard came back into its own as a uniquely appropriate way of expressing, in a whole range of pictures and captions, those deeply felt emotions which seemed impossible to express.

Love and Greetings

The first need was to express the poignancy of departure to the War, reflected in the postcards of all the nations. The noble mission of the departing hero was strongly emphasized. He was leaving to answer duty's call, to protect the future of the younger generation, and womenfolk

Per te, per te nato a vivere
in un'Italia più forte, più felice, più rispettata

Le bonjour du "Poilu"

Mes anges chéris, je me bats pour vous.
Soutenu par vos sourires si doux.

WHEN DUTY CALLS

A FOND FAREWELL.

428

426 Posted 4 September 1917 in Florence to England. By Artist E. Mazzoni Zarini. Caption reads, '*For you, born to live in a stronger, happier and more respected Italy.*' Italian.

427 '*The soldier's good-day. My Darling Angels, I fight for you, sustained by your smiles so sweet.*' French.

428 By Artist J. L. Biggar. *British: (Pub. Brown & Calder.)*

429 Wartime lady police auxiliary demands a worried 'victim's' name and address in a Leap Year – proposal coming up? Posted 29 February 1916! Artist Fred Spurgin. *British: (Pub. Art & Humour, London, 'Leap Year series' No 104.)*

430 Posted 1 January 1916. Saying goodbye was the same in every army, as this Lancer shows. *Austrian.*

LEAP YEAR

FRED SPURGIN

I WANT YOUR NAME —AND ADDRESS.

429

430

were expected to bear up bravely. Once gone, the lads had to be reminded that their loved ones had not forgotten them, and those at home wished to know that their lads were missing them. This was often expressed by posed photographs, or artists' impressions, of one half of the pair dreaming of the other, far away. They were stylized and idealized, but exactly appropriate to the spirit of the age. The French were the masters of this 'artistic' form, and the imagination shown in the thousands of poses and sentiments seemed boundless. The British excelled at apt and stirring verses to suit every occasion and every sentiment.

The song series of the Yorkshire firm of Bamforth & Co., long popular with postcard collectors, really came into their own again during the War. James Bamforth started his business in 1870, producing the current 'rage' – lantern slides. Another member of this family business, Edwin, saw the vast potential in the growing craze for collecting picture postcards, and in 1902 came into the market – at first converting the lantern slide negatives into postcards. The firm's most popular and prolific series were of current popular songs and hymns, from *Goodbye Dolly Grey* to *Abide With Me,* produced in sets of two, three and four with a separate card for each verse. The pictures were posed photographs, for which members of the family and workers for the firm often modelled. Some of them were intentionally humorous, but to today's more sophisticated eyes they all seem hilarious, especially the more solemn subjects.

The War might have been staged for Bamforth's benefit, so apt was their individual brand of sentiment, of tying the appropriate pictures to the words. Old favourites, such as *My Hero,* from *The Chocolate Soldier* and *Jesu Lover of My Soul,* were re-photographed with the leading male characters dressed in khaki or navy blue. New songs, like *Tipperary, Take me back to Dear Old Blighty* and *Keep the Home Fires Burning,* (which featured a particular line, *Till The Boys Come Home,* the title of this book) were soon outstanding hits. The sets of cards were sent almost like a serial story, with a continuing message on each card.

Patriotic symbols, like national flags and military decorations such as the Iron Cross, were often incorporated in the design of cards which wished the recipient luck, paid homage to his bravery and longed for a safe return. Greetings winged their way back from all the areas of active service – from the Russian Front, from Mesopotamia and Egypt, from Salonika, as well as from humbler destinations like Sandling Camp – which feature the location as part of the illustration. National honour and pride in the fighting force also mingled with humbler personal sentiments, another area where the French excelled. Seasonal greetings included many of the aspects and trappings of war with their friendly message: soldiers wished their families a Merry Christmas while squinting down the barrel of a rifle, pictures of ships and aeroplanes are squeezed in any spare space, regimental badges frame happy messages. The birthday of national heroes was also a popular subject for the postcard, like the German set illustrating the birthday celebrations of Hindenburg, at which the Kaiser and Ludendorff were present.

Gimmicky themes, like the 'language of stamps' and the '*Poilu*'s horoscope' treat love and admiration with a lighter touch but cards of pairs of lovers always show the male in uniform to stress the desirability of a serving sweetheart.

Our Dumb Friends

Animals played a significant role in the Great War, not least for their value as pets and mascots on which the troops could lavish some of their pent up affection. The animals often, therefore, came in for a highly sentimental treatment on the picture postcard. In their usual style, the French posed animals in what were supposed to be real situations, while the English favoured paintings and genuine action photographs to portray their well-loved animal friends. The variety of pets

"We can't bear arms, but we can bear armies!"

431

431 Artist Arthur Butcher. The drawing is probably of a member of the 'Womens' Volunteer Reserve.' *British: (Pub. Inter-Art Co, London. 'Artistique Series'.)*

432 The People's War 1914/15. A prayer *'For the Son'*. Posted 21 December 1915. On both sides families contributed to the War effort with the lives of their menfolk, almost as if they were dealing in a form of ghastly currency. A family that paid more than once achieved even greater standing in the community. *German.*

433 *'Tidings From Home'*. The Doughboy has just had a letter from home (the envelope is between his feet) and it has prompted thoughts of the girl he left behind. The card jogs that girl to write. *American: (Pub. Merval Corp, New York.)*

434 Posted 26 April 1916 in Milan. A morale-boosting card celebrating the comradeship of the Alpine troops and the family circle waiting at home. *Italian.*

Völkerkrieg 1914/15   Für den Sohn

432

Tidings from Home.
I wonder what the ache is
In the region of my heart?
Is it that you and I
Are miles and miles apart?

433

434

Frohes Wiedersehen

435

Letter to my Father Soldier

MY DEAR PAPA,
I write to tell you your little girl is not afraid of the "Zeppelins".
Don't be anxious, if I had to, I should be as courageous as our brave
soldiers.   I send you my best kisses   Your loving daughter.

436

F. M. Bredt   Feldpost

437

438

439

435 A German Naval Officer bids farewell to his sweetheart. The Devil may have the best music but the Germans seem to have the smartest uniforms. Posted in the UK 3 September 1915! *German: (Pub. Hermann Wolff, Berlin.)*

436 French, with English overprinted caption and printed message assuring her father that his *'little girl'* is not frightened of Zeppelins. Trade with Paris remained possible throughout the war. *French: (Pub. Lapina, Paris. Guerre Patriotique 1914.)*

437 An idealistic encouragement sent to a Lieutenant in the field by his sweetheart. The girl is looking at his picture as she writes. Posted 11 July 1916, just 10 days after the start of the Battle of the Somme. Artist F. M. Bredt. *German: (Pub. Munchner Kunst.)*

438 Posted 21 February 1917 from a soldier boy to his mother. Message reads, 'We *are all going tomorrow before the Colonel for inspection. I think we are going away shortly shall not like that part so well'.* Many of those who went to war were so young that they were not married and the major female figure in their lives was their mother. *British: (Pub. Bamforth.)*

439 *'Our little lad. Defend us my child, have good heart, be brave.'* French: *(Pub. Dix.)*

440 Artist A.A. Nash. Posted 21.1.17 from an aunt to her nephew with the message, *'This Daddy is telling his little children about the war. He is dressed something like your own Daddy isn't he?'* The caption refers to Neuve Chapelle, a battle of March 1915. **British: (Pub. Inter-Art Co.)**

441 *'At the Grave of a Comrade.'* 22.3.16. The comradeship of shared danger created close friends and their loss was hard to bear. German regiments were quick to erect formal grave markers early in the war, though that soon became impractible. *German.*

THE STORY OF "NEUVE CHAPELLE!"

440

„Am Grabe der Kameraden"

441

and mascots reads like the contents of a menagerie, and includes goats, cats, rabbits, hens, owls, magpies, mules, parrots, monkeys and, of course, dogs. These motley animals were cherished in trenches, in R.F.C. messes, in ships and in military hospitals, where cheerful singing canaries were particular favourites. In more concrete ways, animals played many practical assisting parts in the war effort. At first all the combatants on the Western Front, and on the Russian Front, brought up their traditional cavalry regiments. The Russians had the Cossacks, the Germans the Uhlans, the British had the Lancers and the Indians the Bengal Lancers, while the French, Belgians, Austrians and Canadians all had experienced cavalry regiments. In the early days of the War there were many cavalry engagements, where all the dash and bravery of mounted warfare won many skirmishes. There were, however, none of the epic face-to-face mass cavalry charges of previous wars. The deadly efficiency of ever improving machine guns made this type of warfare too costly. As the War burrowed into the earth and bogged down in the trenches; as the terrain became pitted with shell craters, tangled with barbed wire and churned into a sea of mud, the horse became a behind-the-line fighter, useful as ever when motor vehicles were in short supply, often unreliable and difficult to repair, in pulling guns, supply and hospital waggons and the favourite transport of the officer.

The Cossacks had a reputation as excessively brave but equally simple folk with their more sophisticated Allies. In December 1915 a British War magazine printed the story of a Cossack who, shortly after it was reported that the German Kaiser was on the Russian Front, came into camp, 'driving before him a distressed Prussian Captain whom he had captured during

TILL THE BOYS COME HOME (1).

They were summoned from the hillside, they were called in from the glen,

And the country found them ready at the stirring call for men ;

Let no tears add to their hardship, as the soldiers pass along,

And although your heart is breaking, make it sing this cheery song

BAMFORTH COPYRIGHT.   BY KIND PERMISSION OF ASCHERBERG, HOPWOOD & CREW, LTD.

442

442 No 1 in the Series which gives this book its name. The phrase was the title first given by composer Ivor Novello to the tune that became *'Keep the Home Fires Burning'. British: (Pub. Bamforth.)*

443 'Mis-pah', or 'Miz-pah' is the name of many Biblical locations, including the pillar built by Jacob to witness his covenant with Laban, who then pronounced a blessing. '*The Lord watch between me and thee when we are absent from one another*' which is what '*Mispah*' has come to mean. *British.*

444 Just what Tommy wants to hear, set out in verse using words his girl would be too shy to use – '*love*', '*my heart*', '*fond and true*' and they come from the place he hopes to return to – Blighty. *British: (Pub. Beagles.)*

445 The spirit of France asks grace for a vanquished German. '*France will never be a voracious wolf*' – in contrast to the barbaric Hun of course. *French.*

the day's work.' "I've caught him", he announced.' "I knew him by his moustache." And he produced from his coat an old picture postcard showing the Kaiser's face'. One of the most terrible tasks for cavalry men during a battle was the agony of the mutilated horses, who 'screamed in pain like a child,' as one hussar described his mare, both forelegs shot off at the knee. Many brave men wept as they put their beloved mounts out of their misery.

The Army Veterinary Corps used the same system as the Army Medical Service – of first aid posts, clearing stations and base hospitals for their animal patients. In the first year of the War over 27,000 horses had been treated and they also required their own medical supplies, as well as mobile forges to shoe them and adequate feed to keep them fighting fit.

Dogs were also put to many uses on both sides during the War. Their intelligence and eagerness to learn enabled them to be trained to carry light supplies, ammunition and messages, under heavy gunfire, through smoke and over obstacles. They were harnessed to

443   444

pull small carts, used as guard dogs and by the Red Cross and the Medical Services. Pigeons proved invaluable for getting messages through when more technical methods were impractical or had failed. Tanks carried them, as did many aeroplanes. In June 1918 a pigeon released from an air patrol shot down over the sea returned to base with this message: 'Machine turning over to port. Have jettisoned everything. Am on wing tip, sea calm. Machine has seemingly steadied. Nothing in sight. Send small craft at once. My love to my Mother. Tell her I am not worrying. If the machine sinks, I will swim to a buoy close by.' Alas the sequel of the story did not survive. As gas became a real hazard to animals as well as men, horses and dogs were fitted with gas masks and pigeons carried in gas-proof boxes. Caged mice and canaries were used by sappers tunnelling in the maze of underground dugouts and passages that riddled the Western Front to warn of foul air, and ferrets were trained to hunt the army of rats that ran through the trenches. Rabbits and hens were kept behind the lines to provide good fresh food – so animals had many uses, as food, friends and fighting allies to the men of the First World War.

445

446

447

446 Message reads, '*I am sorry to said (sic) that I can't see you tonight for I am on guard and it is my duty to do it.*' British: (Pub. E. Mack.)

447 A noble theme, Joan of Arc prays to God for protection of France in 1914, with a down-to-earth message on the reverse. '*But's appetite has doubled in one week. So much that the cooks have indented for new Dixie to cook his share of Stew in. What I wonder is how will he earn enough to pay his landlady for board when he returns to Civvy life.*' French.

448 The great occasion of Hindenburg's 70th Birthday on 2 October 1917. The Kaiser named Hindenburg as a *'National Hero'*, posters commemorating the birthday were displayed, souvenirs sold and documentary films made. The Kaiser here bids farewell (after lunch?) to Hindenburg who is in the car, and appears to be encouraging Ludendorff to leave as well. *German.*

449 *'The Reservist's Farewell.'* The armies of the four German kingdoms had their own traditions but in general a Reservist was someone with officer potential who opted for a one year term of service, during which he paid all his own expenses including uniform. Those who did not become officers then had a six year Reserve obligation. The use and obligations of Reserve Forces are current topics in the UK. By prolific Viennese Artist (often of children) Karl Feiertag. Posted Vienna 4.11.15. *Austrian: (Official Card for the War Fund Office.)*

450 *'The* [wounded] *Son'.* The language of loss is international. *German.*

451 Christmas 1915, from a camp photograph. An extraordinary range of items hangs from the ceiling and the group does not look too cheerful. On the right hand side the shape of the one coal-burning stove can just be made out and one of the authors knows from personal experience, that even when the top of the stove is red hot, the hut is still freezing cold. *British.*

452 The language of stamps for soldiers. Be careful where and how you place your stamp on the envelope. Posted 10 April 1916. *British: (Inter-Art Co.)*

Der 70. Geburtstag des Generalfeldmarschalls v. Hindenburg

Nach dem Geburtstagsmahl beim Kaiser. Der Kaiser verabschiedet sich von Exz. v. Ludendorff

448

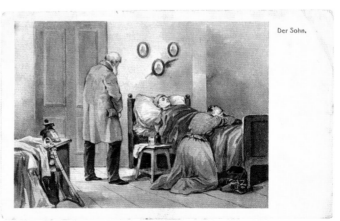

Der Abschied des Reservisten

449

Der Sohn.

450

453 The Naval *'Language of Stamps'* is exactly the same as the Army's version. There was also a *'Language of Flowers'*. *British: (Pub. Inter-Art Co.)*

454 Card by Artist G. D. Armour. Sent from 'The Balkans' Christmas 1917, dated 30 November. Major, later Lt-Colonel, George Denholm Armour, commanded a Remount Squadron of the British Salonika Force. His drawings were published in *Punch* during and after the war. *British: (Pub. the Survey Company, Royal Engineers).*

451

455 *'Christmas Greetings from Bagdad'*. Bagdad was the HQ of the Turkish forces in Mesopotamia and the attempt by the Indian Expeditionary Force to capture it in 1916 failed. It fell in March 1917 to the British under General Maude who is buried in the local CWGC Cemetery. *'Presented by the Women of the Bombay Branch.'* Written 12 November 1917. *Indian: (Pub. Times Press, Bombay.)*

456 A blind soldier in the blue 'casualty' dress sadly recalls his sporting days. A printed message on the back explains that blind soldiers *'learn to be blind'* at St Dunstans and asks for *'Contributions'*. By famous military Artist, Richard Caton Woodville. *British: (Pub. National Institute for the Blind for soldiers at St Dunstan's.)*

452

457 From a personal photograph, a *'Hands Across the Sea'* card, a type popular in the early years of the 20th Century when many family members emigrated from the UK to the Dominions. On the reverse a sailor writes to his girl friend, Emily, apologising that he *'could not get onshore last night'* so had asked his pal, Harry, to send it for him. *Canadian.*

453

454

BAGDAD

With Best Wishes for Xmas and the New Year

Presented by the Women of the Bombay Branch.

455

"MEMORIES."
From the painting by R. Caton Woodville

456

Over the Sea
I send you
The clasp of a
friendly hand,
And the wish, May
Luck attend you
For the sake of dear
freedom's Land.
from

457

A Loving Message

A little card sent thro' the post,
Straight to the one I love the most,
Bringing a message fond and true,
Telling of how I long for you.

458   **459**

458 A soldier bids farewell to his sweetheart while another girl friend puts the traditional farewell flower-decorated helmet on his head. Artist B. Wennerberg. *German: (Pub. Albert Langen, Munich.)*

459 Simple sentiment in rhyme and picture that generally said most of what the sender felt able to say. The Censor made sure that no real ship names were visible on hats. *British: (Pub. Millar & Lang.)*

460 *"'Elizabeth Shrapnell", a child found by 1914 soldiers in the ruins of a burnt out house.'* This (and similar touching tales of orphans being adopted by soldiers) is a much-told early WW1 story. This case was the subject of a book by Bernard Bernauw. Another famous case was that of *'The Daughter of the Bedfordshire Regiment'*. Purportedly a 4–year old girl found, probably in May 1915, by a 'Phillip Impey' of the Bedfords on the front line. She was then adopted by the Battalion and lived with them for 6 months. Impey was killed and, now named 'Phyllis Trench' or Phyllis Impey', the girl was taken to Bedford. Research on this story is ongoing. Today there is a suspicion that such stories were concocted for propaganda purposes. *Belgian.*

Enfant trouvé par les soldats de 1914 dans les ruines d'une maison incendiée

Elisabeth Shrapnell
kind gevonden onder de puinen van een af-
gebrand huis,"door de soldaten van 1914„

460

461

ARMY, NAVY AND RESERVE

462

461 This is a sought-after type of card as it has been sent from a German prisoner of War Camp and carries both the Camp stamp and a London cancellation. The Camp was at Dyrotz, some 20 miles west of Berlin, and several different artist-drawn cards from prisoners are known. The artist here is Cecil A. Tooke of the Royal Naval Division, a prisoner. *British-German.*

462 American soldier and sailor eye up the same girl. Like all soldiers they did the same thing when they went to war. *American: (Pub. Illustrated Postal Card Co, New York.)*

463 Greetings from Egypt to '*Someone dear at Home.*' The Trust published many different types of card including some that the soldiers would not have shown their mothers. *British: (Pub. The Cairo Postcard Trust.)*

464 William Henry Taylor and Margerette Pricellas Lush, married at Wye Cathedral on Monday May 3rd 1915. *British: (Pub. Goodman, Manchester.)*

463

464

465

466

465 Christmas in the Trenches 1914. Here the officer is using his cane to conduct his men in singing – probably a hymn. There are open cardboard boxes in the trench suggesting that presents have been opened, there is a small decorated tree and the soldier opposite the officer is playing a squeeze-box. *German: (Kriegs Karte. Official War photograph, Pub: Gustave Liersch, Berlin.)*

466 A very '*posh*' Christmas card 1916 from Private S. Shakeshaft, 6354 in the 2/4th Alexandra Princess of Wales Own Yorkshire Regiment. This was a Territorial Battalion of a Regiment popularly known as 'The Green Howards'. *British.*

467 A French soldier writes '*Papa*' on the front of this '*Farewell*' card dated 18 February 1917. The Italians certainly boasted fine uniforms and until the Germans arrived in 1917 had more or less held their own against the Austrians on the Isonzo and Asiago. Posted in Milan. *Italian: (Pub. Eliocromia Fumagalli.)*

468 '*Belgian refugees write their location on fences in Flushing so that their friends may find them.*' *British. (Pub. War Series.)*

469 '*I think this is awfully good and so do Phyllis and Duke. Isn't this like us? As we used to be?*', writes Katie to '*Dearest Hubby*', Pte H.W. Wicks in France on 13 June 1918. She is sending him a parcel of underwear, vest, pants, shirt, polishing brush. She is '*so distressed*' about his leave, which appears to have been cancelled. '*I have so looked forward to it.*' *British: (Pub. Inter-Art Co.)*

470 Card sales '*devoted to the fund for disabled and invalided soldiers of the Lowland Regiments.*' The card recognises '*Lowland Regiments Badge Day June 19th 1915.*' Over 7,000 collection boxes were issued in Glasgow on the day. Posted 16 June 1915. *British.*

467

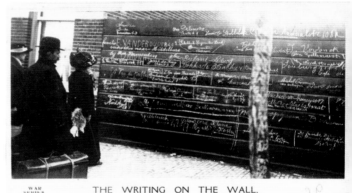

WAR SERIES.　　THE WRITING ON THE WALL.
Refugees write their location on fences in Flushing so that their friends may find them.

468

IT WAS WORTH GOING THROUGH FOR THIS!

469

LOWLAND REGIMENTS BADGE DAY: JUNE 19TH, 1915
TO ASSIST SOLDIERS DISABLED AND INVALIDED AT THE FRONT.

1. ROYAL SCOTS GREYS
   (2nd Dragoons)
2. H.M. SCOTS GUARDS.
3. ROYAL SCOTS.
4. ROYAL SCOTS FUSILIERS.
5. KING'S OWN SCOTTISH
   BORDERERS.
6. CAMERONIANS
   (Scottish Rifles)

M'LAGAN & CUMMING, EDINR.

470

471

CARTA PARA A FAMILIA
Conductor d'artilheria britannica
descançando junto ao seu cavallo

472

471 Placard reads, '*Please help my comrades at the Front. I am 25 years old and rejected, but my friends were taken and with thousands of other horses are suffering and dying TO HELP WIN THE WAR FOR YOU.*' The handlers wear the uniform of convalescent soldiers. *British.*

472 From a propaganda series using a basic template on flimsy card, with an insert block that can be printed in any language. This one in Portuguese shows a British artilleryman writing a letter to his family while resting with his horse. Horses remained a major prime mover throughout the war. *British.*

473 The German people thank their armed forces. Official Christmas Card for troops in the field. Posted 23.12.15. It is important that armies overseas believe that their Home nation is behind them. Without that support morale can degenerate very quickly as it did eventually for the Americans in Vietnam. *German.*

474 The Germans in particular used dogs extensively to carry messages and medical supplies, they were useful as guards and of course as mascots. A very posed picture, the shallow trench and soft hats suggest that it was based upon a training exercise or a skirmish in the early days of the war. *French.*

475 *Russian troops in France. 'Vania, the mascot of the Regiment.'* The first Russian troops arrived in Marseilles in April 1916. The Tsar had provided them in return for equipment and weapons. They then fought around Suippes, suffering some 500 casualties. On hearing news of the 1917 Russian Revolution in March 1917, revolutionary fervour spread among their ranks and many later mutinied in the area of La Courtine in the Limoges. In September 1917, 7,500 mutineers surrendered (some being killed) and

were interned. On 12 September 2012
a memorial to them was inaugurated
in the Cemetery at La Courtine. The
message is in French and dated 16
March 1917. It does not mention the
Russians. *French: (Pub. E.L.D.)*

476 Artist Frederic Regamez. A
patrol of French dragoons surprises
a company of the famed Uhlans. Von
Richthofen, the Red Baron, started
the war on just such patrols and the
first British shots of the war were in a
similar encounter just outside Mons,
where there is a memorial to the event.
French: (Pub. E Le Deley.)

477 The extraordinary military career
of '"Snowball", born Flanders 9 Jan
1918. Lost in British Retreat 23 March
1918. Recovered by Maj Watson MC,
27 March 27 1918. Took part in the
British advance Aug–Nov 1918. Gassed
20 Oct 1918. Army of Occupation
1919.' *British: (Pub. W.H.Needs,
Woodbridge.)*

478 Sold in aid of the Blue Cross
(Animal Medical Society). Poignant
moment, all too common for the
cavalryman in WW1, recorded in
the well-known picture by Artist
F. Matania. In WW2 the American
cartoonist Bill Mauldin caricatured
the scene but replaced the horse with a
jeep. *British: (Pub. 'The Sphere'.)*

479 Foxes, bears, wild boars and other
unlikely animals were also tamed and
made into pets. They, like the cigarette
in the soldier's mouth, offered comfort.
British: (Pub. Vivian Mansell.)

480 *'Dogs are man's friends. The
wounded are succoured by them when they
are laid low.'* The Germans called them
'medical dogs'. However dogs have been
used offensively probably since ancient
times. *French.*

473

474

475

1914-15... Une patrouille de Dragons culbute
un peloton de uhlans
1914-15... A patrol of dragoons tumbles a
uhlan company

477

"GOOD BYE, OLD MAN."
Reproduced by permission of " The Sphere."

478

My Mascot

479

Les chiens sont les amis de l'homme.
Les blessés sont secourus par eux quand ils sont terrassés.

480

5 Back at Home: Women at War

Loveliest of Fifty Thousand

BATTALION WATCH

Advice to the Boys at the Front

THE Germans refuse to believe that an American army is in France. We would suggest that you PROVE it to them by going ON TO BERLIN

Back at Home

In France and Germany the general belief held in 1914 was that the War would be fought only between the opposing armies. But this was a wrong assumption : for this war was to be a total war which demanded total commitment of civilian population to the struggle, even the sacrifice of their lives. This new battlefield needed a name. It was called the Home Front.

Death opened the British Home Front in Scarborough and Hartlepool on 16 December 1914. A German naval force bombarded the two towns and killed some 130 civilians, injuring around 600. Before the year was out, German aeroplanes had raided East Anglia, and assault by aeroplanes was to build up in intensity over the War years until in 1918 a force of almost 50 bombers would be sent against London.

481 The German Navy opened the Home Front on 16 Dec 1914 by shelling and killing over 130 inhabitants around Scarborough and Hartlepool. Some 600 more were injured. The war had now crossed the Channel. Things would never be the same again. *British: (Pub. J. Ashworth, Scarborough.)*

481

482 '*Ramsgate Air Raid,* [by a Zeppelin] *May 17th 1915. Damage at Albion Place and some of the Bombs.*' Ramsgate claimed to be '*the most raided part of Britain.*' Bombing raids and shells caused further damage and casualties in 1916, 1917 and 1918. *British.*

483 'Recruiting day in Caterham 14 April 1915.' Enlistment was voluntary in Britain until 1916. This was one way to get recruits. The pipes are there in numbers, the flag is flying and the nurses lined up behind. Who could resist? *British: (Pub. Caterham Fancy Stores.)*

Ramsgate Air Raid, May 17th, 1915. Damage at Albion Place and some of the Bombs.

482

In January 1915 the Kaiser agreed that London should be bombed. The first Zeppelin raid took place over the East End on the night of 31 May 1915. Sylvia Pankhurst, middle daughter of Mrs. Emmeline Pankhurst, the leader of the fight for women's emancipation, was a welfare worker in the East End and in the middle of the raid. Feelings ran high, and bush fire rumours spread that Germans living in London had signalled to the airships. The angry crowds began to look for German-owned shops, smashing their windows and destroying their stock. Miss Pankhurst described what happened to one woman the crowd caught: 'A woman was in the midst of a struggling mob; her blouse half-torn off, her fair hair fallen, her face contorted with pain and terror, blood running down her bare white arm. A big drunken man flung her to the ground. She was lost to sight... "Oh my God! Oh! They are kicking her", a woman screamed.'

The initial impact of the War was to solve a lot of problems throughout the belligerent countries. Europe generally was restless with the growth of the political Labour movements, the Trade Unions seeking a better deal for the mass of the people, and with high unemployment. Germany introduced immediate conscription and a political truce known as the *Burgfrieden* was agreed between the parties. The major opposition party in the Reichstag was the Social Democrats, who opposed the War, but finally agreed, providing that it was 'defensive'. Nevertheless there were demonstrations against the War right at the beginning. In France too, conscription was immediate and a *Union Sacrée* was declared similar to Germany's *Burgfrieden*. Here and there demonstrations erupted against the War, mainly as a result of the lingering effects of the Dreyfus Affair. Dreyfus, a soldier and a Jew, had been wrongly convicted of betraying military secrets to Germany in 1894 and was sent to Devil's Island. Even when the falsity of the accusation became known, the French High Command tried to suppress the facts. In 1906 Dreyfus was declared innocent, but the whole episode sustained a vein of anti-militarism up

Caterham Fancy Stores.   Recruiting Day Caterham Apr. 14th. 1915.   4562

Irish Rebellion. May 1916.
Soldiers holding a Dublin Street.

484

IRISH REBELLION, MAY, 1916.

SIR ROGER CASEMENT,
Executed in London. August 3rd, 1916.

484a

484 Irish Rebellion. May 1916. *'Soldiers holding a Dublin Street.'* The armed rebellion, known as the 'Easter Rising', began on Easter Monday and was put down in seven days. A machine gun is clearly visible here in the centre. *British: (Pub. The Daily Sketch.)*

484A Sir Roger Casement sought to obtain Irish independence and before the war had forged links with pro-Irish groups in America and through them contacted the Germans. The latter announced their support for the Cause on 20 November 1914. He was captured in April 1916 and was hanged on 3 August. *Irish: (Pub. Powell Press, Dublin.)*

485 *'We have to apologise for the lack of photographic detail, but this photo was secured under exceptional difficulties by our Special War Photographer after 11p.m.'* Rumours swept Britain in 1914 and even a German spy reported seeing Russians with snow on their boots crossing Britain by train for France. *British: (Pub. Photochrom.)*

486 The famous London store devotes its window to a display of maps, bulletins etc, as it had previously done for the Balkan War. Posted 31 Aug 1918. *British: (Pub. Selfridge & Co, Oxford Street.)*

The only authentic Photo of the Russians passing through.

We have to apologise for the lack of photographic detail, but this photo was secured under exceptional difficulties by our Special War Photographer after 11 p.m.

485

SELFRIDGE'S "War Window"

In this window were displayed maps, bulletins, etc., of the Balkan War. It is now being used for the same purpose during the present great War.

486

487 *'The whole Damm Family'* (a popular postcard family from the 1900s on), including Baby Damm and the Damm Dog, get involved in the war effort. *British: (Pub. Regent Pub. Co.)*

488 Official card given to wounded soldiers returning to Blighty. Reverse carries instructions on how relatives may obtain cheap railway tickets to visit the wounded. The more severely the man was wounded, the cheaper the ticket. Army Form W.3229. *British.*

Railway Facilities for visiting Soldiers in Hospital in the United Kingdom.

FREE WARRANTS.—If the soldier is in a *grave condition*, the Medical Officer in Charge of the Hospital is authorised to issue a Free Railway Warrant to one relation to visit him, provided that the relation is not in a position to pay the fare.

Should the Medical Officer in Charge of the Hospital telegraph to the next-of-kin to proceed to the hospital without delay, a refund of the cost of the railway fare will be made under the condition laid down in para. 1.

CHEAP TICKETS.—Medical Officers in Charge of Hospitals are authorised to issue Vouchers for Cheap Tickets, which allow the double journey at the single fare, to soldiers' relations under the following conditions:—

    A. That the journey is not less than 30 miles in the outward direction.

    B. That tickets will be issued for not more than two adults, or one adult ~~and two children~~ ~~under~~

Only one visit is allowed in each case, unless the Medical Officer in Charge of the Hospital should consider a second visit desirable.

N.B.—Applications for Vouchers should be addressed to the Medical Officers-in-Charge of Hospitals, to whose discretion the issue is entirely left.

Ce bel épis, par le soleil ambré,
Fera une tartine bien dorée.

9

489 The French boy is telling the German that he has good bread from the French golden corn – insinuating that the German does not. He didn't, either, he almost starved. Sawdust sometimes substituted for flour. *French: (Pub. C. Pirot. Boulogne.)*

490 *'Her Cross'*. A widow, mourning over her husband's gallantry award of a cross, has her own cross of his loss to bear. Many such young widows in all combatant nations never did marry again, either because they were faithful to his memory or there were not enough men left to go round. In the reception centre of the largest British War Cemetery in the world at Tyne Cot near Passchendaele is a quotation from such a fiancée – 'The thought that Jock died for his country is no comfort to me. His memory is all I have left to love'. *British: (Pub.S.H. & Co.)*

491 At first the civilians listened to the soldiers telling the only real news from the front, but inevitably the stories became embroidered and told only in the hope of a free pint. *British: (Pub. Tuck.)*

Her Cross.

0

FIGHTING HIS BATTLES OVER AGAIN

1

to 1914. One of the most sought after postcard sets, although well outside the First World War period, is that of 12 cards produced in Venice at the turn of the century by G. Sternfeld, which chronicle the whole Dreyfus story, including the writer Zola's involvement in his defence.

In Britain, too, there was opposition to the War and individuals like Bertrand Russell, Ramsay MacDonald and Keir Hardie spoke out against it. The Trade Unions agreed to give up their hard won right to strike and the Women's Suffrage Movement declared a truce until the War's end. The Irish Home Rule problem, although it submerged for a while, boiled up later in the Sinn Fein Rebellion on Easter Monday of 24 April 1916, when armed Sinn Feiners seized public buildings in Dublin and declared the formation of an Irish Republic. The Irish Nationalist, Sir Roger Casement, had been captured on 21 April 1916 when landing in Ireland from a German submarine after a mission to Germany to persuade Irish prisoners to fight against the British. He was convicted of treason and hanged on 3 August 1916.

Within weeks, Germany and France each had a million men under arms. In Britain there was no conscription and the army depended upon volunteers. They flocked to the recruiting stations encouraged by civic receptions and marching regimental bands, accompanied by flags and bunting. Everywhere there was excitement and rumours flew thick and fast.

Spies are not likely to be pictured on postcards, and publicity about espionage is always negligible and facts totally unreliable. However the German agents in Britain in 1914 did seem to be naive. One, Karl Ernst, communicated with his contacts by postcard using a very simple childish code, making it easy for counter-intelligence to keep tabs on him. Postcards with coded messages were used for privacy from the very beginning of the postcard in 1869, but coded cards of the 1914-18 period have a particular fascination in that when decoded they could uncover a trail of espionage and intrigue.

Rumours and spy mania gripped all countries, fluctuating in intensity throughout the War. Reaction to the enemy provoked much name changing to less alien and more friendly forms. In Britain, Bernstein became Curzon and Rosenheim became Rose. The French considered changing Eau de Cologne to Eau de Provence, and when Italy entered the War on the side of the Allies, German restaurants changed 'Italian salad' to 'traitors' salad'. But more tangible results of the War were soon abundantly plain. There were the maimed and crippled, and the widows and orphans. In Britain whole villages and communities had joined up together in Pals' battalions. Football teams and cricket teams had joined in Sportsmens' battalions. They had died together too, and left great gaps in the lives of small communities that could never be healed. In France and Germany conscription prevented the forming of such battalions and the localizing of casualties, yet very soon, there too, the wounded were a common sight, along with widows' weeds and black armbands. During hostilities just how many men were killed and wounded, and the truth of how the War was really progressing, never reached any of the Home Fronts. Reporters were not officially allowed in the front lines until late in the War and even then all their reports were edited and censored. The first casualty in war is said to be truth.

Recruiting remained necessary in Britain until January 1916 when conscription was introduced. The social pressure exerted on men to enlist was virtually unbearable. The postcards graphically record the persuasions – *wear khaki and girls will love you; wear khaki and you'll be a man; only slackers don't volunteer. Where will you look when they give the glance that tells they know you funked?* Most insidious of all was the white feather, symbolizing cowardice, handed out by women to men who had not volunteered. But very soon, particularly in Germany, there were other things to worry about. Before the War was out Germany was on the verge of starvation, its people thin and worn, existing on a diet of turnip in place of potato and needing a doctor's prescription to get eggs. Even in 1914 Germany introduced government controlled War Bread

H.M. The King's Visit to a Shell Filling Factory.

492

WHAT A LIFE! LLOYD GEORGE GIVES THE KID
THIRTY BOB TO COME INTO THE WORLD, AND LORD DERBY
GIVES THE FATHER TWO AND NINE TO GET OUT OF IT!

493

492 The leaders constantly visited the munition factories. The chemicals used in filling shell cases in Britain turned the skin bright yellow, getting the women workers concerned the names '*Yellow Girls*', or '*Canaries*'. British. (*Pub. E. Milner. Finchley.*)

493 Artist A.E. Lloyd George's maternity benefits ('*Thirty bob*') and insurance contributions are contrasted with Lord Derby's recruiting campaign of December 1915 when men signed on for 2s/9d recruitment fee and first day's ration money. The underlying message is the insensitivity to the use of the headline. '*Enormous Casualties.*' *As figures gradually mounted they* came to mean less and less at home. The comment on the back is '*NUF SED*'. *British.*

494 Artist Reg Carter. Written just before the outbreak of war, the message on this card is very anti–Lloyd George. '*I thought you'd like this as it is so good of him… Awful freak! I expect you'll burn it*'. Lloyd George's message here is '*The Better Land*', referring to his unpopular 1909 '*People's Budget*'. He would be even more unpopular in 1919 when his 1918 promise of '*A fit country for heroes to live in*' (often misquoted) was made a mockery by the penury of many ex-servicemen. *British: (Pub. E. Mack, Hampstead.)*

"I hear thee speak of a Better Land,
Thou callest its Farmers a
happy band!"

494

496

497

95 Economy was urged in all things, particularly in Germany and Britain who both relied on imports which, for the latter, had to come in by sea infested with German submarines. This appeal had a limited audience as few members of the general public had motor cars. *British.* *(Pub. H.B. Series, London.)*

96 Mr & Mrs David Lloyd George and their daughter, Megan, pose for The Welsh Troops Picture Post-Card Day in aid of the National Fund for Welsh Troops. Lloyd George was very active in raising a Welsh Division. Some 100,000 men had enlisted before May 19 1915 and by war's end about 272,000 Welshman had served, approximately 35,000 being killed. *British.*

97 The age limit for conscription was raised to 50 in May 1918 following the German '*Great Offensive*' in March which caused heavy British casualties. *British: (Pub. Wildt & Kray.)*

We'll Shed the Old
          And Don the New
For we're Going to See
          This Business through.

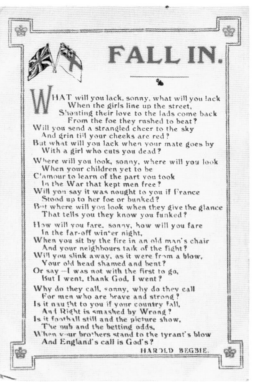

FALL IN.

WHAT will you lack, sonny, what will you lack
When the girls line up the street,
Shouting their love to the lads come back
From the foe they rushed to beat?
Will you send a strangled cheer to the sky
And grin till your cheeks are red?
But what will you lack when your mate goes by
With a girl who cuts you dead?

Where will you look, sonny, where will you look
When your children yet to be
Clamour to learn of the part you took
In the War that kept men free?
Will you say it was nought to you if France
Stood up to her foe or bunked?
But where will you look when they give the glance
That tells you they know you funked?

How will you fare, sonny, how will you fare
In the far-off winter night,
When you sit by the fire in an old man's chair
And your neighbours talk of the fight?
Will you slink away, as it were from a blow,
Your old head shamed and bent?
Or say—I was not with the first to go,
But I went, thank God, I went?

Why do they call, sonny, why do they call
For men who are brave and strong?
Is it naught to you if your country fall,
And Right is smashed by Wrong?
Is it football still and the picture show,
The pub and the betting odds,
When your brothers stand to the tyrant's blow
And England's call is God's?

HAROLD BEGBIE.

498

"PLAYING AT SOLDIERS."
Boy Scout : " We've had enough of his GAS. What else can we do with him ?"
Tommy : " You mind him till I fetch my brother to breathe on him and give
him the MEASLES !"

499

Now then ! less cackling there—
get on with that shell-making.

500

---

498 More heavy pressure to join up in a poem by Harold Begbie – *'Is it naught to you if your country fall?'* Begbie wrote a book, *'On the side of the Angels'*, supporting the legend of the apparitions at Mons. *British: (Pub. Regent Pub. Co., London.)*

499 The Germans introduced gas on 22 April 1915. Kitchener's call for 100,000 men now needed reinforcing with another 100,000. Artist C. Gurnsey. *'Boy Scout: "We've had enough of his Gas. What else can we do with him?" Tommy: "You mind him till I fetch my brother to breathe on him and give him the MEASLES"'.* Posted 11 November 1915. Three years still to go. *British.*

500 *'Witty Series'* No. 231. Lack of shells for the British army (the Shell Scandal of 1915) in France led to the appointment of Lloyd George as Minister for Munitions, coalition Government and the eventual defeat of Asquith's Government. *British*: (*Pub. Bamforth.*)

Appeal dismissed—to be called up at once!

501

WAR ECONOMY,

can be
done
without.

502

"Every Copper Helps."

503

501 A tolerant comment on the *'Shirker'*, a more common reaction was one of disgust, particularly by women who prided themselves on the number of their menfolk in khaki. The word 'Appeal' refers to an application to avoid military service. Artist D. Tempest. Posted 23 September 1917. *British: (Pub. Bamforth.)*

502 The profiteer and wastrel. A hated figure throughout Europe who grew prosperous on the War effort. *British: (Pub. Millar & Lang.)*

503 Early in 1914 Britain created a volunteer force of special constables, known as *'The Specials'*, for home duties. They were part-timers and wore an identifying blue and white armband. Artist F. Gilson. Posted 20 April 1918. *British.*

and as the War went on, it became viciously adulterated. Unscrupulous bakers added sawdust and chalk, but even approved materials included peas and beans, while attempts were made to develop fat substitutes from rats, mice and cockroaches. This fact was seized on by the British and distorted and magnified to become one of the great propaganda successes of the War. The concept of boiling animal corpses to produce much needed fats and glycerine was converted into the goulish practice of boiling human corpses (of fallen German soldiers). This was reported in *The Times* and the *Daily Mail,* the source of the story supposedly being a despatch in the Berlin *Lokal-Anzeiger* of 10 April 1917. The translation of this report reads: 'There is a dull smell in the air as if lime were being burnt. We are passing the great Corpse-Conversion (or Utilisation) Establishment *(Kadaver-Verwertungs-Anstalten)* of the Army Group. The fat that is won here is turned into lubrication oils and everything else is ground down in the bones mill into a powder, which is used for mixing with pigs' food and as a manure. Nothing is to be allowed to go to waste ...' Not a mention of boiled soldiers, and the German defence hinged on assurances that *Kadaver* only applied to 'animal dead'. But the mud stuck and the story was not refuted until long after the War.

Butchers' shops featured black crows by 1917 and the country suffered government inspired meatless weeks. *Ersatz,* meaning 'artificial or substitute' became part of the common language, and over-eating was discouraged by suggesting not only that it was against the country's interests, but also that it caused baldness! Similarly, later in the 1940s, the British were to claim that 'carrots enabled people to see in the dark' in an attempt to encourage carrot eating during a period of potato shortage in the Second World War.

In the First World War Britain came to the edge of starvation. In January 1917 Germany announced that it would sink any ship of any nationality that was trading with the Allies. Up to that time a large proportion of Britain's imports, upon which she was totally dependent, had been brought in on American ships and the Germans had left them alone for fear of bringing the United States into the War. By April 1918 the situation was so serious, due to the enormous tonnages of Allied ships sunk by the U-boats, that all main foodstuffs were rationed. If the sinking had continued at the same rate the War could have had a different ending. However the introduction of the convoy system checked and then began to decrease the sinkings, and the food crisis was over. In Germany, however, there was to be no respite from the powerful blockade of the British Navy that was, in the end, to prove one of the determining factors of the War.

In France most staple foods eventually had to be rationed, although there were no shortages comparable to those in Germany. Prices rose dramatically, right from the start of the War, and there was much complaining and agitation by the civilian population at *La Vie Chère* (the dear life), and this added fuel to one of the phenomena of the War which arose in each of the three major European combatant nations. That phenomenon was the alienation of the fighting soldier from the civilian.

Conditions of life at the Front were understandable only if experienced. Behind the lines, life was different. There was hardship, certainly, but those with money to spend spent it as an antidote to the stress of war. By 1916 over 100 night clubs had mushroomed in Soho, vibrating with the sound of jazz which had just come over from America. The working people were better clothed than they had ever been before and conscious of new freedoms. The soldier coming home on leave from the horror of the trenches could not adjust to what seemed to him a life of laxity and ease. The civilians, concerned with their own problems of material shortages and long working hours, found no time to make the proper effort to listen to the returning soldiers, and many a man felt glad to go back to fight. French postcards often reflect this problem, which is

WE CAN'T ALL BE SOLDIERS
BUT WE CAN ALL FIGHT.

504

505

Lost his Meat Card.

506

504 Part of the continual campaign to remind the country that this was a total war in which everyone was involved, including those on the Home Front. *British: (Pub. Millar & Lang.)*

505 *'Our father has given his life. Will you not donate some money. SUBSCRIBE'* (to War Bonds).Posted Genova 14.11.18. Italian.

506 By January 1918 all the main foodstuffs were rationed. In London there were two meatless days a week – in Germany there were meatless weeks. Artist G.L. Stampa. '*British.*

A 4lb Loaf of War Time Bread
(Eat half a pound a day)
Some Margarine, and
Butter Beans.
A'int Bad Grub anyway!

507

Darling, you are worth your weight
in coal!

508

"OH DEAR! HOW I SHOULD LIKE TO REDUCE THE WAIST!"

509

507 Typical war-time diet – bread, margarine and butter beans. *British.*

508 Comique Series' Card No. 2307. The winter of 1916/17 was a very cold one. German households were very short of coal because it was needed for the War effort and Britain was so short that she stopped her exports to France, leaving her ally short too. *British. (Pub. Inter-Art Co.)*

509 A pun on the word 'Waste'. A well-used poster in WW2 proclaimed *'Waste Not, Want Not'*. *British: (Pub: H.B. Series, London.)*

510 A comment on rising prices. In Germany eggs were so scarce in 1918 that a doctor's prescription was needed to buy them. Posted at an Army Post Office, 9 June 1918, passed by Censor 1368. *British: (Pub. Millar & Lang.)*

511 A bad potato harvest in 1916 produced shortages throughout Europe in 1917. The word 'MASH' has a second meaning – in modern parlance 'to chat up'. *British: (Pub. Wildt & Kray.)*

surprising in view of the tightness of the French censorship, although if they are viewed as an admonition to the populace and a note of understanding to the troops, they perhaps make sense.

Another problem for the soldier was the fidelity of his wife or girl friend back home. The employment of women in almost every area of war effort gave them greater freedom than ever before, and now they earned good wages too. All the countries noticed the new moralities and the sudden jump in illegitimate births. Picture cards meant to reassure the boys at the Front showed girls refusing civilian suitors, but there were to be many broken hearts over the years.

There were general campaigns against waste in all materials. The Kaiser, President Poincaré and their Majesties King George V and Queen Mary set examples in economy in all things. Germany, pitifully short of raw materials, had metal collections to which citizens gave their precious possessions to be melted down for the war effort. Leather had to be replaced by cardboard in all except the most expensive goods and everywhere prices began to rise and to overtake the new wages. In the factories the men and women worked long hours, producing the means of war. All the leaders toured the work places, keeping up morale and encouraging even greater efforts. Drink was a problem everywhere. In France, absinthe drinking was banned and in all countries regulations were introduced to govern the drinking of both men and women, those regulations in Britain being the foundations of our current licensing laws. King George and Lord Kitchener pledged themselves to give up alcohol as an example and 'treating' in public houses was forbidden. Brandy was unobtainable in Britain from the end of 1916 without a doctor's prescription, and this has probably given rise to the saying still used today that a drink is 'for medicinal purposes only'. Temperance campaigns, back to religion movements, all sought to correct what many thought was the collapse of working class morals and standards.

510   511

Civilian Rival: *I thought you were dead."*
Man from the front: *you'll find that I'm very much alive and kicking too, if you're not off,*

512

Is blue your favourite colour?
I see girls go in for it a lot
now-a-days!

513

The War, with its voracious appetite for munitions and all the trappings of battle, gave birth to a vast labour force, and to new opportunities for profit. One of the most hateful figures to appear at home was the Profiteer, waxing fat on the suffering of others, and matched only in public dislike by the 'Conchie' or conscientious objector. Conscientious objectors were not at all understood and were treated as cowards and traitors. They were frequently beaten and subjected to many other unpleasant and cruel physical assaults. Many were sent to non-combatant corps, but were used to dig trenches and put up barbed wire, which put them right in the danger zone. Stories were also told of 'Conchies' being tied to posts in No-Mans Land. In America objectors were protected by law from serving in combatant units, while in Britain special local tribunals were set up to judge each individual case. These tribunals were frequently inept and biased against the applicants.

The European Socialist movement had been generally against the War from the beginning. The initial appeal of nationalistic interest created the truces of the *Burgfrieden* and the *Union Sacrée* but as the years went on, unrest grew and Germany and France in particular, were subject to strikes and demonstrations for peace. Bethmann-Hollweg, the German Chancellor, appealed to the Allies for peace in both 1915 and 1916, but his terms were not acceptable and his attitude to the War forced his dismissal by Hindenburg in 1917. In Russia, mounting unrest with poverty led to the first revolution in March 1917 and anti-war feelings to the Bolshevik revolution of October 1917. This success of people's Socialism against the established order caused ripples of fright throughout Europe and all governments tightened their grips on their peoples. Clemenceau, known as 'the Tiger' for his ferocious attacks on politicians, took over

The Knut and the Nut.

Clik

The "Knut," being sloppy and slack,
All love for his country doth lack;
But the "nut" is all right,
For he's anxious to fight,
And they'll find him a hard one to crack.

514

La Vie chère.

183

Ohé! les ceux d'l'arrière; v'nez donc
un peu par ici, les pruneaux y sont pour rien!

515

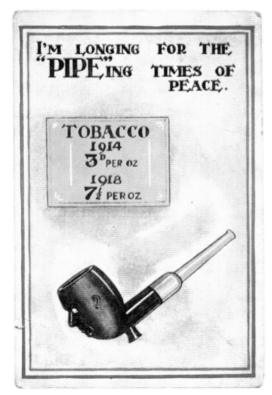

I'M LONGING FOR THE
"PIPE,"ING TIMES OF
PEACE.

TOBACCO
1914
3ᴰ PER OZ
1918
7½ PER OZ

516

512 A sign of relaxing moral standards. The soldier at the front was always afraid that one of the men who had stayed behind would steal 'his girl' – and they often did. '*War Babies*' increased in number each year and women with '*Khaki Fever*' flocked to the Army camps. *British.*

513 Addressed to a Miss Smith on 8 November 1918, three days before the Armistice, the message reads, '*My word, you aren't half doing it some you naughty girl. Do you like blue?*' Blue was the uniform colour of the Special Constables, the Navy and the Wounded. *British: (Pub. Bamforth.)*

514 The '*Knut*' smoked incessantly and found almost everything too much trouble. The name probably derives from a popular revue, '*Gilbert the Filbert*'. The original Gilbert was Basil Hallam Radford, a balloon observer in the RFC who was killed on 20 Aug 1916 when his parachute failed to open. He is buried in the CWGC cemetery at Couin. Posted 9 September 1914. *British: (Pub. The War Cartoon Studios, London.)*

517

"MAN POWER."

518

H. Larwin gem.   Auf dem Stephansplatz.

[handwritten text]

519

515 Rising prices particularly in Paris caused civilians to complain about '*La Vie Chère*', The Expensive Life. The French soldiers were angry at what they considered to be the civilian's narrow-minded concern with his own lot. The caption reads in effect, '*Hi, you at the back, come and see how you'd like it here.*' *French: (Pub. S.I.D. Paris.)*

516 A complaint about the rising cost of pipe tobacco in 1918. In the four years of war it had risen by 250%. The caption uses the popular device of a double meaning. *British: (Pub. H.B. Series, London.)*

517 Delightful card by well-known and sought after artist, Mauzan. Sadly many marriages or engagements made on leave were quickly shattered when the husband was killed on returning to the front. Many widows never remarried and became 'maiden aunts'. Posted to England 22 February 1915. *Italian.*

518 Card No. 423. Artist Harold Earnshaw. The fresh-faced young soldier is the admiration of a host of well-dressed ladies – another reason to join up! *British: (Pub. C. Pulman Ltd.)*

THE STYLE FOR MEN
La mode pour les hommes.

520

Der Graben in Wien im Siegesschmuck

521

 NATIONAL RELIEF FUND
TREASURER
H R H THE PRINCE OF WALES
ON EVERY CARD SOLD ONE
HALF PENNY GOES TO THE FUND
PATRIOTIC PICTURE POSTCARD
SERIES Nº1 AUTHORISED BY THE NATIONAL RELIEF FUND

REGISTERED
DESIGN

522

A votre bon cœur!_
Celui que vous enverrez
sera toujours le bienvenu_

523

519 Two wounded soldiers return to Stephansplatz in Vienna, their plight emphasised by the rainy weather. Money from the sale of such cards went to the Red Cross. Posted 23.10.16. Artist. H. Larwin. *Austrian: (Official Red Cross card.)*

520 Khaki Series No 1056. Artist Fred Spurgin. Posted on 18 January 1916, the month when a Bill to introduce Conscription was passed. It came into force on 2 March 1916. Pressure to volunteer was then redundant. *British: (Pub. Inter-Art, London.)*

521 Der Graben (one of Vienna's smartest streets) decorated for a fund-raising fair in support of the war effort 1915. Oddly, in view of how the war was being fought at the Front, '*graben*', means 'trench'. Artist Georg Gerlach. Official Red Cross Card No 205. *Austrian: (Pub. War Welfare Office.)*

522 Official Postcard for the National Relief Fund, Series No 1, posted 6 October 1914 in Belfast. The Prince of Wales was a popular figure for fund-raising drives. In similar fashion Hindenburg was used in Germany, see Card No 174. *British: (Pub. Patriotic Postcard Series, London.)*

523 Each Nation used the postcard to raise funds. *'An appeal to generosity, whatever you send will always be welcome.'* Posted 27 February 1917. *French.*

524, 524A Both sides of a very personal fund-raising postcard. Actor Edgar Curtis sells his portrait postcard for 'The Performers' Tobacco Fund *'for the benefit of the brave men at-the-Front… The Military Authorities have kindly undertaken to collect and deliver the parcels to the Front free of charge… from Martins Ltd of Piccadilly.'* *British.*

525, 525A There was a national revival of religious belief (cf the saying *'There are no atheists in the trenches'*) during the war. Spiritualism was also popular, with the bereaved (including Sir Arthur Conan Doyle and other notables) attempting to get in touch with their loved ones killed at the front. There were plenty of fraudulent mediums ready to take advantage of grief. The reverse carries a message and picture of *'A Notable and Noble Example'* – Lord Roberts. *British.*

526 *'Witty Series'* No 172. In London the underground stations acted as shelters during air raids and people were advised to go into them during Zeppelin raids. *British: (Pub. Bamforth.)*

524

Mr. Edgar Curtis is selling his photographs for the benefit of the brave men at-the-Front

The money received is devoted to sending 1/- parcels (really 3/6 worth) of tobacco and cigarettes through "The Performer" Tobacco Fund.
And one of these photographs is enclosed in each parcel to liven up a Dug-out.

Will you help to make the men happy?

The more photographs you buy the more cigarettes will be sent, and the more men you will make happy.
As nearly all the leading artistes are selling their photographs through "The Performer" Tobacco Fund, **you can make a souvenir collection** by sending your remittance direct to :—

Hon. Treasurer,
"The Performer" Tobacco Fund,
18, Charing Cross Road,
London, W.C. 2

5/- will buy a collection of **20** artistes
every one different, and post free
10/- will buy a collection of **40** artistes
every one different, and post free
21/- will buy a collection of **100** artistes
every one different, and post free
£5 will buy a collection of **500** artistes
every one different, and post free

"The Performer" Tobacco Fund is a branch of the Newspapers Patriotic Tobacco Fund, which is approved by the War Office and licensed by the War Charities Act, 1916.

For 1/- we send 'Smokes' that would cost you 3/6 if you bought them in a shop at home

A special arrangement has been made with Martins Ltd., 210, Piccadilly, London, W., to pack and despatch these 1/- parcels duty free from in bond, thereby enabling "The Performer" Patriotic Tobacco Fund to send for 1/- what would cost 3/6 if bought in a shop at home. And the Military Authorities (through the Director General of Voluntary Organisations—Sir Edward Ward) have kindly undertaken to collect and deliver the parcels to the men at the Front free of charge

524A

QUEEN'S HALL, Langham Place, W.
(Sole Lessees: Chappell & Co. Ltd.)

MONDAY, JUNE 7th, at 3 p.m.

THE NATIONAL REVIVAL OF FAMILY PRAYERS UNITED MEETING
MONDAY, JUNE 7TH, AT 3 P.M.

Chairman:
THE ARCHBISHOP OF CANTERBURY

Speakers:
THE BISHOP OF WINCHESTER,
THE LORD KINNAIRD, K.T.,
THE CHAPLAIN-GENERAL—
BISHOP TAYLOR SMITH,
SIR JOSEPH COMPTON RICKETT, M.P.
And Others

ADMISSION FREE BY TICKET (to all parts of the Hall).
☞ EACH TICKET REPRESENTS A RESERVED SEAT.
A limited number of special front Reserved Seats (Sofa Stalls and Grand Circle) at 1/- each.

Applications for Tickets and all communications should be addressed to
19, RUSSELL SQUARE,   HENRY MARTYN GOOCH
LONDON, W.C   (General Secretary)

525

A NOTABLE AND NOBLE EXAMPLE.

Copyright.   Russell & Sons.

THE LATE FIELD-MARSHAL EARL ROBERTS, K.G.

"We have had Family Prayers for fifty-five years. Our chief reason is that they bring the household together in a way that nothing else can. Then it ensures the servants and others who may be in the house joining in prayers which, for one reason or another, they may have omitted saying by themselves. We have never given any order about prayers; attendance is quite optional, but, as a rule, all the servants, men and women, come regularly on hearing the bell ring."

Extract from the last letter of Lord Roberts to Lord Curzon of Kedleston: read in the House of Lords, November 18th, 1914.

WILL YOU FOLLOW THE EXAMPLE?

525A

in France as Prime Minister and stated his policy in a set of rhetorical questions; 'My Home Policy? I wage War. My Foreign Policy? I wage War'. Only in Britain under the impetus of Lloyd George, who had taken over from Asquith as Prime Minister in December 1916, was there still a near unanimous feeling of 'we'll see it through to the end' and this became a catch phrase seen on countless postcards.

The War forced governments to introduce controls on almost all activities – Ministries of Food, Ministries of Production, Ministries of Manpower, which were cornerstones of the socializing of European life after the War. Many of the organizations established then have never been dismantled and the old freedoms never regained. Many simple ideas were born from the necessity of war that remain with us today – daylight saving, or British Summer Time, the idea of a Londoner, William Willett, was introduced in 1916, and the allotments came into being that same Christmas. In order to pursue the War the governments needed enormous sums of money and for the first time these were raised from the populations by increasingly heavy taxation and by the issue of government bonds by a Ministry of Savings – many were the ideas used to collect money. One of the most popular in Britain was the 'Tank Bank'. This was a tank in Trafalgar Square from within which War Bonds could be purchased. Many others were to be found around the country, as well as 'Submarine Banks'. The effectiveness of the British National War Bonds is described by a contemporary article, dated August 1918: 'Since October 1917 when these bonds were first put on sale the people of the United Kingdom have found one thousand million pounds sterling, more than the whole of the National Debt as it stood in 1914 ... and it was raised after other big sums had been found and therefore at a time when one would reasonably expect people to have but little cash to spare.'

How dare you walk on our front door!

WARNING
THE PUBLIC ARE ADVISED TO LIVE IN THE CELLARS DURING ZEPPELIN RAIDS
BY ORDER

526

OUT FOR VICTORY.

THE ALLOTMENT HOLDER.
Too old to fight, but doing his bit to beat the U boats.

527

First bit of luck I've had for years— she's going to buy one.

ZEPPELIN
·RAIDS·

RESPIRATORS
AS USED AT THE FRONT

A SURE SAFEGAURD AGAINST POISONOUS GAS BOMBS

528

527 Artist L.Ravenhill. *'Dig for Victory'* was a well-known WW2 slogan. It was just as relevant in WW1. The card is one of a series that illustrates how the war effort can be aided at home. *'Too old to fight ...'* says the caption but Conscription would call upon 50 year old men. *British.*

528 The downtrodden husband is a standard humorous stereotype and here he is used to devalue the menacing Zeppelin with what might be called an 'unexpected consequence'. *'Witty Series'* No 194. *British: (Pub. Bamforth.)*

529 The London and provincial theatres continued to flourish during the war, providing much-needed light relief for local inhabitants and soldiers on leave. A popular show was Albert de Courville's Hippodrome Revue called *Joy Bells*, starring George Robey. He had also produced a Bairnsfather revue, *Flying Colours. British: (Pub John Waddington, London.)*

530 One of the most popular shows was Charles B. Cochran's production of *The Better 'Ole*, a play based on Bruce Bairnsfather's immortal characters, Bill, Bert and Alf which toured the country in 1917. *British: (Pub. Grand Theatre Derby.)*

Postcards played a very large part in the money raising process in every country. All sorts of cards were sold with either all or part of the proceeds going to War Bonds or charities, and an intriguing and historical collection could be made concentrating just on the 'Fund Raisers' of the combatant nations. The picture postcards crystallize the elements of the gigantic changes that turned Europe from autocracy to democracy in five momentous years. Each card tells a story that is an integral part of the time and of all the other stories, and yet can often be selected for individual study. Somehow, amidst all the change and turmoil, life went on in the hope of a new tomorrow, but sadly when the War was over the old problems came back – unemployment, strikes, poverty and social inequality. But after 1919 the picture card no longer made social comment as it had before, newer media made communication quicker and wider. The radio and the telephone spread rapidly and the postcard died in the world's first total war.

When the Germans asked for an Armistice in 1918 it was not because they had suffered a military defeat. In the period between the two great wars the Germans were to proclaim to the world and to their own soldiers that their fighting troops had remained undefeated. The Germans had been defeated at home. The people had lost the will to continue to suffer the privations of war.

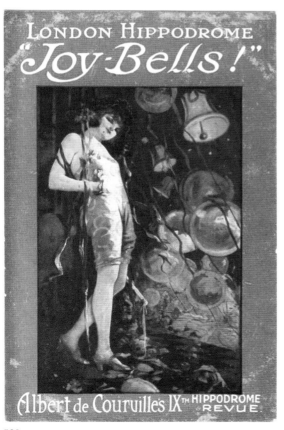

529   530

Women at War

The First World War did more to advance the cause of women's emancipation than decades of feminist agitation. By the time the Armistice was signed, women over 30 in Britain had the vote (their North American sisters would soon also be enfranchised) and women in Britain, France, Belgium, Germany and America had successfully taken the opportunity to prove that they could carry out almost any work a man could do. The German Hausfrau was industrious, obedient and lacked feminine glamour and allure and her role as subservient to the dominant male was generally accepted by both sexes. Despite the fact that conscription had left Germany woefully short of manpower to carry out essential jobs, the thoroughly domesticated image the Fatherland had created for its womanhood debarred her from them. In the early months men were brought in from the country, but eventually there were no spare men available and Germany was forced to consider her women as an acceptable labour pool.

531 During the War, Christabel, along with other members of the N.W.S.P.U. (National Women's Social and Political Union) including her famous mother, Mrs Pankhurst, did much to help the War effort – but they still wanted the vote. *British.*

532 The problems of war-time drunkenness gave these good ladies much to demonstrate about. For the Allies and the Central Powers alike it became a serious problem, both in men and women (many of whom were earning for the first time and could therefore afford to buy a relaxing *'tipple'*). In Britain many official bodies, like the Y.W.C.A., the Y.M.C.A. and the Salvation Army, ran 'dry' canteens to discourage alcoholism. *British.*

VOTES FOR WOMEN.

Photo. by Kay. Manchester.

Miss **CHRISTABEL PANKHURST**, LL.B.

Organising Secretary, National Women's Social and Political Union, 4, Clement's Inn, Strand, W.C.

531

In France the male attitude towards women was the antithesis of the German view. The Frenchwoman was required to be, and enjoyed being, essentially feminine and deliberately attractive. She preserved her mystique by keeping well clear of traditional male activities and when France too was faced with an immense hole in its essential working force because of conscription, there was tremendous male resistance to women filling that hole. More independent than her German counterpart, the Frenchwoman at first agreed to take on only permitted light jobs, but she soon realized that the harvest had to be gathered in, guns and bullets had to be made, and there was only herself to do these things. Therefore she did them, and flaunted masculine disapproval.

Neither France nor Germany started as far along the road to female emancipation, and neither finished with such concrete gains in terms of suffrage and union support for women workers as did Britain. In August 1914 the fight for women's suffrage in Britain had passed from being a joke to being a serious political issue which was causing the Government grave concern. When war broke out, the various rival factions called a truce to pull together for the war effort. The main group was the Women's Social and Political Union (WSPU), run by Mrs. Emmeline Pankhurst, her daughters Christabel and Sylvia, the Kenney sisters and other notable agitators. The Pankhursts were particularly active during the War. Christabel and Mrs. Pankhurst did separate lecture tours in the United States to whip up concern and funds for 'poor little Serbia'. Mrs. Pankhurst, whose personal magnetism was enormously strong, travelled the U.K. indefatigably, making recruiting speeches. When Lloyd George became Minister of Munitions he gave the WSPU a grant of £2,000 to help finance their tremendously successful recruiting campaigns. Mrs. Pankhurst even travelled to Russia in July 1917 intending to address the great workers' and soldiers' congress. Forbidden to do so, she returned to Britain in September totally disillusioned with Bolshevism, in contrast to her younger daughter Sylvia who became a rabid

533 Artist E. F. Skinner, Printed note 'Passed by Censor 24/4/17'. The type of shipyard machining job only men would have had a chance to do before the War. In many cases women were let go when the men came home and claimed their jobs back which caused a great deal of friction. *British*.

534 The women are using belt-driven machinery to finish off shell cases. The rapidly moving belts were a dangerous hazard for long hair and all the workers are wearing hats and coveralls. A War Bonds fund-raiser card. Passed by Censor and approved by the Ministry of Information. *British: (Pub. A. M. Davis & Co.)*

535 Women's desire to pull their weight during the War manifested itself in all combatant nations but they were also able to experience a personal freedom that, once tasted, they did not want to lose. *American: (Pub. Merval Corp.)*

536 *'Forward Children!!'* 'Children' means *'Children of the Nation'*. The gallant charge at the top of the card epitomises the French policy of *'attaque á l'outrance'*, all-out attack. From the *'European War of 1914-15'*, Series. The French flag triumphs over the German standard. Mlle Chenal of the *Opéra Comique* declaims the French National Anthem. 30.7.15. *French: (Pub. Rossi-Lespinne.)*

537 Card home from a British soldier showing a *Poilu* between spells in a first line trench. Message on reverse reads, *'...don't you think this chap makes a fine girl. He is one of the French soldiers and this is how they amuse themselves.'* Bert-Gyll is actually one of the performers in a regular morale-boosting open-air theatre held behind the lines at Commercy, which included sporting events and film shows. *French.*

533

534

535

Mlle CHENAL, de l'Opéra-Comique.
Allons Enfants...   Forward Children !!.

536

Guerre 1914-1915

" Poilu's-Park ". - La Grande Divette
Le Poilu Bert-Gyll entre deux séjours aux tranchées de 1ère ligne

537

Socialist during the war. Her sympathies were shared by the eccentric sister of Sir John French, Charlotte French Despard, a vegetarian who always wore a black lace mantilla and who formed the Women's Freedom League. The family military tradition was continued by French's other sister, Catherine Harley. She became an administrator of the Scottish Women's Hospital and served with the French Expeditionary Force in Salonika. Awarded the *Croix de Guerre*, she was killed in March 1917 in Serbia.

The War soon became an outlet for the indefatigable enthusiasms of the upper-middle and aristocratic classes of womanhood especially in Britain. Their first action when interested in any cause was to form an Association, League, Movement, Corps, Society or Guild of other willing female enthusiasts, backed by the occasional male patron with influence in the right places and or capital. They achieved miracles of fund raising, organization, recruitment, and made a truly effective contribution to the war effort. Happily some of them and their feats of valour have been recorded on the picture postcard, to add another category of wartime cards. Nowadays cards on such topics as suffragism are rare, eagerly sought after and therefore extremely valuable. They provide a unique historical record of a fascinating era and are well worth patiently seeking out to enhance a collection.

Dedicated lady aristocrats were also active on the Continent, especially in Belgium, where, for example, the Baroness de la Grange became known as the 'Mother of the British Army' when she converted her fine château for use as billets, and Princess Marie de Croy courageously helped Edith Cavell in sheltering fleeing Allied soldiers attempting to cross the border. Actresses in all the countries also did their bit by putting on charity shows, touring the Front

MADAME PARSONS AND HER POPULAR FAMILY, INCLUDING THE 7 LITTLE
LANCASHIRE LASSES, THE 2 LANCASHIRE LADS AND THEIR SOLDIER
DADDY, SGT. PARSONS, A.O.C.

538

538 Madame Parsons appears to have done more than her bit in providing future WAACS, WRNS or Munitionettes. The seven sisters (Seven Little Lancashire Lasses) and their mother performed a patriotic song and dance stage show. *British: (Pub. John Waddington.)*

539, 539A Sold to raise funds for Red Cross. By W. W. Werestchaguine, entitled '*The letter will stay unfinished*' [the patient is obviously dying]. The French sender points out that the profits will be used for the widows and orphans of the War. *Russian.*

540 Reverse reads, '*Mdlle [sic] Irma Lorraine is selling her photographs to provide gift parcels of cigarettes and tobacco for the brave men at the front. The amount received for the photographs is acknowledged in "The Performer" week by week*'. See also Card No 524. *British.*

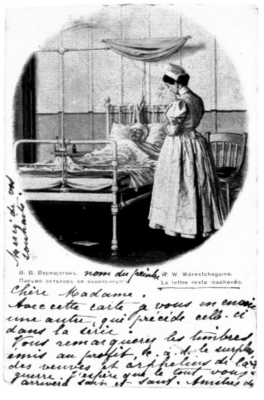

539

539A

Irma Lorraine

P 781

540

with concert parties and selling postcards of themselves (often dressed in khaki) to raise money. When genuine female stars were not available, the troops put on their own shows behind the front line dressed in drag for female parts.

The less ostentatiously extrovert and administratively talented found an extremely worthy outlet for their desire to do their bit by joining the ranks of the Voluntary Aid Detachment. Already formed before the War, the V.A.D. was able to put a hospital unit together and despatch it at the request of the Belgian Red Cross, to Brussels by mid–August 1914. VADs were drawn from the aristocracy, the Universities and from the whole army of unmarried and unoccupied young ladies of good family who had often never done a day's work before the War. They did a superb job in boosting the tiny ranks of fully trained professional nurses. They served bravely and loyally, often in indescribably bad conditions, for gruelling long shifts in England, France, Belgium, Italy, Salonika, Russia, Rumania, Malta, Egypt, Gibraltar, Mesopotamia, India,

541 Artist E. Muller depicts Belgium giving the Kaiser a bloody nose as Luxembourg weeps. Although the Belgians put up a brave defence, only two parts of their country were not occupied – the area north of Dixmuide and the Salient around Ypres defended by the BEF. *French.*

542 Used in France. Smart young ladies rushed to join the auxiliary forces and other organizations, like the V A.D., to do their 'bit'. A title could be an impediment to getting a job, as the aristocracy were often considered effete *and 'stupid'* – according to Lady Iris Capell. She changed her name to Catherine Iris Adams in order to work as a nurse, but later furnished herself with a reference from Lady Iris Capell. *Written 27 April 1918. French.*

543 A supposedly common wartime phenomenon: a German soldier leaves in his wake a bevy of ladies with his illegitimate offsprings. Similar cards can be found for most of the warring nations. *German.*

544 Part of a set of British propaganda cards, the captions printed in many languages, showing the gallant British on active service. Published late in the War on thin, coarse card, reflecting the paper shortage. This one is in Russian, posted from a soldier in the Army of Occupation, 23 March 1919. It shows a British Officer wounded in a motor car accident. *British.*

545 Australian women volunteered enthusiastically to be nurses at home and some served as such in the Australian Army though they had to be single or widowed. Over 2,000 served overseas. Australian Red Cross Nurse by Artist Kay Edmunds. 1915. *Australian.*

Belgium protests.   — La Belgique proteste.

541

Mobilisation féminine.
Féminine Mobilisation   2656

542

Vater werden ist nicht schwer
Vater sein dagegen sehr......

543

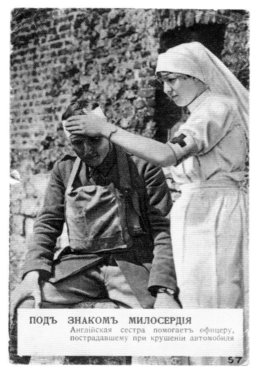

ПОДЪ ЗНАКОМЪ МИЛОСЕРДІЯ
Англійская сестра помогаетъ офицеру,
пострадавшему при крушеніи автомобиля

544

545

The Red Cross Girl.
A pretty sight, I tell you,
Is a Red Cross girl to see;
While I support the colors
'Tis she who supports me

546

and in internment camps in Switzerland and Holland. The nursing VADs, the nurses of the Red Cross, and the many other official nursing bodies who took an active part in the fighting zones provided far more than a mere medical service. They added the feminine touch, the sympathy and gentleness and the humour that the troops of both sides, battered and wounded in body and mind, so desperately craved. They were favourite subjects for picture postcards and tended to be viewed in a rather idealized way as 'Angels of Mercy'.

Many of them were killed on duty, or wounded, and their decorations for valour and dedicated service range from the Russian Medal of St. George, the *Légion d'Honneur* and the Croix de Guerre to the Serbian Order of St. Sava and, less often as Britain tended to be rather niggardly when it came to awarding women with medals, the Military Medal. Their patients, damaged by gas, shell-shocked, with stinking, gangrenous wounds, were not pretty to treat. The nurses referred to them as 'our boys' and cherished them unstintingly.

The three arms of the British service each eventually had a women's branch. The Women's (later' Queen Mary's) Army Auxiliary Corps was formed in 1917. The W.R.N.S, under the direction of Dame Katherine Furse, was formed on 13 April 1918 and offered jobs for cooks, waitresses, shorthand typists, motordrivers, ledger clerks and for those with 'technical qualifications'. The W.R.A.F. was also formed in mid-April 1918, a fortnight after the R.A.F. More than 100,000 women enrolled in these auxiliary services and rushed into unbecoming uniform – a form of dress which the Frenchman abhorred for his women and which he firmly discouraged them from donning. The Americans, however, quickly formed female arms of the services. The U.S. Navy and Marine Corps recruited nearly 13,000 women and there was also a U.S. Women's Motor Corps and many American nurses came over to Europe to look after their own troops. American women at home were filled with patriotic fervour and worked hard at fund-raising and munition making once America came into the War. The Y.W.C.A. was another group active on both sides of the Atlantic, and in Britain women could also join the Women's Land Army, the Women's Legion Motor Transport Section, the Women's Royal Volunteer Service, the Women's Reserve Ambulance (or Green Cross) Society, and the Women's Police Volunteers (renamed the Women's Police Service in 1915).

The policewomen did an outstanding job. They were largely used to tackle the serious problem of promiscuity, drunkeness and general licentiousness, often known as Khaki Fever. They patrolled known trouble spots (like The Strand, which they called 'The Devil's Promenade') with tremendous bravery. The National British Women's Temperance Association had to work overtime. But when not taken to excess one of the greatest services that women provided to the men at War was the comfort of love and gaiety and relaxation when they came home on leave from the trenches, by simply being feminine. The War did much to counteract the old double standards of permissiveness for men and sheltered restriction and limitation for women. During the War, with most able-bodied men absent for long periods and often for ever, women in all the combatant nations let their hair down at such an alarming rate that it became a genuine headache for all the wartime governments. The need for their labour, to women who had never had any job opportunities in the past, gave women an importance and sense of purpose they had never enjoyed before and a heady freedom. They dug the trenches for the Hindenberg Line defences, they drove buses and trams, brought in the harvest, worked in quarries and as dockers, they dug graves, lit lamps, delivered the mail, painted houses, learned how to weld and work copper. For the most part they loved every back-breaking, hand-blistering moment, for they were important workers in their own right. The novelty of women doing manual work and of wearing trousers and other unfeminine working gear was eagerly recorded in many fascinating series of 'Women at War' postcards in all the nations at war.

THE TOUCH OF AN ANGEL'S HAND.
L'ange de nos blessés.

547

IN HOSPITAL — RECOVERING

548

"The Patient is not yet out of Danger."

549

546 Many American nurses came over to Europe in 1917 to look after their own boys with the Red Cross, but from 1915 the, 'American Field Service', a group of volunteer ambulance units, operated with the French Army and they have a memorial at Pont à Mousson. *American: (Pub. Merval Corp, New York.)*

547 By Artist Arthur Butcher. Posted 3 July 1918. Message reads, '*I am now at the 14th General Hp. B.E.F... Wish I was this man and you were the nurse.*' Passed by Censor 3008. *British: (Pub. Inter-Art Co.)*

548 While professional nurses were able to cope with the desperate injuries that some soldiers suffered, many volunteer nursing assistants, full of a desire to help, found the reality of injury too much to bear. The blanket is red so as not to show blood stains – see No. 547. *British.*

549 A blue suit, white shirt and red tie is the uniform of the convalescent soldier. The outfit, known as 'The Hospital Blues', was made of flannel and fitted rather like pyjamas. It was not generally worn by officers who wore instead a white armband bearing a red crown. *British: (Pub. E. Mack.)*

For Mercy's sake.   Au nom de la charité.

550

"ON SERVICE"

551

Most importantly of all, women made munitions. At first conditions in the factories were appalling, with wages a mere pittance and hours impossibly long. 80 hours a week in 12 hour shifts, with a take home pay of nine shillings a week was not unusual. Girls travelled away from home for the first time to work and slept in barrack-like dormitories. Crêches and nurseries were set up to woo mothers to work. Gradually conditions and pay improved as active feminist socialists like Mary Macarthur, Secretary of the Women's Trade Union League, fought for their sisters' rights. But a woman's pay was always below that of a man's for the same job and as soon as the men came back for their jobs after the war, there was massive unemployment among female workers. The glory was short-lived, but the great revolution in female job opportunity opened doors for the persevering few who refused to go back to domestic slavery or genteel governessing as the only alternatives. The terrible shortage of marriageable men after the fearful losses of the War meant that marital security was not available to a large number of women. At last a career was now a respectable alternative and a more attractive one to many progressives who were reviewing the whole institution and validity of marriage. Tremendous inspiration for women wanting to make their contribution to the War came from the very top in most countries – from the Royal lady workers. In Britain Queen Mary worked tirelessly to put the women's voluntary organizations on an efficient basis and she ran her own Queen Mary Workshops' for needlewomen in the East End. She encouraged her rather moody man by cheering letters during his frequent absences and when he was badly hurt after a fall from his horse when touring the Western Front, she deputized for him on many engagements. Her tea parties at Buckingham Palace were a great source of excitement and enjoyment for convalescent soldiers. Her daughter,

552

553

554

550 To a wounded soldier all nurses probably looked like this. By Artist Arthur Butcher in *'Our Own Girls'* Series. *British: (Pub. Inter-Art Co.)*

551 By Artist Harold Copping. Posted 15 November 1918, just after the Armistice, from a hospital in France. Reverse bears printed sentimental tribute to the modern *'Red Cross lady of the Lamp'*. The sender comments, *'Well! We have won out at last and of course we are all pleased ... Note what praise the V.A.D.s are given above. Ha Ha. He!!!'* Passed by Censor 3008. *British: (Pub. Tuck.)*

552 *'The Blessing during the Action'*. The catholic French were more likely to have a mystical or religious element to their cards, as here, with rosary and cross very evident. The 'Nuns' or 'Sisters' respond to a 'Calling' and dedicate themselves to those in need. *French.*

553 By popular American 'kids cards' Artist, C.H. Twelvetrees. At the end of the war Twelvetrees gained the title of 'America's Champion Postcard Artist' and could regularly be seen in Central Park, New York, sketching children at play. Here once again we have the gentle use of a double-entendre. *American.*

L'ÉTERNELLE PETITE GUERRE

" Attaque de front "

555

Si la jambe est en bois, le cœur ne l'est pas

556

MISS VESTA TILLEY IN KHAKI

The proceeds of the sale of these cards will be handed by Miss TILLEY to one of the War Relief Funds

557

554 By sought–after 'pin–up' artist, Xavier Sager. *'One often has need for one more wounded than oneself.'* Is the nurse holding up her thumb to be bandaged by her patient? Written on 2 September 1917 the message just says 'Daddy' in English. The patient, not in blue, is shown as an officer. *French: (Pub. A. Noyer, Paris.)*

555 Also by Xavier Sager, entitled *'The Eternal Little War – Frontal Attack'*. The card was sent to London via a Field Post Office in June 1917 and passed by Censor 4812. The blue overcoat is typical dress for the French Poilu and can be seen on many village war memorials. *French: (Pub. A. Noyer, Paris.)*

556 Another by Xavier Sager. *'If the leg is wooden, the heart is not.'* Coming to terms with such an injury was an overwhelming challenge, not only for the soldier but also for his loved ones. Posted to London via a Field Post Office and passed by Censor 4812. See card No. 555. Both cards were sent to a 'Miss Johnson' and their subject suggests that the sender was himself badly injured. *French: (Pub. A. Noyer.)*

Greetings from one of your fair Allies.

558

I'M NOT GREEDY - BUT I LIKE A FAIR W.A.A.C

559

557 Vesta Tilley, the most famous of all male impersonators, dons uniform to raise money for the War. The caption says, *'The proceeds of the sale of these cards will be handed by Miss Tilly to one of the War Relief Funds'*. Posted April 1915. *British: (Pub. Davis. Allen & Sons.)*

558 This card has no particular axe to grind, just a pretty lady to raise morale all around. Artist Barribal, a friend of cartoonist Captain Bruce Bairnsfather, specialised in drawing elegant ladies and based all his drawings upon his wife, 'Babs'. *British: (Pub. Inter-Art, London.)*

559 A typical British pun. Reg Maurice the artist, drew a range of saucy sea-side-type postcards and was fond of using puns. *British: (Pub. Regent Pub. Co.)*

560 The caption reads, *'German aggression in 1914 having taken up many male personnel one can see, even in Arvert, a woman employed by the Railway as a railwayman. Very active, she works valiantly.'* Arvert is well away from the war, way down in the south-west of France near the mouth of the Gironde. *French: (Pub. F. Braun, Royon.)*

561 One of a set of 3 French cards recording the heroic exploits of a certain Sister Julie at Gerbeviller on 24 August 1914 who sent the Germans packing to protect her patient and was decorated for her bravery. *French.*

Princess Mary, donned the uniform of the Red Cross and accompanied her mother on many of her morale-raising tours.

The German Kaiserin was active in supporting her husband's war effort, as was the Queen of the Belgians, Elisabeth. She founded a school for Belgian orphans as one of her many contributions. Queen Marie of Rumania was the eldest daughter of Alfred, Duke of Edinburgh, Queen Victoria's second son. She married Prince (later King) Ferdinand of Rumania in 1895 and took a tremendous interest in her new country. During the War she worked actively with The Red Cross, setting up a hospital in the Palace. Towards the end of the War she told a British reporter: 'It has been difficult for the King and me. He is a German. I am English. But we have never let our difficulties stand in our way. We are both Rumanian. That is our safeguard'. Postcards of these gallant Royal ladies are becoming increasingly sought-after and form an important part of the 'Who's Who in the Great War' picture gallery.

Miss Olive Dent, author of *A VAD in France* published during the War, prophesied on the day War broke out: 'This is going to be a woman's, as well as a man's. War.' How right she was.

560

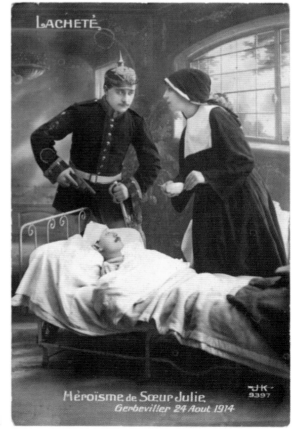

561

BACK TO THE LAND!

562

Sinn Fein Rebellion, Dublin
Rebel Countess leaves after Court-Martial
The Countess Markiewicz leaving after Court-Martial.
She is here seen seated with a Wardress in the
Red Cross Waggon which took her away

563

564

562 WW1 version of 'Dig for Victory' by well-known 'kids" Artist, Agnes Richardson. Privations brought on by the war continued for some years afterwards and so the propaganda cards continued to be of morale value. Posted 14 August 1919. *British: (Pub.Inter-Art Co, London.)*

563 Rare postcard of *'Rebel Countess Markiewicz'* being escorted from her Court-Martial for her part in the Sinn Fein Rebellion. Her death sentence was commuted to 'life' and she was released in 1917 as part of the General amnesty. She would later serve more time in prison for anti-British activities. *Irish: (Pub. Valentine, Dublin.)*

564 Card from a personal photograph. The Police woman's chief job was a *'morality'* patrol in the main areas of drunkenness and *'loose'* behaviour. *British.*

565

566

567

565 Card from a personal photograph of a W.A.A.C. (Women's Auxiliary Army Corps set up in 1917 with volunteers) in uniform. In 1918 the Corps was given the honour of having its name changed to *'Queen Mary's Army Auxiliary Corps'*. Its initial purpose was to release more men for active service. *British: (Pub. USA Studios, London.)*

566 Personal photograph of a Land Girl in uniform. The message reads, *'With best love and sincere regards, from your bed-mate.'* Women workers often left home for the first time during the War and slept in hostel accommodation. By the end of the war the Women's Land Army numbered over 250,000. *British: (Pub. Wicken Studios, Bangor.)*

567 The wartime woman soon learned to drink and even smoke and with her new-found freedoms sexual immorality became a widespread problem. Today the caption would be considered very doubtful but in 14–18 probably not! *British.*

Guess, we'll all do our bit!

568

Kitcheners "Knuts"

569

L'ANGLAISE

Les Femmes Héroïques

570

568 Caption on reverse, '*Miss U.S.A.*'. Posted 30 May 1918, as America was about to make a significant contribution to the fighting in France. On the back is an imperative overstamp, '*Buy War Bonds NOW*'. *British: (Pub. Tuck.)*

569 A '*Knut*' is a chic young thing, generally male and cigarette-smoking. This one has joined Kitchener's New Army. See card 514. The pyramid in the background is presumably an acknowledgement that at the beginning of the war Kitchener was British Consul-General in Cairo. Life in Cairo was pretty racy so this Knut needed to be careful. *British: (Pub. The Barty Pub.Co.)*

570 By Artist Emile Dupuis in '*Heroic Women*' Series. Posted 28 December 1915 on active service. Message reads. '*Had a ripping time at Christmas. Have not forgotten you at home.*' Girls left behind would not be too pleased to get such a message, especially if the sender was stationed near, or on leave in, Paris. *Passed by Censor 346. French: (Pub. Visé, Paris.)*

AS MULHERES teem desempenhado um papel importantissimo no exercito industrial da Grã-Bretanha, que sem cessar trabalha na producção de munições. Perto de meio milhão de mulheres se emprega hoje nas varias industrias de guerra e, é de notar, que antes da guerra nem uma só mulher era empregada em dois terços dos 500 processos de fabrico de munições em que actualmente trabalham.

571

572

La toilette avant la bataille
(Shaving before the battle)

G. W. D.

573

OUT FOR VICTORY.

THE FARM GIRL.
Who is doing her bit to feed us all.

574

OUT FOR VICTORY.

THE MUNITION GIRL.
"England expects every woman to do her duty."

575

I'VE COME TO HELP
OUR BELGIAN BOYS.

576

SAUCY SALLY
STITCHING SHIRTS
FOR SAILORS.

577

"Doing her Bit"

THE LADY "BOBBY"

578

571 Publicity card with text in Portuguese showing British women helping with the war effort. Much British printed propaganda was produced in neutral Portugal though it is not clear why this card would have been printed in Portugese. *British.*

572. Austrian women, like their counterparts in the other belligerent countries, were co-opted to work as tram conductors, postal workers, land girls and other vital jobs. Posted 31/8/16. *Austrian.*

573 In France women acted as temporary landladies as British troops were billeted in their homes and, despite the appalling number of casualties, authorities still felt that this kind of idealistic image aided morale. *French.*

574, 575 Artist L. Ravenhill's *'Out for Victory'* Series. These two show *'The Farm Girl'* and *'The Munition Worker'*, essential jobs for which there was no longer enough men to carry out. *British.*

576 *'For The Cause'* Series. The promotion of the idea that the war was in pursuit of a 'Cause' probably originated with Government propaganda policy as a way of getting the Nation to pull together. In modern Prime-Minister-Parlance, *'We're all in this together.' British: (Pub. Tuck.)*

577 Posted 4 September 1916 in Redditch, Midlands. Message reads : *'What do you think of the Zepps last night.'* This refers to the largest airship raid of the War when 14 crossed the English coastline, one of them being destroyed by Lt. Leefe-Robinson (qv). *British: (Pub. Regent Pub. Co.)*

578 By Artist Flora White. Posted August 1917, the month when the battle of Passchendaele was getting underway. Flora was a Brighton artist whose family owned a stationer's business in the town and she painted hundreds of this type of card. *British: (Pub. Photochrom Co.)*

579 Card by well-known Artist, B. Wennerberg entitled *'On Leave'*. The young lady proudly admires her sweetheart's Iron Cross. The decoration as a mark of military endeavour probably originated with the Prussians and there are a number of levels equating to the type of courage being recognised. *German: (War Postcard, Pub. Hesse & Co, Leipzig.)*

579

Schwesters Geburtstag.

580

La Femme et la Guerre.   Woman and the War.

LEROY. — Le Magasin d'Habillement. — The Quarter Master.

581

580 Another card by B. Wennerberg, whose bathing beauties were popular all over the Continent and in Britain before the War. The caption reads, '*Sister's Birthday*'. Wennerberg was a Swedish artist who studied in Paris and in Munich where he settled in 1898. *German: (War Postcard. Pub. 'Lustigen Blatter', Berlin.)*

581, 582, 583, 584, 585, 586, 587, 588, 589 Superb French set by Leroy of '*Woman and the War*'. *French: (Pub. P.J. Gallais, Paris.)*

La Femme et la Guerre.   Woman and the War.

LEROY. — La Mère adoptive. — The adopted Child.

582

La Femme et la Guerre.   Woman and the War.

LEROY. — La Marraine. — The Marraine.

583

584

585

586

587

La Femme et la Guerre.   Woman and the War.

LEROY. — L'Infirmière. — The Nurse.

588

La Femme et la Guerre.   Woman and the War.

LEROY. — Travaux des Champs. — Farm Work.

589

590 Women at work – Postman, Chimney Sweep and Window Cleaner – all traditionally male jobs. New Year card for 1916.Posted 29 December 1915. *German.*

591 Queen Mary, with King George V, visits one of her favourite causes, QMWAAC, in Aldershot, 31 June 1918. The importance of the role of the Royal Family as a figurehead of the 'Cause' was well understood by both the King and the Queen. British.

592 Printed message written by Queen Mary on 26 April 1918 on behalf of the women of the British Empire. The heartfelt letter reads, *'To the men of the Navy, Army andAir Force, I send this message to tell every man how much we, the women of the British Empire at home, watch and pray for you during the long hours of these days of stress and endurance. Our pride, in you is immeasurable, our hope unbounded, our trust absolute. You are fighting in the cause of righteousness and freedom, fighting to defend the children and women of our land from the horrors that have taken other countries, fighting for our very existence as a people at home and across the seas – you are offering your all, you hold back nothing, and day by day you show a love so great that no man can have greater. We as one send forth with full heart and unfailing will the lives we hold most dear. We too are striving in all ways possible to make the War victorious. I know that I am expressing what is felt by thousands of wives and mothers when I say that we are determined to help one another in keeping your homes ready against your glad home coming. In God's name we bless you and by His help we too will do our best. Mary R.' British: (Pub. Tuck.)*

593 Explanatory leaflet inside packet from which this card comes explains: *'This picture was painted as a memorial of the work done by women during the Great War… women and girls take up the tools laid down by (the men). In the eight or nine figures nearly all branches of work are represented…. On the extreme right an older woman … hides her eyes with her hand, unable to bear the sight of her son going off, who has left his children to her care.'* The artist, Lucy Kemp-Welch, is best known for the illustrations she did for the Anna Sewell's *'Black Beauty'* in 1915. *British: (Fine Arts Pub. Co.)*

Glück ohne Ende
Zur Jahreswende!

590

Inspection of QMWAAC by Their Majesties at Aldershot.
Presentation of Miss Pierce.

591

FOR FREEDOM

592

By permission of the Gresham Committee.
" Women's work in the Great War, 1914-1918."
By Lucy Kemp-Welch.

594 Queen Marie of Rumania, granddaughter of Queen Victoria who worked actively with the Red Cross during the War. Her country had entered the war against the Central Powers (Austro-Hungarians) by invading Hungary on 27 August 1916. *British*: (Pub. Rotary *Photo-Co.*)

595 Princess Mary, daughter of King George and Queen Mary of Great Britain, she accompanied her mother on many wartime engagements. She became Commandant of the British Red Cross whose uniform she is wearing here. After the war she became Honorary President of the Girl Guides. *British: (Pub. Beagles.)*

596 The much-respected British Queen who took an active role in organizing women's war efforts. The message reads. 'Dear Aunt this is one for your collection which I am sure you would like.' *British*: (*Pub. Valentine.*)

594

595

596

QUEEN ELISABETH

HELP THE BELGIANS 2ᴰ

NOVELTY PHOTO.

597

597 Queen Elisabeth of the Belgians was the daughter of the Duke of Bavaria before her marriage to King Albert. She renounced her country of birth at the outbreak of war and worked tirelessly for Belgium throughout it. Fully qualified as a doctor of medicine, she was decorated by King George V with the Royal Red Cross (1st Class). *British*.

598 Kaiserin Augusta, the first wife of the Kaiser, with the German Crown Princess and Prince Joachim, places wreaths on the grave of a soldier killed on the Russian Front. The caption says, *'Faithful Remembrance'*. *German*.

TREUES GEDENKEN

598

6 Pin-ups & Heroes
Silk Cards

Heroes

Despite the machines and the mechanical sophistication of the War, the occupation of the enemy's trenches could only be done in the end by man to man combat. In that combat, men for brief moments lifted themselves out of the common herd and performed extraordinary deeds of valour and became heroes. There was no monopoly by any nation of the emotional impetus which turned men into supermen and the artists were quick to picture and glorify the deeds. Artists in Germany like Richard Assman, Arno Grimm and Paul Leuteritz, in France like Albert Beertz and Georges Scott and in Britain like Dudley Tennant, Richard Caton-Woodville, Stanley Wood and Pearse, all show an astonishing similarity of presentation – only the nationality of the hero is different. The heroes here are Allied and their stories are told in the way they might have been told in contemporary accounts.

Todger Jones, V.C. of the Cheshires. No incident of the Great War so fired the imagination of the British people as that by which Private A.A. Jones, Cheshire Regiment, better known to his comrades as Todger Jones, won the Victoria Cross, for there is a grim humour about it. On the Somme, snipers were doing considerable damage to his comrades. Todger went out alone, and although one bullet went through his coat and another through his helmet, he succeeded in locating and killing three snipers. Going on he reached the enemy's trench and found several dug-outs full of Germans. By threatening them with bomb and bayonet he compelled 102 of them, including three officers, to surrender, and single-handed marched them back to the British lines with their hands above their heads.

The Boy Scout Hero of France. During the German advance in the Vosges an *Eclaireur* (French Boy Scout) was captured. He was asked to indicate the position held by his countrymen. He defiantly replied, *Je suis francais,'*(I am a Frenchman). This sealed his fate, for at once they put him against a telegraph pole and called out a firing party. As the German Officer rapped out the word of command, the young hero whipped of his hat and crying out *'Vive La France'* received his baptism of fire.

Jack 'Boy' Cornwell: When the light cruiser, *Chester*, steamed sadly in the Humber after her terrible ordeal in the battle of Jutland she carried amongst her grievously wounded a boy of only 16 years. In the midst of the battle this gallant lad stood alone by his gun, quietly awaiting orders though mortally wounded. He died on 2 June 1916 and was awarded a posthumous V.C.

The Immortal Story of L. Battery: During the retreat from Mons, L. Battery of the R.H.A. was resting briefly near Néry in the early morning of 1 September 1914. Without warning the pursuing German Cavalry Division arrived and fell upon them with artillery and machine gun fire. After the first bombardment just one of the six 13pr guns remained usable and the only men left in action were Captain Bradbury, three subalterns, Battery Sergeant-Major Dorrell, Sgt. Nelson, Driver Osborne and Gunner Darbyshire. The Germans had ten field guns and two machine guns in action against the lone 13pr and soon the subalterns were all dead and Captain Bradbury wounded twice. B.S.M. Dorrell took command and they knocked out a pair of German guns before Sergeant Nelson was severely wounded. The three remaining men fired the gun until it was almost too hot to work, and they continued to fire when reinforcements arrived and drove the Germans off. Driver Osborne and Gunner Darbyshire were awarded France's highest decoration for bravery in the field, the *Médaille Militaire.* Sergeant Nelson and B.S.M. Dorrell (who became a Lt. Colonel)

599 This card was presented free with *'The Rover'* comic paper. The Artist is Richard Caton Woodville. The East Surreys, pictured here at Contalmaison during the Battle of the Somme, were not the only footballers at the front. The London Irish Rifles used footballs at Loos in September 1915. *British.*

600 Series II. Card No. 16 – a much-reproduced postcard. The caption reads: *'A gallant rescue under fire. This man saved 20 lives like this.'* The soldier's mother bought the card and wrote to the *Daily Mail* to identify him. He was Driver Tom Spencer R.C.A., who was later decorated. *British: (Pub. Daily Mail.)*

601 The heroic and famous stand of L Battery, RHA, during the Retreat from Mons. The three men behind the gun will be B.S.M. Dorrell, Gunner Darbyshire and Driver Osborne. Lying injured on the ground is Sgt. Nelson. The censor (No. 1696) has erased the name of the location of the episode – Néry – on 1 September 1914. Posted 9 July 1915. *French: (Pub. E. Le Deley, Paris.)*

602 G & P Series. Card No. 1749. Artist Stanley Wood. *'How Todger Jones of the Cheshires won the V.C.'* – by capturing 102 Germans, including 3 officers, at Morval on the Somme on 25 Sept 1916. In 2013 fund-raising was started to raise a statue of 'Todger' in Runcorn, his home town. *British: (Pub. Gale & Polden, Aldershot.)*

THE EAST SURREY REGIMENT.
Football on the Battlefield at Contalmaison.

599

600

1914... Un grand fait d'armes : L'exploit héroïque de la batterie "L" de l'artillerie montée royale. | 1914... A great feat of Arms : The heroic exploit of "L" battery royal horse artillery

601

both received V.C.s. Captain Bradbury, too, was awarded the V.C. but posthumously, for he died of his wounds. Gunner Darbyshire wrote about the episode after the War and this is what he said about Captain Bradbury's last moments: "... a lyddite shell exploded behind me, threw me to the ground and partly stunned me. When I came round I got up and found that I was uninjured. On looking round, however, I saw that Captain Bradbury was mortally wounded. Though the captain knew that death was very near, he thought of his men to the last and begged to be carried away so that they should not be upset by seeing him, or hearing the cries which he could not restrain.' A hero's words for a hero's deeds.

This small selection of cameos is representative of thousands of equally outstanding acts of heroism, many of them passing unrecorded and therefore unrecognized (usually because all senior witnessing officers had been killed).

602

603

"BLINDED FOR YOU!"
From the painting by R. Caton Woodville.

604

HENRI GEERAERT
Chef-Eclusier
Inondeur de l'Yser en 1914

605

603 G & P Series. Card No. 1750. Artist Stanley Wood. *'How Captain R. J. Young* [Middlesex Regiment] *won the V.C'*. Researches in official Victoria Records have failed to identify this award. However, a Captain R. J. Young of the Middlesex did win an M.C. on 22 September 1916. *British: (Pub. Gale & Polden, Aldershot.)*

604 St. Dunstan's card seeking donations. *'One of the most terrible sights at the front was the long lines of blinded men, shuffling along with a hand resting on the shoulder of the man in front for guidance. Often as many as 20 men would be led in this way by one sighted soldier.'* The Artist, Richard Caton Woodville, is greatly sought-after. *British.*

605 *'Henri Geeraert, Chief Lock-keeper and Flooder of the Yser'* opened the flood gates in Nieuport, letting in the sea and swamping the area to repel the German attack of October 1914. This action allowed the Belgian forces to make a stand on the Yser. *Belgian: (Pub. Mme Lobbestal, Café de l'Eclusier* [on which there is a bust of Geeraert], *Nieuport.)*

PRIVATE H.R.H. THE PRINCE OF WALES,
Officers' Training Corps, August, 1914.

606

"HEROS,.   *M. Wagemans.*

607

DARING DEEDS.

Acting-Sergt. W. Winter (Distinguished Conduct Medal),
1st Royal Berkshire Regt.

For conspicuous gallantry on November 2nd, when he left
his trench at great risk and recovered a machine gun which
had been buried by a shell. He then worked the gun by
himself, the officer and man previously manning it having
been wounded.

608

BRITISH HEROES.

PRIVATE C. H. BOOTH (Distinguished Conduct Medal),
3rd Coldstream Guards.

For conspicuous gallantry in continually undertaking
dangerous duties, especially on November 9, at Polygon
Wood, where he assisted another man to clear a house
occupied by German snipers. He also obtained valuable
information the next day while on reconnaissance duty.

609

BRITISH HEROES.

SERGEANT A. J. MART (Distinguished Conduct Medal),
1st Bedfordshires.
For gallant conduct on November 10 in assisting to
recover one of our abandoned machine guns, killing one
German, who was watching the gun. He distinguished himself previously on dangerous services.

610

OSNAS, THE RUSSIAN HERO, WINNING THE CROSS OF
ST. GEORGE

611

606 *'Notabilities Series'*. Card No. 4308. The Prince of Wales, who would become King Edward VIII and abdicate for Mrs. Simpson, is seen here (marked with a cross below his boot), as a cadet in the Officers' Training Corps. His younger brother, Prince Albert, fought at Jutland on *H.M.S. Collingwood* and later became George VI on Edward's abdication. *British: (Pub. Tuck.)*

607 Card printed on the instructions of Prince Leopold, Duc de Brabant. Artist M. Wagemans. The proceeds from the sale of the cards went to help wounded Belgian soldiers. *British: (Pub. C. W. Jones, London.)*

608 The *'Daring Deeds'* series. Acting-Sergt W. Winter of the 1st Royal Berks wins the Distinguished Conduct Medal (DCM). Artist Alfred Pearse. Pearse, who was a British civilian, was one of three artists appointed in 1918 to chronicle the actions of the New Zealanders in France. The other two were New Zealanders. *British.*

609 The *'British Heroes'* series. Pte C.H. Booth of the 3rd Coldstream Guards wins the DCM at Polygon Wood. The DCM was an award made only to Other Ranks (i.e. not to Officers) and for them it lay ranked behind the Victoria Cross. He also won the Military Medal. Artist A. Pearse. *British.*

610 Sgt A.J. Mart of the 1st Bedfords winning the DCM. The message on the reverse reads. *'Dear Mabel. Thanks for letter if you have no special engagement on Thursday will you call in at mother's. I will tell you all news then. This is supposed to be my cousin Alf. Excuse scribble but I am writing this in office time. With love, Nellie.' Posted 24 November 1916.* Artist A. Pearse. *British.*

611 Leo Osnas, the Russian hero, winning the Cross of St George. Card No. 26. Artist A. Pearse. The story of the bravery of this Jewish doctor (sometimes described as 'medical student') and the award of his decoration from the Tsar himself, appears in several wartime and later historical accounts, notably by Sir Martin Gilbert. *British: (Pub. War Photogravure Publications.)*

612 Gaining the *Légion d'Honneur* for a French Regiment. The concept of Campaign and Bravery awards dates from Roman times. Their purpose is not just to recognise service, or acts, of a notable nature, but also to inspire others to acts of bravery. The aggregation of such awards within a group such as a Regiment contributes to the morale of the whole. *British: (Pub. War Photogravure Publications, London.)*

613 Volunteers of the Czech Army fighting against Austro-Hungarian forces for their independence, 1914. Volunteers in France, Italy and Russia formed '*Legions*' that fought in the war and ultimately won the formation of an independent Czechoslovakia in 1918. *Czech: (Pub. Minerva, Prague.)*

614 '*Galérie Patriotique*' Series. Card No. 669. Artist Georges Scott. '*The Cross of Honour.*' Although his name suggests that Scott was British he was actually French and through his art covered wars as far apart as those in the Balkans in the early years of the 20th Century, to those of the Second World War. *French: (Pub. A. Noyer. Paris.)*

615 The Boy Scout who defied the Germans in the Vosges in 1914. The story is told on the reverse and concludes: '*Verily, if the Blood of the Martyrs was the seed of the Church, may we not believe that from this youth's blood sunk into the roadside, will spring armed resolute men to avenge it.*' Artist Edward Jagger. *British: (Pub.Castle Studios, Hollinwood for the Boy Scout Movement.)*

616 A real treasure, a unique handmade card. It was probably made with others by the local branch of the Star and Garter organization and sold by them to raise funds. The picture (stuck on here) of Jack Cornwell, 16-year old VC, is one taken when he was serving on H.M.S. *Lancaster* before joining H.M.S. *Chester* and small versions of it were handed out to children at schools, or sold for one penny, soon after his death. *British: (Pub. Carbonara, Liverpool.)*

617 *Bugler Henri Grève, Hero of Liège, Louvain and Termonde,* appearing at the Leeds Empire, Oct 25 1914. This chap pops up quite frequently in this pose on postcards but we have not been able to find out any more about him than what we have here. Louvain fell to the Germans mid-August and Termonde in mid September so Henri moved pretty quickly to get to Leeds. *British: (Pub. Carbonara, Liverpool.)*

612

613

D'après l'Illustration   E. Scott

LA CROIX D'HONNEUR

569

614

A HERO'S FATE.
—*After sketch by Edward Jagger.*

615

1916

In Aid of the
"JACK CORNWELL" WARD
at the Star & Garter Home

JACK CORNWELL
V.C.
AGED 16 YEARS
DIED
of
WOUNDS

616

BRIGADIER HENRI GREVE.
Hero of LIEGE, LOUVAIN, MALINES & TERMONDE.

617

Silk Cards

The most colourful cards of the whole war were the embroidered silks. First produced in early 1914, it soon became obvious that this new genre of postcards made the perfect vehicle for the troops on the Western Front to use to express their feelings and they were produced in their thousands until well into 1919. Their production was a great marketing success story: the classic case of finding a need and fulfilling it.

There were three main types of embroidered cards. The most common and still readily available are the frankly sentimental (including greetings cards). They bear symbolic flowers like Forget-me-nots and loving messages to *Dear Mother, My Darling Wife* etc. Cards bearing patriotic messages, like *Might is Right* and *England for Ever*, and the flags of all the Allied nations are not quite so easy to find and are therefore slightly more valuable. Designs made up of large dates for the five years of the War are also priced more highly than the common varieties. The Regimental Crests and Badges, which are the most difficult to find are, therefore, the most valuable. Crests of Regiments of the Line are rarer and more valuable than those of Corps and non-combatant units.

618

619

618 Woven silk cards are much sought-after and this is an extremely rare card of the famous picture by Georges Scott. *'They shall not pass!'*, says the *Poilu*, a clear statement of National intent. Most of the cards like this were sent in an envelope for protection. *French.*

619 Woven silk card. The humanity of the Allies tramples the eagle of German *'culture'* underfoot. The silk for this type of card was mostly made by Nyret Frères, a ribbon-making company founded in 1825, but during the war the final product was published by Deffrène. *French: (Pub. E.D., Paris.)*

620 A Nyret woven silk card of President Poincaré who held that office throughout the war. He felt that the terms of the Peace Treaty were not harsh enough and that Germany should have been made to give up more territory in Europe. *French.*

621 *'The Leaning Virgin of Albert, 1914'*. A legend grew up about the statue on the Basilique, toppled to a perilous-looking angle by a German shell In January 1915. The Allies believed that the war would end the day the statue fell, the Germans that whoever knocked it down would lose. Both were wrong. Machine-woven silk card. These cards of the WW1 period are comparatively rare. Earlier cards by manufacturers like Stevens and Grant were extremely popular. The wartime cards were mostly produced in France. *French: (Pub. E. Deffrène. Paris.)*

620

621

622 Very rare American-themed embroidered silk card, showing a female representation of the USA with a skirt made up of the Stars & Stripes. This lifts to show a pocket which originally contained a small card. It is obviously aimed at the Doughboys (known to the French as 'Sammies, after 'Uncle Sam'), newly arrived in France (c. 1917). *French.*

623 This is a typical embroidered silk sentimental design, one of the many hundreds of such that can still be found. They were embroidered at home or sometimes, as in Ypres, by Nuns, on strips of silk and then cut up to be made into cards. *French.*

624 From Will, on active service, to Lily, Christmas 1918 (surely the best since 1913) from Arras. These cards were expensive and fragile and were either sent in envelopes or taken home on leave. The fact that so many can be found, in pristine condition 100 years on, speaks volumes for the way in which they were treasured. *French.*

622

623

Variations in the basic designs include envelope-like pockets which hold tiny message cards (and these range from simple one colour written messages to coloured and illustrated designs) photographs or miniature silk or lace handkerchiefs. Fine, hand-tinted inset photographs of War Leaders and Generals also appear on embroidered cards and add considerable value. That so many of these embroidered cards exist today, sometimes in perfect condition, is largely due to the fact that they were sent through the post in protective brown, semi-transparent envelopes. Also they were patently of considerable value to the recipient and tended to be kept and treasured where normal cardboard cards would be thrown away in time. The cards were hand-embroidered by women at home, mostly in France and Belgium, often by Nuns, the same design being worked up to 25 times on a continuous strip. The completed strip of organdie was then sent to factories to be cut and mounted. Many little shops in the villages behind the lines stocked a good selection of these bright and attractive cards and the lads would enjoy browsing through them to find exactly the message and picture to suit their particular mood and circumstances. They were not cheap – selling at the equivalent of 25p in today's money which was a great deal out of a soldier's meagre pay packet. They were therefore mostly out of reach of the poorly paid French and Belgian troops. The British soldiers often commented on their prettiness and superiority as they sent the cards, as if subtly pointing out that they were damned expensive! In the final year of the War, the better-off Americans proved the best customers of all, and cards incorporating the American flag were quickly designed and put into production for their benefit.

Much rarer, and of far greater value today, are the woven silk cards. Even during the War they were produced in fewer numbers by far, and cost proportionately more, than their poor relations, the embroidereds.

The colours are more subdued on the woven cards than on the embroidered : black and white cards were often produced with striking effect and reds and flesh tones are the usual contrast. Occasionally a new colour, such as violet, appears on a woven card – as in the rare example which depicts Edith Cavell.

625

625 Woven silk card, made by machine. *French.*

626 Typical description of a Red Cross nurse – and nurses probably received many such cards! *French.*

627 Fine card with Royal Army Medical Corps Crest. Cards with Regimental crests are rapidly gaining in value. Message reads: '*Hope you will like this one.*' *1 Aug 17.* Its original tissue paper protective envelope is present. *French.*

628 Rare card with two hand-tinted photographs of the King and Queen of the Belgians. Sent from husband to wife, the message reads: '*My dearest wife, What a joy to me to be able to give you pleasure in sending these cards to you. I trust you will like them and get them quite safe.*' *French.*

629 Glorious deep red Flanders poppy. '*Envelope*'-type with tiny card inside saying '*Home Sweet Home*'. *French.*

630 The ubiquitous good luck symbol. Sent from 46 Infantry Base Depot, B.E.F. *French.*

631 French, British and Belgian flags on an embroidered silk card. There were many different publishers of these cards and it is rarely possible to identify them as they were often very local. French.

632 Vibrant colours and inset hand-tinted photograph of be-medalled '*Marshal French, Campaign 1914-15*'. *French.*

633 Message reads: '*A small token from France*', 1.12.15. *French.*

634 Handsome crest of the Royal Engineers. Regimental crests increase the value of these cards and the more obscure the regiment the higher the value. They probably cost more too to buy originally. *French: (Pub E.C. Boulogne.)*

635 Good luck symbols. The flags show that America had not yet joined the Allies, but see 638. *French.*

636 Card in mint condition, found in its original brown transparent envelope. Crest of the Royal Garrison Artillery. The motto says, '*Where might and glory lead*'. 5 June 1916. *French.*

637 '*Envelope*'-type, with another little card saying '*Love and Kisses*' in pocket. Sent from George who was '*still in the pink.*' Many soldiers were illiterate and a card like this addressed openly to a mother was probably the highest expression of love that could be imagined. *French.*

638 '*Envelope*'-type with tiny card saying '*Greetings from France*' in pocket. Now the American flag has joined those of the Allies so the card will have been made in late 1917 or in 1918. *French.*

626

627

628

631

629

630

633

634

632

636

637

635

638

Pin-ups

The first pin-up is as difficult to identify as is the first picture postcard, although the actual word 'pin-up' probably originated in the Second World War in connection with the regular issue of pictures of scantily dressed girls in the American Army weekly, *Yank*. Perhaps early cave drawings served the same purpose as pin-ups – elevation of the spirit.

The development of today's pin-up begins with the invention of photography in 1839 and very quickly photographers took to making pictures of beautiful women. As photography improved technically and it was possible to produce many prints from one negative, so a wider distribution of pictures took place. It was natural that women in the public eye, like stage performers, should frequently be the subject of such pictures, hence the connection between show business and the pin-up picture.

The postcard around 1900 was probably the major communication medium, and rotary printing processes enabled photographic cards to be churned out in their millions. The stage stars featured in droves on these cards, vying with each other to look the most appealing and using theatrical roles and costumes as excuses for baring their flesh.

639

640

641

642

643

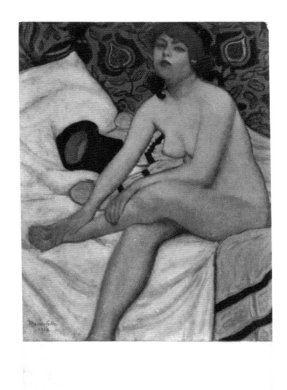

644

645

64

647

646

650

65

53

654

649

652

655

656

Victorian morality in Europe, particularly in Britain, did not allow public display of sensual or suggestive poses. About the most daring pictures generally available were those where living models pretended to be classical figures in well known poses. Even though they sometimes went so far as to whitewash themselves to resemble the marble of the originals, they could not be entirely nude. It was left to the French to lead the way forward and this occurred not through the photograph, but through imaginative drawings of idealized young ladies wearing very few clothes. The magazine, *La Vie Parisienne*, founded in 1863, initiated and developed the genre, the drawings ranging from the gently suggestive to the frankly erotic.

It was from the initiative of *La Vie Parisienne* and from the familiarity of the theatrical picture postcards that the beautiful pin-up cards of the First World War had their origin. The millions of men away from their homes and their women for the first time in their lives,

Sei wieder gut!

639 Pin-ups' (literally cards that were pinned up) were hugely popular amongst the young, isolated male audience that made up the armies in the field. Many of the designs drew inspiration from Parisian magazines and to the innocent volunteers from Britain who had no home exposure to such things they were intensely exciting. Card No. 6. Series 3317. Artist San Marco. *Italian: (Pub. 23 March 1917. Milan.)*

640, 641, 642, Series 1332 Three of a set of 5 *'Artistic Postcards'* in brown envelope produced to encourage the sale of National War Bonds. Probably a copy of a Continental set. *British: (Pub. Alphalsa Pub. Co.)*

643 *'September'*, part of set of *'The Months'* by Mauzan. A Frenchman by birth, Mauzan moved to Italy in his 20s and during the war drew many hundreds of postcards. He also drew posters and after the war he established his own poster business in Argentina. Posted 23.3.17. *Italian: (Pub. Uff Rev. Stampa, Milano.)*

644 *'The Yellow Dressing-gown'* by Artist Armand Rassenfosse. Produced for the 1914 International Art Exhibition, Venice. The red hair and style owe much to Lautrec's brothels paintings. The painting was made in 1912. *Italian. (Pub. Bestetti e Tuminelli, Milano.)*

645 *'At her Toilette'* by Artist Ney. Series 29. This would definitely have been a strong candidate to be pinned up in a trench. The cards were sold in sets, and complete ones in their original envelope can still be found. They were treasured! *French: (Pub. Delta, Paris.)*

646 *'Oui, je t'attends.'* (Yes, I am waiting for you.) Artist Raphael Kirchner, the undisputed originator of the 'Pin-up'. Many of his designs began life as posters for *'La Vie Parisienne'*, an operetta. *French: (Pub. L-E, Paris.)*

647 *'Poisson d'Avril'*. The fish is the French symbol for April Fool's Day. Artist Raphael Kirchner. *French: (Pub. L.E., Paris.)*

648 By sought-after specialist in *Art Deco*-style lovelies and fashion (but see also propaganda Cards No. 197 & 198), Artist Tito Corbella. He was born in Tuscany and studied In Venice. Sent home from France 10.3.18. *Italian.*

649 Series 29. *'A sa Toilette'* Card No. 144. Artist Ney. *French: (Pub. Editions Delta.)*

needed sensual consolation. Their only source of pictures was the picture postcard and there in France was the background and the talent to give them idealized, erotic representations of their wildest dreams: and there in France one man above all others was to produce the pictures that everyone wanted. Ironically he was Austrian. His name was Raphael Kirchner.

Kirchner was born in Vienna in 1876 and later moved to Paris. He drew for *La Vie Parisienne* together with artists like Mucha, all of whom were greatly influenced by the work of British artist Aubrey Beardsley, who had created an 'art nouveau' style of his own. Mucha went on to concentrate on posters and Kirchner was drawing for postcards by 1901. His cards are treasured items for collectors today, the earliest being in the Japanese idiom that was fashionable at the beginning of the century. The model for all his cards was his wife Nina, and following his death in August 1917 she first tried to commit suicide and then went out of her mind through excessive use of drugs.

650, 651, 652 from 1917 Series by Artist Vittorio Rappini (1877-1939), also known for his beautiful Egyptian scenes. *Italian: (Pub. VisoRevisioneStampa, Milano.)*

653 Advertisement card for Wellcome shoe heels, which are pictured on the reverse. '*Peaceful Shells*' Series, a magnificent phallic symbol. Notice the tiny victorious Allied plane and the German pilot falling out of his. Card No. 685. Artist Xavier Sager. *French.*

654 Another in the '*Peaceful Shells*' Series. Card No. 686. Artist Xavier Sager. *French.*

655 Artist Alice Luella Fidler, '*American Girl*' Series No. 46. There are 34 cards in the series. Postcard numbers often defy logic as they do here. Alice was one of three sisters from New York all of whom drew 'pretty ladies'. 'Fidler' is sometimes seen as 'Filder'. *American: (Pub. E. Gross Co.)*

656 Artist Pearle Fidler. '*American Girl*' *No. 101.* 'Fred' sent the card from France to Sheffield while 'OAS' on 3 November 1918. Barely a week to go. See card 655. *American.*

657 '*Be good again.*' The child is being bribed with sweets – but what for? Artist Günther Nagel. Nagel continued to draw propaganda designs into the Nazi period. *German: (Pub. A.Sch. & Co.)*

658 '*Pride*' from the '*Capital Sins*' *Series.* Artist Raphael Kirchner. Pinholes clearly visible (original of course). The highly successful Kirchner, who used his wife Nina as his model for many of his designs, died of appendicitis in New York in 1917. *French: (Pub. L-E., Paris.)*

659 'La Jolie Maud'. Also with pin holes. *French: (Pub. L.E., Paris.)*

660 '*Avarice*' from the '*Capital Sins*' Series. Note the pin holes on the card. *French: (Pub. L-E., Paris.)*

661 Series XIII. Card No. 1. Hand painted. Artist W.Zabczinsky. *French: (Pub.CBB.)*

662 *Cupid's Week* Series. '*Thursday*'. Card No. 5003. The sad message on the back begins, '*Dear Kay, You are the mean bugger for not writing…*' Receiving mail from home was an important element of morale and it was not unknown for soldiers to share their mail with chums who had none. Prolific glamour Artist Suzanne Meunier. *French: (Pub.L.E., Paris.)*

658

659

660

661

662

Kirchner's cards of the war years are not so draughtsmanlike as his earlier cards. They are more direct, easier for the soldier to identify himself with than the ephemeral beauties of *La Vie*. Other French artists drew girls – Sager, Hérouard, Fontan, and Italians too, like Mauzan and Rappini – but Kirchner was the favourite, his were the cards that were pinned up in the trenches. His cards were the original pin-ups.

The Tommy called Kirchner 'Kirsonner' and young officers had competitions to see who could collect the most cards. In the 3 July 1916 issue of the *Kemmel Times*, a trench newspaper, Gilbert Frankau wrote a poem entitled *The Nuts of the Old Brigade*. It was a lament for lost Gunner companions and one of the verses went like this:

'O where is Bob of the big moustache?
An alien adjutant shoots
For the Major-man that I used to know
With his Kirchner ladies all in a row
And his seventeen pairs of boots.'

663   Series 29. Card No. 143. '*Intimité.*' Artist Xavier Sager. Very little is known about Sager. It is believed that he was born in Austria but spent the last years of his life in the United States. He died in 1930. *French: (Pub. A.O.E. Paris.)*

664   '*Les Zeppelins à Paris*'. Card No. 35. Paris cellars look more attractive than London ones. Black stockings seem very popular. Notice pin up holes. Artist Raphael Kirchner. *French: (Pub. L.E., Paris.)*

663

664

7 Cards from the Queen's Collection

Cards from the Queen's Collection

"THE POSTCARDS IN THIS CHAPTER ARE REPRODUCED BY GRACIOUS PERMISSION OF HER MAJESTY THE QUEEN, AND ARE FROM THE PHOTOGRAPHIC COLLECTION IN THE ROYAL ARCHIVES AT WINDSOR CASTLE."

Her Late Majesty Queen Mary was an avid collector of Christmas cards – the eventual size of her collection was to be 18 albums – and in 1917, knowing of her interest in cards, a postal censor presented her with a collection of confiscated picture postcards. They do contain some harshly anti-British cards – presumably why the censor confiscated them –and some rare Dutch cards that are bitterly anti- war in character. The majority of the cards (which include postally used – often to America – cards and also unposted cards) are not only in perfect condition, but are of types that are not often found in this country in such a large quantity collected together in one album.

Queen Mary was deeply involved in every way in the War firstly as a mother, with two sons on active service. The Prince of Wales (later to become King Edward VIII) served as A.D.C. to the C.I.C. in France, then as Staff Captain to the G.O.C of the Mediterranean Expeditionary Force and finally as General Staff Officer to Lord Cavan in Italy. His enthusiasm and desire to be in the thick of things was a continual headache to Lord Kitchener (who dreaded the embarrassment H.R.H. would cause should he be taken prisoner) and to his protecting aides. Prince Albert (later to become King George VI) was a Midshipman on H.M.S. Collingwood when war broke out

England and the Merchant Flag Humbug.

665, 665A, 665B, 666 *'England and the Merchant flag Humbug.'* There is nothing to identify the country of origin on the reverse of this postcard, but it was probably produced by pro-Germans in America before she entered the War. It is a rare and valuable mechanical card which exposes England's tricks of disguising her warships as merchant ships and of changing her flag from the Union Jack to the flags of the Central Powers or of neutral countries. The wheel at the bottom right hand rotates to change the flag from (1) the Union Jack to (2) the Italian flag (before Italy joined the Allies) and (3) the Hungarian flag amongst many other possible variations.

667 Official Red Cross Card. Germany recognizes Italy's intrigues and perfidy but *'Certainly the day of Revenge will come.'* German.

668 Symbolic representation of the War, decorated with nails. Card designed and sold in aid of the War Orphans of the elementary school in Dierhagen on the Baltic. The basic design was used by other towns. *German: (Pub. Bering, Essen. 1916.)*

669 *'God With Us.'* 5pf card, whose proceeds went to the Soldiers' Welfare Committee. Artist H. Landgrebe. *German: (Pub. Doring & Huning, Berlin.)*

670 *'Think of the Red Cross'* - i.e. give them your money instead of spending it on drink. Excessive drinking was tackled by the propagandists on behalf of the Governments of both sides. *German: (Pub. Niedersedlitz, Dresden.)*

665A

665B

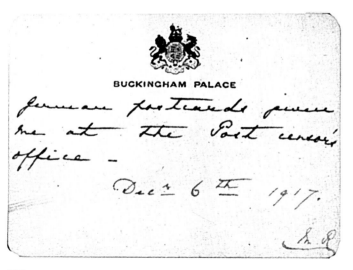

666

and he arrived back from sick leave in time to fight in the Battle of Jutland. He described the Battle to his parents as '... a great experience to have been through'. Secondly, Queen Mary's involvement as Consort to a King who felt sincere personal concern for his subjects at war (civilian and in the Services) was arduous. The Royal Couple made literally hundreds of visits to hospitals, munitions factories, bomb damaged areas throughout the War and through the length and breadth of the country (and also abroad as far as the King was concerned). When the King fell off the horse loaned to him by General Haig during a visit to the troops in France and was severely injured (with extensive bruises and fractured pelvis) she undertook many of his engagements alone during his lengthy and difficult convalescence.

The King and Queen set personal examples of economy, sobriety and thrift throughout the War. Like the rest of their subjects they were issued with ration cards and they 'dug for Victory' at Sandringham. Drunkenness had become such a serious problem in 1915 that the new Minister of Munitions, Lloyd George, appealed to the King to make a Royal gesture of abstinence.

Another way the Royal Family found of showing their genuine concern was to hold tea parties for the wounded at Buckingham Palace. When home on leave the Royal Princes served at the tea table and members of the Family who were available would attend.

Thirdly, as an intelligent and active person in her own right, with strong ideas on the contribution that women could make, Queen Mary worked tirelessly to put the women's voluntary organizations on an efficient basis. She also encouraged her daughter. Princess Mary (whose gift to the troops of a brass tin of tobacco at Christmas was much appreciated) to 'do her bit'.

Kriegswahrzeichen

genagelt zum Besten der Jugendspende
für Kriegerwaisen von der
Volksschule Ostseebad-Dierhagen

Entwurf Professor Edmund Körner, Essen-Darmstadt

669

670

671 '*God Punish England*' is the message on the menacing Zeppelin. Reverse states: '*German Schools Association Card 723.*' *German: (Pub. Josef Eberle VIII.)*

672 '*God Punish England and Destroy Italy.*' It is hardly surprising that the Censor thought fit to confiscate such a virulently anti–Allied card. *Austrian: (Pub. Brüder Kohn, Wien.).*

673 '*Firm and True is the watch on the Rhine. Bombardment of Fortress Reims.*' The Iron Cross decorates the border. The most popular symbol of Germany's military might, it found its way on to all manner of articles, from mugs to brooches. *German. 1914.*

674 *Field Postcard with Regimental Postmark.* Posted 30 April 1916. The famous 42cmm gun – the '*Big Bertha*' of 1914–18. It was the Germans' use of such weapons that overcame the Belgian forts in 1914. *German.*

675 '*Now I can breathe freely again, dear Fatherland*', says the blond Teuton as he breaks the iron band of England, France and Belgium. Artist I. Mermagen. *German: (Pub. Peter Luhn. 1915)*

676 On reverse '*War Postcard No. 77.*' Artist '*P.O.E.*' – the German equivalent of Mabel Lucie Atwell? The English would have asked themselves if the young soldier wasn't taking advantage of the white flag! *German.*

677 On reverse '*War Postcard No. 48.*' Artist '*P.O.E.*' '*Tell us about von Hindenburg.*' Hindenburg was revered in Germany as was Kitchener in Britain. *German.*

678 The Kaiser pays homage to a soldier fallen '*On the Field of Honour.*' *German: (Pub. Albert Fink, Berlin.)*

679 The Kaiserin does likewise. *German.*

680 Posted in Budapest and addressed to the U.S.A. Justice redresses the unfair balance of the numerous Allies against the 3 Central Powers (Germany, Austro–Hungary and Turkey). *Hungarian.*

671

672

673

674

675

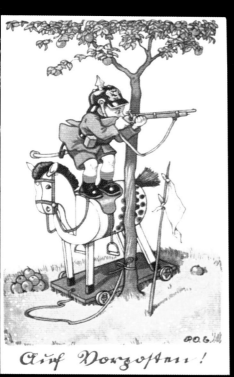

Auf Vorposten!

676

AUF DEM FELDE DER EHRE

...DENKEN

679

678

Erzähl' uns was vom Hindenburg!

677

680

I've done my bit

Welcome Home!

As the bugles clarioned the Cease Fire along the Western Front at the eleventh hour of the eleventh day of the eleventh month of 1918, Canadian troops of the 116th Battalion reached the spot, 8 km N.E. of Mons, where Corporal Thomas was reputed to have fired the first British shot in the Great War on 22 August 1914. As the church bells of villages throughout France and Belgium pealed in joy and the civilians wept with relief, the troops on the battleground received the news in almost bewildered disbelief. A British soldier hearing the news in a Belgian village later wrote: 'We were really too stunned for much gesticulation ... of all the incredible

681 Marshal Foch's carriage in which the Armistice was signed (shown here In the Army Museum at Les Invalides in Paris). In 1940 Hitler insisted upon taking the French surrender in the same carriage (then at Compiègne). *French: (Pub. The Society of the Army Museum, Les Invalides.)*

682 *'Now thank we all our God'.* Like the Prime Minister Lloyd George, many people's first action on hearing the news of the Armistice was to give thanks at a church service. *British.*

683 Around these tables sat Clemenceau, the French Premier, Doktors Bell and Müller who signed for Germany. President Wilson of America, Lloyd George, Prime Minister of Great Britain, and their entourages. *French.*

681

682

682

announcements that had ever been made to us, this left us the most staggered. It must only be a dream! Surely we should hear the distant sound of guns in a minute or so, which would prove we had been deluded!'

But it was true. Since the spring of 1918 events had inexorably been leading to the collapse of Germany and the end of hostilities. On 8 January, President Wilson proclaimed his famous '14 points' for Peace. In July and August the Germans launched their last major offensive at the Second Battle of the Marne, responded to by a successful French counter offensive. During August and September the Allies achieved great gains at Amiens, Bapaume and Arras, with the Americans playing a major role on the Saint Mihiel Salient. On 27 September the advance to victory began and on 29 September Bulgaria was granted an Armistice by the Allies. On 27 October, Ludendorff, his efforts to make the High Command aware of collapsing German morale ignored, resigned, and two days later mutinies broke out in the German Navy.

At the end of the month the Kaiser fled from Berlin to Hindenberg's headquarters at Spa. On 30 October Turkey was granted an Armistice, followed by Austria on 4 November. Germany stood alone. The Chancellor, Prince Max of Baden, sick with flu, was persuaded to press for an Armistice. Marshal Foch was authorized by the Allies to accept an Armistice delegation from the German Government which on 10 November steamed into a railway siding in the Forest of Compiégne at 7.00 a.m. The Allied train, containing Marshal Foch, General Weygand and Admiral Sir Rosslyn Wemyss, lay in a nearby siding. The historic carriage was preserved as a museum and many postcards exist of it. The original was destroyed in The Second World War and a replica now stands in its place.

The two delegations met at 9.00 a.m. Admiral Wemyss reported later that: 'All the Germans are very much distressed – naturally so – Erzberger showing most nervousness but Winterfield and Vanselow looked the most distressed ... Erzberger is a common looking man, a typical

Signature of Treaty of Peace of the Great War   La Signature de la Paix de la Grande Guerre
Palace of VERSAILLES. Hall of Mirrors   VERSAILLES - Galerie des Glaces
La Table historique

684 Artist's impression of the historic scene of signing the Armistice in the railway carriage at Compiègne. Admiral Wemyss (wrongly spelled on the card) commented later on Erzberger's bourgeois appearance. *French.*

685 *'The Day of Deliverance. Inhabitants of a liberated French town welcoming the arrival of French troops.' British: (Pub. Delta Fine Art Co.)*

686 The first Doughboys returning to the USA. *American: (Pub. US Signal Corps. Bureau of War Photography.)*

684

685

686

German bourgeois.' Upon seeing the terms, the Germans asked for an extra 24 hours to consider them, but the original deadline of 11.00 a.m. on 11 Monday was adhered to. Meanwhile the German Empire was fast disintegrating. On 9 November Germany was declared a Republic. The Kaiser had eventually and grudgingly taken the advice of Prince Max and of Hindenberg and abdicated, and in turn Prince Max gave way as Chancellor to Herr Ebert. On Sunday 10 November, the Kaiser, urged by Hindenberg, left Spa for the Dutch border town of Eysden, where his train was held up for six hours waiting for permission to cross into Holland. Arriving finally with his party of 20 at Count Bentin's chateau at Amerongen, the Kaiser is said to have demanded of his host, 'Now give me a cup of good English tea.'

Back at the Forest of Compiégne the Allies were informed at midnight that the German envoys wished to meet. The two sides conferred all through the night and the Armistice was finally signed at 5.10 a.m. on the following morning, an event recorded by a photographer and soon on sale as postcards. After the momentous signature. Admiral Wemyss remarked:'... it was a queer feeling that I had that the War was at last over and that bloodshed would cease at 11 o'clock.'

'Armistice' was a new word to use for ending a war. Technically it means 'a suspension of hostilities'. 'Peace' or 'Victory' were more accustomed terms, but this time there was so much to resolve, with so many participating Allies to be appeased, that the terms of an equable peace treaty would obviously take many months to finalize. Armistice, therefore, implied the interim period between the cessation of hostilities and the signing of a peace treaty. The terms of the Armistice itself were uncompromisingly strong for Germany. Although not technically 'defeated' it amounted to unconditional surrender and left Germany virtually without Army, Navy or Air Force. The Armistice was originally to be of 36 days duration with an option to extend. This option was taken up on 13 December 1918 and renewed on 16 January 1919 and 16 February 1919.

At home in each of the Allied countries the joy and jubilation emulated the euphoria of the first intoxicating rush to take up arms. A distinguished journalist, Michael Macdonagh, described the scene in London where there prevailed : '... an irresistible impulse to let business go hang, to get into the streets and yell and sing and dance and weep – above all to make oneself supremely ridiculous'.

In Belgium the much-loved King and Queen, who had shared so many of their subjects' tribulations, made a triumphal re-entry on horseback into their liberated capital. The official Victory Marches did not take place until the signing of the Peace Treaty was concluded – in July 1919 – but many such triumphal processions took place after the Armistice and provided a popular theme for postcards.

In Germany the demoralized and dispirited remnants of a once fine Army straggled home – those, that is, who had not already deserted in their thousands. All attempts at an orderly retreat and discipline were abandoned by disillusioned officers and there would inevitably have been a widespread mutiny in the Army as well as in the Navy had not the Armistice just arrived in time to avert it. The bitterness of defeat was almost unnoticed by the civilians, so great was the relief that the War had finally ended and they could look forward to an end to their bleak existence of starvation and lack of most basic creature comforts. The Allied Army of Occupation was almost welcomed, especially in areas where Bolshevik uprisings threatened the undermanned and disorganized resources of German law and order. And then the 'boys' and the 'poilus' started to dribble home. Demobilization was slow and cumbersome and compulsory service did not finally end until 1 April 1920. The fortunate families who had a loved one to welcome home often had to wait many months for their reunions, but happy and excited reunions they still were and they

687 The Belgian Unknown Warrior was chosen by Raymond Haesebrouch, a blind soldier, from five unknowns at Bruges station, 10 November 1922. *Belgian.*

688 *'Victory Day in Cambridge'.* Card by Harry A. Maden. Soldiers from the U.S.A., the British Empire and other Allies join Boy Scouts, WAACS, the wounded and civilians in celebrations, which the Padre finds alarming. Note the effigy of a German soldier. *British.*

687

689 Under the terms of the Peace Treaty, Alsace-Lorraine was returned to France. The card shows the Alsace-Lorraine delegation at the Cenotaph during the Victory Parade, Paris, 14 July 1919. *French: (Pub. E. Le Deley.)*

690 Tombstone of the British Unknown Warrior in Westminster Abbey. He was disinterred from the Ypres area and brought home in great and reverential pomp, the coffin covered by the flag that had covered Edith Cavell's coffin when it too was brought back. *British.*

688

691 The French Unknown Warrior under the Arc de Triomphe. The body was chosen by Private August Tain, who fought at Verdun, in a ceremony organized by André Maginot, then Minister of Pensions. Eight unidentified bodies were exhumed at random from the main zones of war, and transported to Verdun where Private Tain placed a bunch of flowers on the coffin of his choice. *French.*

LES FÊTES DE LA VICTOIRE A PARIS — 14 JUILLET 1919
Devant le Cénotaphe - La délégation Alsacienne-Lorraine

689

made a happy subject for the spate of colourful postcards, often by famous artists like Mabel Lucy Atwell, Tempest and AE in Britain, which feted the glad moment.

After the first days of jubilation however, a weird sense of anti-climax was prevalent. Michael Macdonagh expressed it thus: 'A melancholy took possession of me when I came to realize ... that a great and unique episode in my life was past and gone. Our sense of the value of life and its excitements, so vividly heightened in the War is, with one final leap of its flame, about to expire in its ashes. Tomorrow we return to the monotonous and the humdrum.' The unique sense of comradeship would never be repeated for the troops, nor the exciting sense of pulling together for a Cause for civilians, nor (for many years again to come) the almost total freedom of job opportunity for the women. Not only did women resent giving back their jobs to the men they had replaced, but a whole new problem arose in the placing of the demobilized Women's Auxiliary Forces and the thousands of women munitions workers in jobs to match the freedoms and responsibilities they had enjoyed during the War.

The final signing of the Peace Treaty in Versailles' Hall of Mirrors (a suitably imposing setting as commemorative postcards show) on 28 June 1919 gave a temporary 'lift'. A Council of Ten Allies (two each from Britain, France, America, Italy and Japan) met in January 1919 to draw up the conditions and the final decisions were made by a Council of the Big Three – President Wilson of America, Clemenceau the French Premier, and Lloyd George, the British Prime Minister. On 7 May the Draft Treaty was presented to the German delegates and on 22 June the German National Assembly at Weimar voted in favour by 237 votes to 138. The terms echoed those of the Armistice. Surrendered territories were shared out between the Allies – notably Alsace-Lorraine to France – but even Portugal received territories in East Africa and 0.75 of

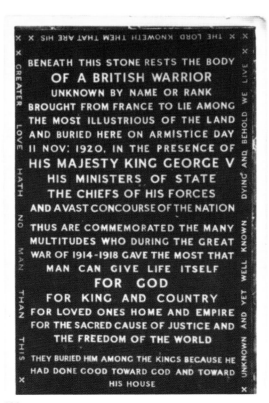

692 In '... *some corner of a foreign field that is forever England'* lies the grave of Lt W.E. Parke, 2nd DLI, Mentioned in Despatches, died 13 Oct 1914. His grave is tended by a local girl. The grave is now in Outtersteene Comm Cem, Bailleul. *French.*

693 The grave of a West Kent soldier – and with a very Germanic cross – could Pte. Lawrence have been buried by a chivalrous foe? Only two soldiers named Lawrence from that Regiment are listed by the CWGC. One died in 1918 and the other one four years earlier on 29 September 1914. On the basis that by 1918 elaborate crosses for individuals were no longer put up, then 'our' soldier is probably Harold Fredrick Lawrence and he is commemorated on the Loos-en-Artois Memorial. Thus his grave was lost in later fighting, a fate that befell many temporary markers. *French.*

694 At the Armistice, Prisoners of War might have easily been forgotten. This card was produced by the Association of Men of Kent and Kentish Men to raise funds to send members of the 'The Buffs' and Royal West Kents, parcels of food etc. *British: (Pub. Illustrated London News.)*

692

693

694

the monetary repatriation payable by Germany. This amounted to 20,000,000,000 gold marks. Many articles of the Treaty were never implemented, one of the casualties being President Wilson's pet scheme, the abortive League of Nations. In the Treaty, the Kaiser was publicly arraigned for his 'supreme offence against international morality and the sanctity of treaties.' Military tribunals were to try persons accused of acts of violation of the laws and customs of war, but the Netherlands refused to surrender the Kaiser and he was never tried. He lived out his days in peaceful luxury at the Castle of Doorn, where he died in June 1941 and is buried.

The Official Peace was the excuse for another round of celebrations and victory marches, ceremonies of commemoration, the erection of war memorials and symbolic funerals for 'unknown soldiers' in all Allied countries – and the production of series upon series of postcards to immortalize the junketing and the solemn occasions too.

And then came the awful reckoning, the dreadful realization of the unbelievably high figure of the dead and the wounded. Published figures are often contradictory, but the total dead was probably in the region of 8.5 million – Russia and Germany losing over 1,700,000 each, France and Austria nearly 1.5 million, the British Empire forces just under 1 million. The bare figures cannot begin to tell the story of grief and irreparable loss, of bereaved families, firms, clubs and even whole towns, where groups of relatives and friends joined up together and were slaughtered *en masse*. Stark photographic postcards of fields of crosses and newly made cemeteries, of reverential memorial services and monuments to soldiers of many regiments and towns throughout the world, bear witness to the national and international mourning for the dead.

VICTORY MARCH OF THE ALLIED TROOPS IN LONDON.
JULY 19th, 1919.
THE PROCESSION IN THE MALL

HOMMES 40
CHEVAUX 8

GOOD
BYE-E-E.

695   696

695 Parade in London of Allied troops on 19 July 1919 to celebrate the signing of the Treaty of Versailles – until which the Allies were still technically at war with the Central Powers. *British: (Pub. Beagles.)*

696 The standard troop transport railway carriage, with room for 40 men or 8 horses. The cheery soldier on his way home is saying *'Goodbye to all that'*. Message on reverse, dated 22 February 1919, *'This is what I have said to the old camp. Love from Daddy.'* *British.*

697 Original Memorial to the Anzacs in Port-Said. It was unveiled on 23 November 1932 and was meant to represent an Australian and New Zealander dismounting their horses in order to engage the enemy. It was destroyed during the Suez riots in 1956. Replicas have been erected in both Australia and New Zealand but the Nations disagree about what the figures represent. The horses were modelled on 'Bess', the only horse that left New Zealand in 1914 and returned home at the end of the war. *Egyptian: (Pub. Lehnert & Landrock, Cairo.)*

697

698

699

Is there room for Willie there?

700

698 *'OBEY.'* Battle Honours of the 52nd Italian Alpine Infantry Regt up to 1918. *Artist Ferrari. Italian: (Pub. V.E. Boeri, Roma.)*

699 Patcham's Indian Chattri (Cremation Memorial), dedicated by the Prince of Wales, 1 Feb 1921. It stands above Brighton (where many Indian soldiers were treated in the military hospital) on the South Downs and is on the cremation site for many of the 800,000 Indian soldiers who fought for the Allies in WW1. Local photographer's card. *British.*

700 The Kaiser abdicated in 1918 having lost the confidence of his country and armed forces. He found refuge in Holland and died in exile in June 1941, age 82. British: (Pub. Bamforth.)

701 A strangely prophetic card, posted as early as 24 December 1914, but accurately anticipating the Kaiser's exile at Doorn in Holland. The reported atrocities by German troops had destroyed any sympathy that there might have been for the German cause. *British.*

"NOBODY LOVES ME."

701

By permission of the Gresham Committee
"National Peace Thanksgiving Service at St Paul's Cathedral, A D 1919"
By Frank O. Salisbury

702

702 Explanation on sheet in original packet of postcards reads: '*This picture shows their Majesties, King George and Queen Mary, the Prince of Wales and other members of the Royal Family attending the Divine* Service *held on the steps of St. Paul's Cathedral on the 6th July 1919, for a National Peace Thanksgiving. In the foreground is the Archbishop of Canterbury pronouncing the Blessing, on the left of the picture is the Bishop of London. In the background is the Lord Mayor of London attended by the sword-bearer and members of the Corporation of London.*' Artist Frank O. Salisbury. *British: (Pub. Fine Arts Pub. Co.)*

703 One of the most reproduced paintings on postcards in the first decade of the century, Reynolds' '*Heads of Angels*' incorporated in a 'Peace' design. *British: (Pub. Valentine.)*

704 Delighted Doughboy returns to the U.S.A. (Cleveland, Ohio) in 1919. *American: (Pub. Jewish Welfare Board, US Army and Navy.)*

705 Unexpected consequences for Tommies returning home! *British.*

706 The wounded will still need care by such organisations as the St John Ambulance Association. The message reads, '*I bought this off a Boy Scout when in port on the* Grampian *July 1915.*' *Maltese.*

703

704

705

706

WHEN TOMMY COMES MARCHING HOME
AGAIN !

707

HOME SWEET HOME

WE COME.

WE'LL ALL BE GLAD, DEAR SOLDIER LAD
WHEN YOU RETURN HOME SAFE ONCE MORE
AND HERE'S A VIEW TO SHOW TO YOU
THE WELCOME YOU'LL GET AT THE OLD FRONT DOOR!

708

WISHING YOU A JOLLY XMAS.

CHEERIO

WE ARE ALL BACK AT OUR OLD JOB.

709

The simile of the flower of young manhood of a whole generation destroyed is poignant, and the aptness of the association of the blood red Flanders poppy as a memorial to the dead is immortalized in Col. John Macrae's verses:

"In Flanders fields the poppies blow
Between the Crosses, row on row
That mark our place and in the sky
The larks, still bravely singing, fly!
Scarce heard amid the guns below

We are the Dead. Short days ago
We lived, felt dawn, saw sunset glow.
Loved and were loved, and now we lie
in Flanders fields."

John Macrae died of pneumonia, at Wimereux, on 28 January 1918.

The tragedy of the irreplaceable dead is only surpassed by the tragedy of the fearfully wounded survivors. Estimates based on the British Ministry of Pensions figures twenty years after the War reveal the appalling reality. The State then provided pensions for 442,000 who, because of their injuries, were totally incapable of working. The injured included amputees, the blind, the deaf, those unmentionably maimed in body and mind from gas, shell shock or the sheer horror of months in the trenches or ships under fire, or days in flimsy, inadequate aeroplanes. Their support cost Britain £2,000,000,000 a year. Many contemporary songs, poems and politicians' speeches vowed that 'We will remember them'. The proof that we all too soon forgot is the Second World War.

TO THE GLORY OF GOD & IN MEMORY OF THE OFFICERS · WARRANT OFFICERS · N·C · OFFICERS & MEN OF THE DEVONSHIRE REGIMENT · WHO LOST THEIR LIVES DURING THE WAR 1914-1918

707 Tommy wears a German helmet trophy. The troops did not come rushing home as soon as the Armistice was signed; demobilization was slow and cumbersome and compulsory service did not end until 1 April 1920. *British: (Pub. E. Mack.)*

708 By well-known comic artist, *'A.E.'*, in a style which foreshadows the future of the picture postcard as a, 'seaside', genre but the image of 'Home' is what kept so many men going during the war. *British: (Pub. H.B. Series, London.)*

709 A *'wishful thinking'* card. Unemployment was a serious postwar problem and the women did not want to give up their jobs. Posted 24 December 1919. *British.*

710 From a private postcard. The 2nd Devons were presented with the *Croix de Guerre* for their gallant stand on the Aisne on 27 May 1918. The Citation reads:'.... *the few survivors of the battalion, though isolated and without hope of assistance, held on to their trenches north of the river and fought to the last with an unhesitating obedience to orders.'* The Memorial is in Exeter Cathedral and is one of hundreds that would be erected in the post war years. Sadly, those not in such prominent places fell into disrepair and in the metal shortage period of WW2 and then in the 2000s were taken for their scrap value. *British.*

711 Memorial to 54,896 British soldiers who had lost their lives at Ypres and who had no known graves. To this day the Last Post is sounded every night under the Gate by Belgian buglers on silver

711

712

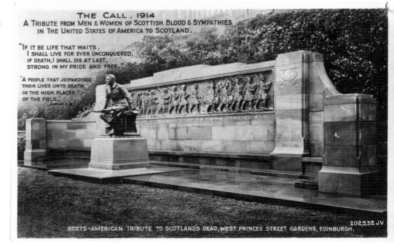

713

I was fairly taken off my feet
when he came home.

714

bugles given by the Queen's Royal (West Surrey) Regt. When the authors first visited Ypres regularly in the 1970s, they would often be alone with the buglers. Currently it is difficult even to see them because of the number of spectators. *British: (Pub. Samuels Ltd.)*

712 War Memorial to German soldiers at Aachen railway station. Railway stations were of course the hubs to and from which soldiers travelled. *German.*

713 Scottish Regiments performed some of the most gloriously heroic deeds of the War, with the resultant loss of many lives. This Memorial in Edinburgh was raised by *'Men and women of Scottish Blood & Sympathies in the United States of America.'* British.

714 By Artist D. Tempest. Posted 14 August 1918, a prophecy of the Armistice 3 months later. *British: (Pub. Bamforth.)*

715 The message, to a Miss May Kirkland, is clearly from a soldier on his way Home after the Armistice. It reads: *'Hope you didn't bubble over in the train on Saturday and that you found a letter containing the news awaiting you. Have you seen it in any paper yet? If so which and when? Two people told me they saw it but I haven't managed to yet…I'm not sure if I will get home on the 4th …I do hope it's like this (the weather) when I'm at home.'* British: (Pub. Inter-Art Co.)

BACK TO BLIGHTY!

715

Index

Illustration numbers appear in **bold**

INDEX OF POSTCARD ARTISTS, DESIGNERS AND PUBLISHERS